Marginalized, Mobilized, Incorporated

MODERN SOUTH ASIA

Ashutosh Varshney, Series Editor
Pradeep Chhibber, Associate Series Editor

Editorial Board

Kaushik Basu (Cornell University)
Sarah Besky (Cornell University)
Jennifer Bussell (University of California, Berkeley)
Veena Das (Johns Hopkins University)
Patrick Heller (Brown University)
Niraja Gopal Jayal (Jawaharlal Nehru University)
Devesh Kapur (Johns Hopkins University)
Atul Kohli (Princeton University)
Pratap Bhanu Mehta (Ashoka University)
Shandana Khan Mohmand (University of Sussex)
Ashley Tellis (Carnegie Endowment for International Peace)
Steven Wilkinson (Yale University)

The Other One Percent
Sanjoy Chakravorty, Devesh Kapur, and Nirvikar Singh

Social Justice through Inclusion
Francesca R. Jensenius

Dispossession without Development
Michael Levien

The Man Who Remade India
Vinay Sitapati

Business and Politics in India
Edited by Christophe Jaffrelot, Atul Kohli, and Kanta Murali

Clients and Constituents
Jennifer Bussell

Gambling with Violence
Yelena Biberman

Mobilizing the Marginalized
Amit Ahuja

The Absent Dialogue
Anit Mukherjee

When Nehru Looked East
Francine Frankel

Capable Women, Incapable States
Poulami Roychowdhury

Farewell to Arms
Rumela Sen

Negotiating Democracy and Religious Pluralism
Karen Barkey, Sudipta Kaviraj, and Vatsal Naresh

Cultivating Democracy
Mukulika Banerjee

Patching Development
Rajesh Veeraraghavan

The Difficult Politics of Peace
Christopher Clary

Making Meritocracy
Edited by Tarun Khanna and Michael Szonyi

Access to Power
Ijlal Naqvi

The Migration-Development Regime
Rina Agarwala

Capacity beyond Coercion
Susan L. Ostermann

Internal Security in India
Edited by Amit Ahuja and Devesh Kapur

Marginalized, Mobilized, Incorporated
Rina Verma Williams

Marginalized, Mobilized, Incorporated

Women and Religious Nationalism in Indian Democracy

RINA VERMA WILLIAMS

OXFORD
UNIVERSITY PRESS

Oxford University Press is a department of the University of Oxford. It furthers
the University's objective of excellence in research, scholarship, and education
by publishing worldwide. Oxford is a registered trade mark of Oxford University
Press in the UK and certain other countries.

Published in the United States of America by Oxford University Press
198 Madison Avenue, New York, NY 10016, United States of America.

© Oxford University Press 2023

All rights reserved. No part of this publication may be reproduced, stored in
a retrieval system, or transmitted, in any form or by any means, without the
prior permission in writing of Oxford University Press, or as expressly permitted
by law, by license, or under terms agreed with the appropriate reproduction
rights organization. Inquiries concerning reproduction outside the scope of the
above should be sent to the Rights Department, Oxford University Press, at the
address above.

You must not circulate this work in any other form
and you must impose this same condition on any acquirer.

Library of Congress Cataloging-in-Publication Data
Names: Williams, Rina Verma, author.
Title: Marginalized, mobilized, incorporated : women and religious
nationalism in Indian democracy / Rina Verma Williams.
Description: New York : Oxford University Press, [2023] | Series: Modern
south Asia series | Includes bibliographical references and index.
Identifiers: LCCN 2022027317 (print) | LCCN 2022027318 (ebook) |
ISBN 9780197567227 (paperback) | ISBN 9780197567210 (hardback) |
ISBN 9780197567241 (epub)
Subjects: LCSH: Hindu women—Political activity—India. | Women—Political
activity—India. | Bharatiya Janata Party. | Nationalism—India.
Classification: LCC HQ1236.5.I4 W55 2022 (print) | LCC HQ1236.5.I4 (ebook) |
DDC 320.082/0954—dc23/eng/20220709
LC record available at https://lccn.loc.gov/2022027317
LC ebook record available at https://lccn.loc.gov/2022027318

DOI: 10.1093/oso/9780197567210.001.0001

For William
You exist in every page of this book and in every chapter of my being.

Contents

Acknowledgments	ix
Introduction: Women, Political Parties, and Indian Democracy	1
1. Of Histories and Numbers: Hindu Nationalist Political Parties and Women	18
2. Women Mobilized: Three Controversies, Three Prongs of Gendered Mobilization, 1985–1992	48
3. Of Questions and Contexts: Feminist Responses, Scholarly Literatures, and Positionality	72

LOOKING BACK, LOOKING FORWARD

4. Women Marginalized: The All-India Hindu Mahasabha, 1915–1951	97
5. Women Incorporated: The Contemporary BJP, 2013–2016	120
6. Denouement—"The Condition of Its Women": Women's Political Participation and Indian Democracy	147
Appendix A: Interviews	161
Appendix B: 2014 Manifesto Items on Women, Coded	163
Notes	165
Bibliography	175
Index	193

Acknowledgments

This book and I have been accumulating debts for upwards of 10 years. We have spanned two institutions—University of Virginia and University of Cincinnati—that nurtured and sustained us both. The support and counsel of stellar colleagues at both institutions have pulled us both up to higher levels of attainment than we might otherwise have attained on our own. At UVA, where the book began, we owe deep debts of gratitude to Mehr Farooqi, Farzaneh Milani, Geeta Patel, Hanadi al-Samman, Denise Walsh, and Kath Weston. At the University of Cincinnati, we owe much to Richard Harknett, Laura Dudley Jenkins, and Anne Sisson Runyan. I have also been lucky, and smart, to strike up outstanding writing groups that kept me going when I wanted nothing more than to stop; for that, our thanks are owed to Danielle Bessett, Jana Braziel Corkin, Miki Hirayama, Laura Dudley Jenkins, Annulla Linders, Erynn Masi de Casanova, Sarah Mayorga-Gallo, Lizzie Ngweya-Scoburgh Shailaja Paik, Adrian Parr, Olga Sammiguel-Valderrama, and Rebecca Sanders.

Beyond Cincinnati and Charlottesville, neither the book nor I reach this stage without the support and insights—and friendship—of Sikata Banerjee, Amrita Basu, Nandini Deo, and Ashutosh Varshney

I have also been incredibly lucky, and smart, to work with remarkable academic coaches at different stages throughout my career: Rena Seltzer (https://www.leaderacademic.com) and Roxanne Donovan (https://www.wellacademic.com).

The book and I have also benefitted from the help of several wonderful research assistants along the way: Ayesha Casie Chetty, Maya Gulani, Bekir Ilhan, Sarah Imran, Elena Marsteller, Sayam Moktan, and Crystal Whetstone.

Fieldwork in India was supported and enabled by multiple awards from the University of Cincinnati's Charles Phelps Taft Research Center and a Senior Fellowship from the American Institute of Indian Studies. Writing was greatly facilitated by a Summer Stipend National Endowment for the Humanities; a Center Fellowship from the Taft Research Center; and a Jerome and Hazel Tobis Fellowship from the Center for the Scientific Study of Ethics and Morality at the University of California, Irvine.

I have the great privilege of being able to say that both my books were published by Oxford University Press. Our special thanks to Ashutosh Varshney, Pradeep Chhibber, and David McBride and his team.

My family in India has nourished my body and soul, engaged gamely with my (often impenetrable) academic pursuits, accepting it all, and me, unquestioningly and letting me merge work and joy in the best possible ways. I was, and am, lucky to have not less than two homes in India: in Gurgaon, with C. D. Sahay, Neelam Sahay, Anamika Sahay, Shalini Sahay-Bose, Sanjay and Shlok Bose; and in Lucknow, with A. P. Varma, and the late Mamta Varma. Would that Chachi were around to see the completion of this book, to which she contributed so much. And to all my family all around India: thank you for making this work not feel like work with countless meals, trips, adventures, and welcoming my intermittent arrivals with love and warmth and open arms, doors, and hearts—as well as some connections.

My family here in the United States constitutes every good thing that I am. Mom, you are the rock that we all perch on, and I understand better than ever that a daughter doesn't accomplish what I have without the full support and sacrifices of her mother in particular. Dad, I'm sorry I couldn't get this done before you left us. And to my sister Nita, and my brother Suraj, and to Gautam and Annie and Siri and Ishan: thank you for making every day lighter and brighter with your texts and emoji (not to mention the occasional dash of Anglophilia!), and for always cheering on my culinary pursuits. Suraj, what would a conference in San Fran be without you and a Giants game?

And to all those whom I have undoubtedly missed: you know who you are. The absence of your name here is no reflection of the importance of your contribution to this work, or to me.

I'll end with my deepest debts and most fulfilling debts. To my husband William: who is lucky, and smart, enough to have married to their mentor, their best friend, and the love of their life all rolled into the same person? Me. And to my son Jai: you are my heart walking around outside my body. The next one's for you. Or perhaps you'll write one and dedicate it to me first.

Introduction

Women, Political Parties, and Indian Democracy

On December 6, 1992, thousands of Hindu nationalist *kar sevaks* (militant activist "volunteers") converged on the Babri Masjid—a mosque built in 1527 in the northern Indian town of Ayodhya—and tore it down with crude tools like shovels and pickaxes, even tearing at it with their bare hands. The mosque's destruction sparked weeks of religious rioting around the country and shook the foundations of Indian secular democracy. Hindu nationalist women played very particular roles in these events: some exhorted Hindu men to violence against Muslim minorities to defend the faith and protect Hindu women; others literally cleaned up in the streets after bloodletting had occurred.

Less than a year after these events I arrived in India for dissertation fieldwork.[1] The destruction of the mosque is commonly marked as a turning point that launched the political party of Hindu nationalism, the Bharatiya Janata Party ("Indian People's Party," or BJP), to national political prominence. Twenty years later—having returned specifically to study the role of women in Hindu nationalist politics—I watched women, now shoulder to shoulder with men, milling about in the crowd and speaking on the dais at the BJP's campaign kickoff rally in New Delhi for the 2014 election, which the party won in a landslide that surprised even the most seasoned observers of Indian politics.

These two moments in modern Indian politics frame the core questions of this book: How has the participation of women in Hindu nationalist politics changed over time? And what does their changing participation mean—for women, for Hindu nationalism, and ultimately for Indian democracy?

The growing role of women in Hindu nationalist politics has corresponded with Hindu nationalism's rising political fortunes. But the benefits for women are less clear, as the BJP has expanded the role of women without significantly altering regressive gender ideologies that continue to tether women's political voices to their societal roles in the home and family. Access to the public sphere has expanded for some women, and this is not a negligible benefit in a society in which the public sphere remains heavily male dominated. But women's increasing participation has not led to notable advances on women's issues or women's rights more broadly, and has corresponded instead with an expansion of the radical right-wing agendas of the party that are undermining Indian democracy.

Hindu nationalism (or *Hindutva*, which translates roughly to "Hinduness") is at core an ethnic nationalism that holds that the only true Indians are those for whom the Indian subcontinent is both the land of their birth *and* the homeland of their religion: that is, followers of religions that originated in the subcontinent. This would include Hindus, Sikhs, Jains, and Buddhists,[2] while excluding Muslims and Christians as well as Jews and Parsis (also known as Zoroastrians). In this way Hindutva virtually equates being Indian with being Hindu. Despite Hindus being an overwhelming majority in India (around 80 percent since independence in 1947, and about 75 percent in prepartition, preindependence India), Hindutva constructs Hindus as under perpetual demographic threat from minority religious groups.

This book focuses on the political parties of Hindu nationalism in India—including the All-India Hindu Mahasabha (or simply Hindu Mahasabha) and the BJP, its contemporary successor—to show how women have become increasingly involved in Hindu nationalist politics over time.[3] I place women's participation in religious politics in India into historical perspective by comparing three critical time periods: before, during, and since the party's initial rise to national political power during the 1980s and 1990s. In its formative years in the early 1900s, before it initially rose to power, Hindu nationalist politics *marginalized* women. In the 1980s and 1990s, during its initial rise to power, the BJP began to *mobilize* them; and in the contemporary period, since its initial rise to power, it has institutionalized ways to *incorporate* women into its structures and activities. I argue that *incorporating* women into Hindu nationalist politics has significantly advanced the BJP's electoral success compared to prior periods when women were *marginalized* or *mobilized* in more limited ways. For the BJP, women's incorporation works to normalize religious nationalism in Indian democracy; however, incorporation has not been emancipatory for women, whose participation in BJP politics is still predicated on traditional gender ideologies that tether women to their social roles in the home and family.

To make this argument, I draw on significant new data sources gathered over almost a decade of fieldwork in India. I discovered new archival documents, never before examined, on a women's wing of the Hindu Mahasabha in the formative years of Hindu nationalism. In 2013 and 2015–16 I conducted interviews with key BJP leaders, gathered visual campaign materials, and attended major campaign events to construct an unmatched before-and-after view of India's watershed 2014 elections.[4] I deploy these new data in methodologically innovative ways, combining textual analysis and interpretation of primary and secondary sources for the historical periods with mixed-method analysis of qualitative and quantitative data—including interviews, ethnographic observation, visual analysis, and voting data—for the contemporary periods.

This is not a causal or generalizable argument in the narrow positivist sense: I do not argue that increasing participation of women "caused" the BJP to succeed politically. Subsequent chapters will show that the correlation is undeniable and revealing: the Hindu Mahasabha historically marginalized women and was a political failure. As the BJP began to mobilize women in the 1980s and 1990s, it attained increasing political success, culminating in its first stint in power at the center, heading a coalition government, from 1999 to 2004. This was the first non–Congress Party–led government to complete a full term in power since independence. Since that initial rise to power, the BJP achieved an overwhelming and largely unpredicted political victory in the 2014 elections with the incorporation of women into its structures and activities. But as an interpretive case study, this study is not meant, nor should it be read, as a primer for political success for the forces of Hindu nationalism. Rather, I have taken women's participation as a lens through which to trace, analyze, and illuminate the changing political fortunes of Hindu nationalism in Indian democracy. This study thus examines Hindu nationalist politics through multiple lenses of women, political parties, and India as a case study.

Why Women?

Activists and academics began documenting the participation of women in Hindu nationalist politics in India in the 1980s and 1990s, during the BJP's initial rise to power. An early wave of scholarship provided critically insightful analysis in and of that time period (Jeffery and Basu 1998; Sarkar 2001). Scholarly studies sometimes saw such participation as both novel and counterintuitive; they focused on understanding why women participate in such movements, and whether such participation can be empowering for women. I shift the analytical lens to first trace *how* women participate, how their participation changes over time, and what their changing participation means. In this I build on Charles Tilly's argument "that how things happen is *why* they happen" (2006, 410)[5] to suggest that we cannot understand why women participate in Hindu nationalist politics until we first understand *how* they participate, and how their participation has changed over time. And we cannot evaluate whether their participation can be empowering unless we understand what their participation *means*, for them, for the party, and ultimately for Indian democracy. Foundational studies of women's participation in Hindu nationalist politics proliferated during the BJP's initial rise to power in the 1980s and 1990s; the passage of time since then allows a systematic and temporal comparison of women's involvement in Hindu nationalist politics before and since that critical time period. This enables a contextualization of the 1980s and 1990s, dispelling any sense that such participation appeared suddenly and seemingly inexplicably during that period.

Focusing on the role of women in Hindu nationalism over time offers an important lens into how Hindu nationalism mobilizes political support. Hinduism as a religion does not provide an obvious basis for political mobilization. The fragmented characteristics of Hinduism as a religion—the lack of a single authoritative text or ecclesiastical hierarchy, the multisited nature of Hindu religious practice, and even the proliferation of deities, in addition to caste, regional, and linguistic differences—mean that nothing like a "Hindu identity" in a political sense exists a priori (Williams and Moktan 2019). Rather, Hinduism as a basis for political mobilization must be constructed, and mobilizing women became a primary way to do so in the 1980s and 1990s.

Rooted in both religion and nationalism, Hindu nationalism does not espouse a gender-forward ideology or gender-progressive agenda. Nandini Deo (2014) has argued convincingly that Hindu nationalism does not have a consistent gender ideology but instead tacks to whatever gender rhetoric suits their political purposes at any given time. For this very reason, studying women in the movement and how their roles have evolved can provide unique insight into how Hindu nationalism mobilizes political support.

The political science literature on women's political participation has cycled through multiple phases (Whetstone and Williams 2019). After initially ignoring women, then blaming them for their own lack of political participation (Duverger 1955), early attempts to account for women's political participation adopted an "add women and stir" approach: this meant studying women's political participation in the same frames within which scholars had long been studying participation, without fundamentally altering those frames (Sapiro 1998, 67). Political science did finally move to considering structural and institutional aspects of women's participation (Peterson 1992; Randall and Waylen 1998) and has in some ways returned to the idea that women's representation or presence in the public, political sphere matters for women's political participation. This is evidenced by the large and still-growing literature on gender quotas (Krook and Zetterberg 2014; Franceschet et al. 2012) as well as work on symbolic, descriptive, and substantive representation of women (Schwindt-Bayer and Mishler 2005; Celis and Mugge 2018).

Mainstream studies focus on specific political activities to measure women's political participation. These include voting, donating to political causes, volunteering in political campaigns, running for office, making and signing petitions, participating in civil society organizations, and participating in demonstrations and boycotts. These standard ways to measure women's political participation tend to derive from Western contexts and are largely quantitative. Such measures do describe the participation of women in the BJP—and are covered in Chapter 1—but only as a first cut. To rely on such measures alone as a means to understand women's participation in the BJP is to miss deeper levels of meaning and impact. For example, by standard measures, we can quantify the extent of BJP and Hindu nationalist women's participation in demonstrations, but that does not capture the use of gendered language to incite men to violence against Muslim minorities before and during such demonstrations. Even in an established democracy like India, voting data alone cannot capture the deeper ways women's issues were deployed to make the BJP a viable national political party. This study, as an interpretive case study and temporal comparison, captures those deeper meanings.

Why Political Parties?

In addition to focusing on women, this book focuses on political parties as distinct from the social movement organizations of Hindu nationalism. Hindu nationalism in India comprises three national organizations, along with numerous regional and local parties and organizations. The

BJP, a political party, is the political wing of the movement. It was founded in 1980; its predecessor parties were the Bharatiya Jana Sangh (from 1951 to 1980) and the Hindu Mahasabha (from 1915 to 1951).[6] The Rashtriya Swayamsevak Sangh ("National Volunteer Organization," or RSS) is a domestic social movement organization and the anchor organization of Hindu nationalism. Founded in 1925, the RSS seeks to regenerate and strengthen the Indian nation (defined as a Hindu nation) individually, person by person, from the ground up. The RSS explicitly disavows direct political activity in that it doesn't run candidates for office—that is the job of its political wing/party, the BJP—but it is a deeply politicized organization in every other sense of the word. The Vishwa Hindu Parishad ("World Hindu Council" or VHP), founded in 1964, is primarily the religious and international wing of the movement. Together these three organizations, along with local and regional counterparts, are known as, and often call themselves, the Sangh Parivar, or "Family of Organizations."

Much work on Hindu nationalism in India tends to collapse these organizations together, treating them as essentially interchangeable. Indeed, they can be difficult to disentangle in practice. The organizations work closely with each other, and their membership overlaps significantly. For example, many if not most BJP leaders have belonged or do belong to the RSS; and the RSS and VHP provide critical mobilizational support for BJP campaigns and candidates.

Yet despite the complexities of doing so, this study builds on the pioneering work of others who have productively drawn a distinction between the BJP and the political parties of Hindu nationalism, on the one hand, and the social movement organizations of Hindu nationalism on the other (Heimsath 1964; Jones 1989; Basu 2015). Focusing on political parties lets me address a critically important question about how a right-wing, gender-regressive, religious nationalist political party negotiates an inherent tension between its own ideological roots in religion and nationalism (which tend to confine women to the private sphere) and its need, as a political party in a democracy, to involve and engage women in the political sphere in order to win elections. This study explores how Hindu nationalism has negotiated this tension over time.

In this sense religious nationalist political parties pose a unique theoretical puzzle. A religious nationalist political party in a competitive democracy, and one tightly linked with a powerful social movement organization (Schlozman 2015), faces competing incentives. Unlike the social movement organizations of Hindu nationalism, the BJP has to increase its vote count and win votes and elections—and to do so it has an incentive to appeal more broadly across sectors of society than the RSS or VHP may have to. But unlike other political parties, the BJP espouses a gender-regressive, religious nationalist ideology. Amrita Basu (2015) captures this "rock and a hard place" dilemma perfectly when she argues that political parties and social movement organizations face competing incentives: the latter need to keep their members engaged and mobilized—and thus are incentivized to keep radicalizing—while political parties (especially in established, competitive democracies) need to moderate their rhetoric and agendas to widen their base of support.

Indeed, many of my interviewees clearly differentiated between the party and the social movement organizations of Hindu nationalism. Several women BJP leaders emphasized that they had never belonged to the RSS or the social wings of the movement, while others, of course, had belonged to both and in fact had moved into the BJP via their activism in the RSS. Notably, it was national-level leaders in New Delhi who affirmed they were never involved with the RSS, while the state-level leaders in Lucknow were more likely to have come to the BJP via the RSS and their husbands, brothers, or other male relatives (interviews are listed in Appendix A).

An important and growing body of literature focused on religious (or "religiously oriented"; Ozzano 2013) political parties advances the "inclusion-moderation hypothesis," which holds that the participation of more radical religious parties in electoral democracy tends to lead such parties to moderate their rhetoric and agendas (Brocker and Kunkler 2013). This hypothesis originated and was tested largely in the context of European countries; scholars of Indian politics have rightly noted that the case of the BJP does not clearly support the hypothesis (Ruparelia 2006; Basu 2015; Jaffrelot 2013; Flåten 2019). When the BJP governed from 1999 to 2004, the broad consensus among scholars of Indian politics was that ruling in a coalition government kept the BJP from implementing its more radical agendas—thus resulting in some tension with the RSS and its more radical social movement support base (Chakrabarty 2014, 2006; Adeney and Saez 2005). Since 2014, the BJP has held an outright majority in the Lok Sabha (the lower house of India's parliament), so no such constraints existed. Since 2019, if anything, the BJP has turned the inclusion-moderation hypothesis on its head: the BJP's participation in Indian democracy has not led it to moderate its agendas, but rather to consolidate power and undermine democracy itself (Tepe 2019; Varshney 2021)—a point I return to and expand on in Chapter 6.

Recently, Chhibber and Verma (2018) argued that the BJP's dominant electoral victory in 2014 might signal a turning point beyond which the BJP may be hegemonic in Indian politics for some time to come. Events since 2019 certainly seem to confirm this prediction (Vaishnav and Hintson 2019). This makes it all the more important to understand the role of women in the party and how it has evolved over time: how women have helped the party to success, and how the party may (or may not) help women.

Most of the work on women in political parties has focused historically on women in left political parties (Banaszak et al. 2003), arguing that parties of the left have been more likely, and quicker, than parties of the right to include women and integrate gender issues as part of their platform—at least in rhetoric. Other studies find a pattern of women entering political parties primarily through a family link (Freeman 2000). The case of the BJP in India partly supports and partly refutes these arguments. On the surface, BJP leaders explicitly disavow what they call "dynastic" politics, as associated with the Congress Party under—and abjectly reliant on—the ongoing leadership of the Nehru-Gandhi lineage. While it is true that many BJP women did not come into the party through a family link, many others did—through the RSS or the involvement of their husbands and sons.

More recently, scholars of women and politics have turned their attention to religious, conservative, and right-wing parties. This includes a growing literature on women in Islamic political parties (Jamal and Langohr 2014; Yadav 2012; Arat 2005; Clark and Schwedler 2003). A consensus has emerged in the scholarship that the participation of women works to normalize right-wing movements and parties, making them more acceptable in mainstream politics (Blee and Deutsch 2012; Celis and Childs 2018; Och and Shames 2018; Schreiber 2008; Bacchetta and Power 2002). It is in fact a central task of this book to document how the increasing participation of women in the BJP correlates with the party's growing electoral success and institutionalization over time. Yet I argue that in the case of BJP women, while their growing participation (via mobilization and incorporation) may have softened or mainstreamed the public image of the party—itself a debatable issue—it has not corresponded to any moderation of the party's radical agendas.

Why India?

India is a critical case to study religious nationalist politics in a Global South democracy. As two of the most salient forces of modern political life, democracy and religion must find ways to coexist in the modern international political order; both exist in abundance in India. Through the lens of gender, my study explores multiple ways that Indian democracy has accommodated religious politics—from conflicts over Islamic law to the rise and spread of majoritarian Hindu nationalism.

I define religious politics as "the mobilization of religious symbols, discourses, and narratives for political gain—in the case of democracy, for electoral gain" (Williams and Deo 2018, 549). In a word, the BJP has successfully incorporated markers of Hindu nationalism in the everyday fabric of Indian politics. This claim does not assume that the BJP represents or advocates Hinduism as a religion per se, but rather that the BJP represents Hindu nationalism as an aspirational form of Indian national identity that centers Hinduism in the national imaginary; subsumes other South Asian–origin religions under the mantle of Hinduism (Buddhism, Sikhism, Jainism); marks followers of all other religions as second-class citizens, outsiders, or actively subversive of Hindu nationalism; and virtually equates being Indian with being Hindu.

Studying religion and democracy in India (through the lens of gender) serves to correct multiple imbalances in multiple literatures. Scholars of religion and politics have often focused largely on Abrahamic religions (Judaism, Christianity, Islam) and the Western world; and occasionally they do so explicitly (Grzymała-Busse 2012; Lynch 2020).[7] Recent important works in the field grapple with concepts of religious freedom, religious tolerance, and religious rights, as well as secularism/secularization and the political role of evangelicals and the Christian church (Lewis 2017; Grzymała-Busse 2015; Hurd 2015; Norris and Inglehart 2011).

But Hinduism as a religion has several unique characteristics with important political implications that set it apart from the Abrahamic religions. These include its polytheistic character and the lack of a single, authoritative text; its widely varying practice across region, locality, and caste; and its informal, multisited practice wherein core aspects of worship take place outside of formal institutional settings such as temples. As a result of these various characteristics, Hinduism as a religion poses unique obstacles as a basis of political mobilization. People must be convinced that their unity as Hindus supersedes differences on the basis of caste, region, and language, among others. The multiplicity of Hindu texts and deities, in conjunction with the dizzying array of local, regional, and caste-based practices, highlights the hazards of assuming any overriding "Hindu identity": such an identity must be assiduously—and politically—constructed (Williams and Deo 2018). And while this is certainly true to some extent of all religious traditions—and indeed of all identities—the particular characteristics of Hindu nationalism in India highlight the processual aspects of bringing religious nationalism into democratic politics.

Scholars of religion and of women and gender are often not in conversation with each other; India is an ideal case study to bridge this gap. One leading scholar is worth quoting in full on this:

> There is a remarkable extent to which the study of religion and the study of gender have been bifurcated, not intersecting. Scholars of gender . . . have indicated limited interest in religion as a topic of study or area of interest; as they think about gender, they seldom include the relationship of gender to religious context, belief, or religious organizations, or to the theoretical interests of those who study religion. In corresponding fashion, social scientists who study religion have thus far indicated a limited interest in gender as a topic, especially in gender as more than a variable, and have not yet explored the potential usefulness of concepts and analytical tools being developed by gender theories, feminist theories, and theories of sexuality. (Charlton 2015, 336)

Where studies of women/gender and religion do intersect, they focus either on Western contexts or Islam. Studying Hinduism in India corrects both these biases. Political philosopher Carole Pateman (1988), for example, has argued that the marginalization of women from the public, political sphere, and their relegation to the private sphere, was not an accidental byproduct but rather a defining characteristic of modernity. But others have argued that the relegation of women to the private sphere—and in particular their marginalization from nationalist projects—was a Western rather than a universal phenomenon. Jill Vickers agrees with Pateman that in the West, "women's loss of public, civic, and property rights was not an accidental feature of nation-state making and consolidation, but actually central to it" (Vickers 2008, 24). In anti- and postcolonial nationalisms, on the other hand, women were involved from the start: "In many post-colonial countries, women and men became citizens simultaneously . . . and women's participation in national movements often gained them civil and property rights in the new states" (Vickers 2008, 27). Indeed in India, universal adult suffrage came at the moment of independence in 1947 (Sinha 2000; Pearson 2004). Studying India sheds light on complex ways that public and private spheres intermingle to pull women into religious politics in the Global South. My study shows that in postcolonial contexts of the Global South such as India, marginalization is not necessarily the only or even the predominant mode of political interaction between women, religion, and nationalism.

This study also corrects an overwhelming focus on Islam in the study of women/gender and religious politics. Pathbreaking research, such as Saba Mahmood's (2005) study of pious Egyptian women, successfully steps away from Western experiences and conceptual frameworks to focus on Global South contexts. Yet undue emphasis in the broader literature on just one religion—Islam—constructs it as somehow especially oppressive of women (Inglehart and Norris 2003). Studying Hindu nationalism and democracy in India through the lens of gender broadens the focus beyond women and Islam to explore the role of women in religious politics more generally.

Terms and Definitions

The terms I use to capture and convey the meanings of women's participation in Hindu nationalist politics correspond to the three time periods I focus on. For the first time period, I call the general failure to conceive of women as political subjects a model of *marginalization*. I selected this term because of its implications of deliberate intent, suggesting that leaders of the Hindu Mahasabha in the early 1900s—all men—did not simply forget or benignly neglect to think about women. One woman, whose activities I document in Chapter 4, persistently implored them to pay attention to women, and they just as persistently ignored her. Expressions of gender ideology in this period shed light on why the Hindu Mahasabha leaders could not or did not make women part of their political calculations. This cannot be ascribed to innocent oversight; rather it signals the deliberate intent that is conveyed by the term *marginalization*.

I use the term *mobilization* to capture the approach of the 1980s and 1990s. The gendered mobilization I elaborate in Chapter 2 comprises three constitutive prongs: deploying gendered language and discourses; challenging feminism's claims to speak for women; and rallying women into the streets. I sought a term that balanced the idea that something was being *done* to women—they were *being* mobilized—and the recognition that the women themselves had agency and chose to come into the streets—to mobilize—in support of the BJP in the 1980s and 1990s.

To highlight the role of women in the BJP today, I focused on the period immediately before and after the 2014 election. I resisted the term "inclusion" because it seemed more deliberately positive than was warranted. Its implications of inclusivity and integration of women, and women's interests and voices, as significant and constitutive in the BJP's decision-making structures did not accurately reflect my findings. I use instead the term *incorporation* to convey the contemporary role of women in the party's structures and activities. Amrita Basu (1998) has argued convincingly that religious communalism—which Hindu nationalism and the BJP represent—can create limited spaces for women's participation. It is these limited spaces that I call incorporation. This term conveys the sense of something "outside" being "brought" (actively) in—yet it retains the sense of outside and inside as remaining distinct from each other, not becoming one and the same thing. To "incorporate" being defined variously as "to take in or include as a part or parts, as the body or a mass does," or to absorb, assimilate, or subsume,[8] conveys this sense.

The issue of women's agency has been a vexed one for feminist scholars and activists focusing on women's participation in Hindu nationalist politics. The idea that women's participation in Hindu nationalist politics—including antiminority and often violent politics—could empower or liberate women remains anathema to feminist scholars and activists. But to assume that women who participate in BJP and Hindu nationalist politics "don't know" or "don't realize" what they're doing is of course to deny them agency. None of the dozens of Hindu nationalist women leaders I met or interviewed in the course of my fieldwork ever seemed anything but clear-eyed about what it meant to be involved with the party; they did not at all seem "duped," as a nonagentic view might suggest. I do not claim that my study or my terms resolve whether women's participation in regressive, conservative, religious, and often violent politics can or cannot be empowering for women. Rather, with Mahmood (2005) I hold that even to pose the question this way defines empowerment—and thus agency—primarily in terms of resistance. Instead, I seek to uncover and understand what their participation in the movement means to these women and for the party, and what it can show us about the changing role of Hindu nationalism in Indian democracy.

Materials and Methods

I use qualitative and quantitative data and mixed methods—empirical interpretive, descriptive quantitative, and qualitative—to carry out this study. While excavating quantitative data for purposes of descriptive understanding, I employ qualitative and interpretive data and methods to capture forms and meanings of women's political participation that quantitative approaches alone can't. Fieldwork was completed at two sites in India—the capital, New Delhi, and Lucknow, the capital of the northern state of Uttar Pradesh—over the course of four extended trips to India between 2010 and 2016. Uttar Pradesh is the largest state in India and the heart of the "Hindi belt," a cluster of 10 states in north central India in which the primary spoken language is Hindi and which constitutes a key support base for the BJP.

As a temporal comparison, each time period presented unique methodological challenges, requiring different data as well as methodological approaches. For all three periods, I collected primary and secondary materials on the party and its activities—including party agendas, meeting notes and minutes, and newsletters; papers and speeches of party leaders; and newspaper accounts of party meetings and other events. For the early 1900s, I analyze new, never before examined archival materials on a women's wing in the formative years of the Hindu Mahasabha. For both the 1980s and the contemporary period, I conducted 20 distinct interviews with BJP leaders in New Delhi and Lucknow. These included two women (one in New Delhi and one in Lucknow) whom I was able to interview before and after the 2014 election, in 2013, and again in 2015–16. In 2013, before the election, I gathered visual campaign materials and attended major campaign events. I have also compiled significant quantitative data on political parties, women candidates, and women's voting patterns over time. I process these materials through close reading and interpretation of primary and secondary documents; descriptive analysis of quantitative data; and content analysis including visual, narrative, and ethnographic analysis.

The ability to match data and methods to time periods and different political and research contexts enabled me to carry out a comparison of this scope. Thus I used archival sources for the Hindu Mahasabha, and interviews, visual analysis, and ethnographic observation for the contemporary BJP. This kind of comparison can be difficult to undertake, a reason why such studies are rare. This is the first study to undertake such comprehensive, temporal comparison of women's participation in Hindu nationalist politics.

This mixed-method, qualitative, quantitative, and interpretive approach enables me to add a depth of understanding that any one approach could not. Matching materials and methods to time periods lets me construct a temporal understanding of women's participation in Hindu nationalist politics and how it has evolved, and to interpret the meanings of those changing forms of participation for the women themselves and for Hindu nationalism in Indian democratic politics more broadly.

The Rest of the Book

The book eschews a chronological organization for a conceptual one. Chapters 1, 2, and 3 lay the foundations of the study in the 1980s and 1990s, the critical period when the BJP first catapulted to national political prominence and women became involved in Hindu nationalist politics in significant ways. Chapter 1 demonstrates that Hindu nationalism did not succeed politically as long as it marginalized women. It traces the historical evolution of Hindu nationalist political parties, beginning with the Hindu Mahasabha—the first political party of Hindu nationalism in the early 20th century—up to the founding of the BJP in 1980. The chapter then presents descriptive data about women in Indian democracy, including election data and voting patterns, contrasting Hindu nationalist parties with other Indian political parties. In the process, Chapter 1 documents the unrepresentative nature of women's participation in the BJP: women active in the party, especially those at upper leadership levels, represent a thin sample of Indian women at large. Hindu women are the overwhelming majority, with just one or two highly visible exceptions; and they tend to be upper caste, mostly northern and western Indian and Hindi speaking, as well as urban, middle to upper middle class, and educated.

Chapter 2 presents a new framework to understand and analyze the participation of women in Hindu nationalism in the 1980s and 1990s: gendered mobilization. Gendered mobilization comprises three interrelated prongs: deploying gendered discourses about women's rights and women's issues; challenging feminism and its claim to represent or speak for Indian women; and rallying women into the streets. These three prongs of gendered mobilization are analyzed through three critical controversies of the period: a controversy over multicultural protections for minority religious (Islamic) law; a controversy over a modern-day case of sati;[9] and the temple-mosque controversy alluded to at the beginning of this chapter. These controversies underpinned the BJP's ascent to national political power during this period and reflected the increasing politicization of religion in Indian democracy. Yet in terms of its gender ideology, women leaders of the party tended to be those who were desexed in various ways (as celibate renunciates or widows), without significant family responsibilities in the domestic sphere.

Chapter 3 excavates scholarly and activist responses to the gendered mobilization of the 1980s and 1990s to show how women's participation in Hindu nationalist politics—including violence—got constructed as both novel and counterintuitive. Based on these assumptions, the interdisciplinary literature on women and Hindu nationalism came to center on two key questions: *why* would women participate in such a movement, and could such participation be considered empowering or liberating for women? Answers to such questions were not to be found in disciplinary political science literatures of the time on women and participation, religion and politics, or political parties, because these literatures were asking different kinds of questions. I close Chapter 3 by briefly analyzing my own positionality in carrying out the research that underpins the analyses of Chapters 4 and 5.

Tracing women's participation before and after the 1980s shifts the analytical lens away from a primary concern with *why* women participate to understanding *how* they participate in religious politics and what their participation means, for women, for Hindu nationalism, and finally for Indian democracy. Chapters 4 and 5 together place the 1980s and 1990s into historical and comparative perspective by first looking "back," to the early 1900s; and then "forward," to the 2010s. Chapters 4 and 5 present and expound the frameworks of marginalization and incorporation, respectively. I explain how they manifested internally, within the party, through its leadership and governance structures, including the women's wing—what V. O. Key ([1942] 1964), in his classic study, called the party-as-organization; and electorally, examining women as candidates and women's/gender issues in the party platform—in Key's terms, the party-in-the-electorate.[10] Each chapter goes on to analyze what marginalization and incorporation, respectively, meant for women, and what they meant for the party.

Chapter 4 reconstructs the historical role of women in the Hindu Mahasabha. I analyze previously unexamined papers of the party's women's wing and the persistent efforts of one woman, Jankibai Joshi of Pune in western India, to convince party leaders of the urgent need to involve women in the party. Despite Joshi's prescient warnings about the political consequences of ignoring half the electorate, Hindu Mahasabha leaders failed at even token efforts to include women in its structures or activities. I argue that the party's marginalization of women paralleled its political failures; and it reflected a gender ideology that confined women, literally and physically, to the home.

Chapter 5 demonstrates the incorporation of women into the BJP immediately before and after the 2014 elections, through interpretive narrative analysis of interviews with party leaders, ethnographic observation of party events, and visual analysis of campaign materials. The incorporation of women corresponded with the BJP's return to power at the center in 2014. Yet the gender ideologies of party leaders continued to tether women conceptually to the home through the trope of "family support" for women's political activities and the kin-like structures of the RSS.

Chapter 6 concludes by summarizing the key findings of the book and laying out implications of the analysis for how to understand and interpret women's political participation. My analysis suggests that the benefits of incorporating women have redounded more to the BJP than they have to women, as the gender ideologies of Hindu nationalism continue to tether women to their roles in the home and family. My study thus suggests that participation in Hindu nationalist politics is an unlikely path to empowerment for women in the Indian context.

Ultimately, my analysis shows how Indian democracy has negotiated the religious politics of majoritarian Hindu nationalism. Its continued capacity to engage religious politics will be a critical gauge of the institutionalization and resilience of Indian democracy itself. Does my analysis mean that the BJP's ability to gain support for Hindu nationalism is evidence of the resilience of democracy? Or does it demonstrate the erosion of democracy that results from the BJP's undermining of minority rights? My answer is both: while the BJP's ability to gain support from Hindu nationalist women is evidence of the resilience and adaptability of *electoral* democracy as a process, ultimately the BJP's attacks on secularism and minority rights have altered the substantive nature of Indian democracy, reducing it to elections to sustain a minimal definition of democracy without the civil rights and liberties that make those elections, and democracy itself, meaningful. To explain this claim requires covering the basic facts and background of Hindu nationalist politics, which I undertake in the next chapter.

1
Of Histories and Numbers
Hindu Nationalist Political Parties and Women

This chapter lays the groundwork for subsequent analyses by tracing a genealogy of Hindu nationalist political parties followed by quantitative data on women as candidates and voters. I focus on the peak national political organizations of Hindu nationalism in the chronological order in which they succeeded each other: the Hindu Mahasabha, the Bharatiya Jana Sangh (known simply as the Jana Sangh), and today's Bharatiya Janata Party (BJP). These organizations were and are "national" not because their reach stretched across the territory that comprised India during the time they operated. Indeed, an important part of laying out the historical background of these political parties is precisely to analyze their geographical and regional grounding. Rather, "national" here signifies an intent of scope: these organizations purported to represent or speak for Hindus across India without attention to regional differences.[1] The aspiration to speak for all Hindus set apart the organizations I focus on, and might even be considered their constitutive characteristic, or their sine qua non: trying to patch together a "unified," organized Hindu community, eliding or violently obliterating distinctions of caste, sect, region, and language, was precisely their objective.

The first part of the chapter constructs a historical account of Hindu nationalist political parties, relying on close reading of key primary sources, including party documents, the papers of party leaders, and media accounts, as well as secondary sources covering the different parties. Part of the reason to sketch the historical development of these Hindu nationalist parties is to simply lay out the basic names, dates, and events that underpin the arguments to come in subsequent chapters. But it is also to trace a genealogy of sorts, to understand how a specifically political Hindu nationalism evolved and developed vis-à-vis the broader Hindu nationalist movement, and also vis-à-vis Indian democracy and the Indian political system. Of course an important premise of the book is that Hindu nationalist *politics* is not coeval with Hindu nationalism as a social movement—it is an important part of it but not identical to it, and indeed the political parties of Hindu nationalism have at different times had differing levels of disagreement over strategy, approach, and tactics. In fact, we will see in the next section that Hindu nationalism as a social movement initially disavowed politics, and only evolved over time to participate in politics through a political party.

The second part of the chapter lays a numerical foundation for subsequent chapters. I examine quantitative data on women as voters and as political candidates in Indian democracy over time more broadly, and also focus specifically on the BJP where possible in comparison to other political parties. The data for my analyses of voting trends and women's political candidacies have been culled from a range of primary sources, including primary election data from the National Election Studies (NES) carried out by the Center for the Study of Developing Societies in India (CSDS; a premier research institute that has been tracking and gathering Indian voting data since the 1990s); reports of the Indian Election Commission (the nonpartisan body responsible for running Indian elections); and secondary sources that analyzed these data and data from the Census of India.

The historical background and quantitative data, I argue, tell complementary stories about the changing role and participation of women in Hindu nationalist politics. The historical and genealogical story shows how Hindu nationalist politics lagged the growth and development of Hindu nationalism as a social movement: Hindu nationalism as a specifically political project did not fully take off until several decades after the social movement wing had established itself. The numerical story shows how the participation of women provides an important lens into the evolution of Hindu nationalist politics in Indian democracy overall. It does so by paralleling and highlighting broader trends. Both these forms of data—historical and numerical—are integral to the interpretive analyses of subsequent chapters. As argued in the introduction, the historical background or numerical data can tell us, for example, how women voted by party in a given election, but cannot unpack the meaning of gendered campaigns or discourses that mobilized men and women into the streets in support of the movement or into a voting booth to vote for a party. Subsequent chapters will undertake the latter; the remainder of this chapter lays out the former.

Hindu Nationalist Political Parties: What Does History Tell Us?

The political parties of Hindu nationalism evolved chronologically, each the successor of its immediate predecessor. As such, the parties evince both significant continuities with each other as well as distinct differences. In this section I seek to convey both the continuities between the parties and the notable differences between them and the political contexts in which they operated. This genealogy reveals three aspects of Hindu nationalist political parties that are critical to the analyses of subsequent chapters. The first is the continuity between the Hindu Mahasabha, the original political party of Hindu nationalism in the early 1900s, and the BJP, which is the political party of Hindu nationalism today. The second is the "bridging" character of the middle party, the Jana Sangh—which, while an important aspect of the evolution of Hindu nationalist political parties overall, played only a limited role in the evolution of women's participation in Hindu nationalist politics and thus does not constitute a separate case or chapter in the analyses to come. Third, and finally, this genealogy shows how the political wing of Hindu nationalism lagged behind the social movement wing, and did not begin to catch up until it began mobilizing women.

Figure 1.1 shows both the continuity and the separation between the political parties of Hindu nationalism. The graph shows Lok Sabha seats won by each party—the Hindu Mahasabha, the Jana Sangh, and the BJP—in national elections from the first election in 1951–52 through the most recent election in 2019. Figure 1.1 clearly shows that each political party has been more successful than its predecessor. The following pages will analyze the electoral failures of the Hindu Mahasabha, the status of the Jana Sangh as a "bridge" party and its dissolution as a separate party in 1977, and the establishment and subsequent political successes (as well as intermittent failures) of the BJP from 1980 on.

Figure 1.1 thus illustrates a key part of the story of Hindu nationalism as a specifically political formation: its fitful path to political prominence. Rather than a single, continuous upward line, Figure 1.1 shows a series of disjointed lines with notable gaps and falls over time. While the popularity of Hindu nationalism as a social movement has been frequently seen and described by observers and analysts as experiencing steady growth over time, the same cannot be claimed for Hindu nationalist politics. Hindu nationalist politics has had to establish itself, in a series of fits and starts, both as an important

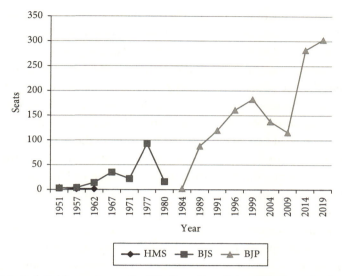

Figure 1.1 Lok Sabha seats won by Hindu nationalist political parties (national elections, 1951–2019)
Source: Compiled by the author.

part of the Hindu nationalist social movement and as a viable political contender on the national level as a political party. There were critical junctures when Hindu nationalism as a political enterprise may have been in danger: in the first decade and a half of independent India, when neither the Hindu Mahasabha nor the Jana Sangh saw significant or sustained political success, and again between 1977 and 1980, when the Jana Sangh was dissolved—by its own decision—into the Janata Party and ceased to exist as a separate party. The story of women's participation in Hindu nationalist politics tracks with the lines in the figure: Hindu nationalist politics was weakest when women were marginalized, in its formative years, and tracked its steepest upward trajectories when women were mobilized and incorporated—in the 1980s and 1990s and the 2010s, respectively.

The Hindu Mahasabha

The genesis of organized Hindu nationalism lay in the formation of regional associations (or sabhas) at the turn of the twentieth century in the Punjab province of northwestern India, where Hindus were economically dominant but Muslims comprised a large numerical majority. The Punjab Hindu Sabha was founded in 1907 in reaction to local and regional events that converged to produce a growing sense of unease among some Hindu communities about the rise of Muslim identity politics and sparked the beginnings of Hindu consciousness in northern India. The most important such event was the founding of the Muslim League, across the subcontinent in the northeastern province of Bengal in 1906. The founding of the Punjab Hindu Sabha spurred the creation of parallel organizations in other provinces; from these regional beginnings the first All-India Conference of Hindus was held in April 1915 and is officially recognized by the Hindu Mahasabha as its first annual conference (Gordon 1975; Baxter 1969).

The Hindu Mahasabha was singularly unsuccessful as a political party from its very inception. Indeed, in the beginning, it wasn't even meant to function as its own party but as a subgroup or pressure group within the Indian National Congress. Most of its annual meetings until 1937 were held in conjunction with the annual meetings of the Congress, and many influential Congress members also attended and participated in the activities of the Hindu Mahasabha. Mahatma Gandhi spoke at the founding meeting of the Hindu Mahasabha in 1915. Dr. Rajendra Prasad, a key Congress leader who became the first president of independent India, was also involved with the Hindu Mahasabha through the 1920s. Lala Lajpat Rai and Madan Mohan Malaviya both served as president of both organizations at different times.

During the 1920s the Hindu Mahasabha slowly changed to a more rigidly communal[2] outlook and began to separate from the Congress Party. This was the period when Hindu nationalism acquired its distinctive features and codified the core of its ideology. During this period, the Hindu Mahasabha did obtain sporadic electoral success through negotiated alliances with other parties (Gordon 1975). But it never achieved sustained electoral success on its own, outside of such alliances. The Hindu Mahasabha formally split from the Congress Party in 1937, with the ascendancy of Vinayak Damodar ("Veer") Savarkar to the presidency of the Hindu Mahasabha. One year later, the Congress Party decided that dual membership in both organizations would no longer be permitted: if one wished to be a member of the Congress, one would have to resign from the Hindu Mahasabha.

Savarkar served seven consecutive terms as president of the Hindu Mahasabha, from 1937 to 1942, and was by far the most important influence on the party from the time he became president until his death in 1966.

He greatly radicalized its agenda and expanded its base of support and operations from north to central and western India. Savarkar's key tract, *Hindutva: Who Is a Hindu?*, was written in the 1920s and represented the first attempt to forge the ideology of a Hindu nation. Savarkar's presidency certainly raised the prestige of the Hindu Mahasabha, but "neither its organization nor its personnel were suited to the demanding tasks of party-building which it faced" (Jaffrelot 1996, 32). The party's primary supporters were conservative notables and princes, who could not expand the base of the party and "whose conservatism and factionalism hampered the development of the organization" (Jaffrelot 1996, 33). As traditional aristocratic-style local leaders whose wealth and status were often dependent on supporting British colonial rule and rulers, not only could they not mobilize the masses (as the Congress Party proved adept at doing) but they were likely to have been threatened by the very idea of such mobilization.

After the 1937 split with Congress, the fortunes of the Hindu Mahasabha came to depend increasingly on its inconsistent relations with a newly founded (in 1925) social organization, the Rashtriya Swayamsevak Sangh ("National Volunteer Organization," or RSS). The RSS was founded in Nagpur, in northern central India, by a physician, Dr. K. B. Hedgewar. Its mission was to unite and organize Hindus, by instilling discipline and national pride from the grassroots, at the individual level, as the basis of Indian nationalism. The RSS quickly became the organizational anchor of Hindu nationalism and remains so today.[3] The RSS was not a political organization in the narrow sense that it did not run candidates for political office. But this was the only sense in which the RSS was not political—it profoundly affects politics in at least two ways: (a) it provides cadres of manpower support for political candidates, leaders, rallies, and events that it supports, as well as volunteers in local communities who provide support and assistance in the event of natural disasters or riots; and (b) almost without exception, every key leader of the other wings of the movement—most notably for our purposes, the BJP itself—has risen through the ranks of the RSS. Accordingly, they not only are imbued with RSS ideology, but as a practical matter retain close personal and professional ties with the RSS leadership structure.

One might assume that the RSS and Hindu Mahasabha would quickly begin working in close concert to advance Hindu nationalism; indeed some historical accounts suggest early RSS leaders understood the need for an explicitly political wing of the movement even as the RSS itself retained, or precisely so that the RSS could retain, the veneer of being a "nonpolitical" organization. But no such coordination came about. RSS leaders came instead to believe that while the Hindu Mahasabha had the right ideas, "a leadership of conviction and realism with a nucleus of followers has failed to emerge" in the party (Baxter 1969, 56). Lalji Tandon, a longtime leader of the movement, told me in an interview that RSS leaders at that time considered the Hindu Mahasabha "too communal" to be successful as a political party.[4] As the RSS gained in strength, the Hindu Mahasabha declined, and the RSS easily freed itself from the Hindu Mahasabha.

The Hindu Mahasabha's last gasp as a political party came under S. P. Mookerjee, its most capable political leader. Mookerjee officially joined the Hindu Mahasabha in the mid-1930s and served as its president from 1943 to 1945. On August 15, 1947, he joined independent India's first government, under Prime Minister Jawaharlal Nehru and the Congress Party, as minister of industries and supplies. The assassination of Mahatma Gandhi in January 1948 by Nathuram Godse—who had previous affiliations with the RSS and the Hindu Mahasabha—sparked moral outrage against the Hindu Right and strengthened Congress secularists to go on the attack against Hindu nationalism. Although no direct involvement of the RSS or Hindu Mahasabha in Gandhi's assassination was ever proven, the government banned the RSS from 1948 to 1949. The Hindu Mahasabha was placed under severe restrictions, and many of its key leaders—including Savarkar—were arrested. That the Hindu Mahasabha managed to avoid being banned was due in significant measure to Mookerjee's advocacy within the government. After Gandhi's assassination, Mookerjee issued an ultimatum: the Hindu Mahasabha must either curtail its political activities or open its membership to non-Hindus, or he would step down. The Working Committee voted against him, and Mookerjee resigned as president of the Hindu Mahasabha at the end of 1948 (Zavos 2000).[5]

Several basic contradictions inhered in the Hindu Mahasabha that worked ultimately to limit and undermine its capacity as a political party. Christophe Jaffrelot has argued that Hindu nationalism as an ideology has itself been rent by a fundamental tension between a Western, egalitarian conception of the nation, and hierarchical and inegalitarian aspects of Brahmanical culture (Jaffrelot 1996). Internally, the Hindu Mahasabha could never resolve its relationship to reform versus orthodoxy within Hinduism. This was embodied in the tug and pull between two broad factions within the party. One was the Arya Samaj faction, based largely in Punjab, which sought to reform and purify certain aspects of Hinduism, including untouchability and the caste system. The other was the Sanatan Dharma faction, drawn largely from the United Provinces,[6] which represented the cradle of Hindu orthodoxy and resisted any attempts at reformism. This faction favored retrenchment on issues like idol worship, the caste system, and Brahman priesthood, and staunchly opposed any moves to reform the caste system or integrate the lowest castes into mainstream Hindu society. Finally, tensions persisted between the social and political activities of the party, and between its local roots and national aspirations.

The Hindu Mahasabha and its leaders, in hindsight, turned out to be on the wrong side of history on multiple issues. The Hindu Mahasabha rejected Gandhian nonviolence, advocating instead "violence organised and disciplined on modern scientific lines" (Jaffrelot 1996, 46). A circular from a provincial Hindu Sabha summed up how the Hindu Mahasabha saw the forces it had to combat: "The Hindus are faced with triple wars:—(i) Congress (ii) the Muslim League and (iii) The British Government."[7] Notice that of the perceived threats, the British came in last. As a result of communications—and actions—like this, the Hindu Mahasabha was often seen as being pro-British. The Hindu Mahasabha opposed the Quit India movement led by the Congress Party under Gandhi that ultimately culminated in independence in 1947. They refused to accept partition even as it became inevitable: a full four years after Pakistan had become an established fact, in 1951, the Hindu Mahasabha amended its constitution to reflect its goal of establishing a Hindu state and reuniting India, by force if necessary. As a result, "The old style of Mahasabha extremism seemed hopelessly outmoded" (Graham 1968, 337).

In retrospect, the Hindu Mahasabha's failures as a political party seem overdetermined. Along with these many elements, a key failure of the party was its marginalization of women, which was out of step with other major political parties of the time—including secular and other religious nationalist parties as well as its own social movement organization. I expand on these points in Chapter 4.

These basic contradictions and weak policy positions of the Hindu Mahasabha were reflected in its consistently poor electoral performance, both before and after independence. It appears not to have contested the 1934 Central Legislative Assembly (CLA) election, as it had not yet formally split from the Congress. In the 1945 CLA election the Hindu Mahasabha did not win a single seat. The party's performance did not improve after independence: in the first elections of 1951–52, the Hindu Mahasabha won a paltry four seats in the Lok Sabha (the lower house of parliament) with less than

1 percent of the popular vote—significantly less than the 3 percent threshold necessary to be officially recognized as a national party by the Election Commission (Lambert 1959).

The Hindu Mahasabha declined steeply through the 1950s, as secularism strengthened, and increasingly began to function as a small, isolated, extremist group. Although it had the longest record of political activity among Hindu nationalist organizations, its leaders seemed more concerned with rhetoric and agitation than with the hard work and details of party building and organization (Weiner 1957). For these types of reasons, the Hindu Mahasabha never became a significant legislative force on its own. S. P. Mookerjee was the most able leader the organization had seen, but he was driven out. While the Hindu Mahasabha continued (and indeed continues) to exist,[8] it ceased to be a politically relevant player in Hindu nationalism or on the Indian political scene after 1951.

The Bharatiya Jana Sangh

Shyama Prasad Mookerjee, who was driven out of the Hindu Mahasabha in November 1948, would become the founder of the Bharatiya Jana Sangh, the political party that succeeded and replaced the Hindu Mahasabha as the primary political vehicle of Hindu nationalism and was the direct predecessor of the BJP. As a leader of national stature, with a strong following in the critical state of West Bengal, Nehru appointed Mookerjee to his first cabinet as minister of commerce and industry. In April 1950, however, an internal disagreement within the government broke out over the Delhi Pact between India and Pakistan regarding migrants, minorities, and refugees between the two Bengals after partition (Graham 1990, 22–23). Mookerjee resigned his cabinet post in protest and began exploring the possibility of forming a new political party. He approached leaders of both the RSS and the Hindu Mahasabha, securing a qualified commitment of assistance only from the former. From his efforts, the Bharatiya Jana Sangh (commonly known as the Jana Sangh) was founded in Delhi in October 1951, just in time to contest the first national elections. By the early 1960s, key Hindu Mahasabha leaders and thousands of members had left the Hindu Mahasabha to join the Jana Sangh (Graham 1990).

Unlike the Hindu Mahasabha, the Jana Sangh saw its electoral performance grow every year between 1952 and 1977 (with the exception of a slight decline in 1971; see Figure 1.1). In the early decades after independence, no party could challenge the electoral dominance and genuine popularity of the Congress Party machine. But Bruce Graham, who charted the most detailed political history of the Jana Sangh, argued that the party faced three particular handicaps: its link to and dependence on the RSS; its reputation for extremism and intolerance; and its obscure leadership, which after the death of Mookerjee in December 1953 had no national reputation or standing at all in the shadow of those who had led the movement for independence (Graham 1990, 53).

Even with these handicaps, however, the Jana Sangh's electoral performance was noteworthy and certainly exceeded that of the Hindu Mahasabha. India's first general election was held in 1951–52, just months after the party was founded. Even in this first election, with so little time to prepare, the Jana Sangh outperformed the Hindu Mahasabha: it won 3.06 percent of the popular vote (just above the 3.0 percent threshold set by the Election Commission to be recognized as a national party), nominated candidates for 94 seats and won three of them, seating three members of parliament (MPs) in the First Lok Sabha. The party incrementally increased these numbers in the second general election of 1957 and again in the third general election of 1962. By 1964, Congress Party dominance had begun to erode, if only slowly. India suffered a humiliating defeat at the hands of the Chinese in the 1962 Indo-China war; Nehru had died; and Congress lost several state governments and by-elections. At the same time, Jana Sangh leaders had come to accept an idea they had previously resisted: that they would be unlikely to take power on their own and would need to forge alliances with other parties.

In November 1953, the Jana Sangh had faced an internal succession crisis with S. P. Mookerjee's death. In a struggle between M. C. Sharma, Mookerjee's chosen successor, and Deen Dayal Upadhyay, the choice of the RSS, the latter won. Upadhyay's philosophy of "integral humanism" shaped Jana Sangh politics for subsequent decades and is still given token recognition in the BJP today.[9] The Jana Sangh's political peak came in the 1967 election, partly through continued defections from the Hindu Mahasabha as well as a few from the Congress Party (Graham 1990, 233–34). In Graham's words, the "Jana Sangh as an electoral force reached its apogee in 1967 and fell away thereafter" (1990, 240).

Its official end came 10 years later, perhaps ironically, when it finally came to power as the largest single-party contingent of the Janata Party, which formed to oppose Indira Gandhi's Congress (I) government after the

Emergency of 1975–77. The Jana Sangh captured 93 Lok Sabha seats in 1977 and held three cabinet posts in the Janata Party government from 1977 to 1979 (Malik and Singh 1994). To do so, however, the Jana Sangh dissolved itself as a separate party (as did all the parties that joined together to form the Janata Party). Although the Jana Sangh's participation in the Janata Party government brought it to national prominence and cultivated many subsequent top BJP leaders, it also spelled its undoing as a separate political party. The Janata Party comprised a wide range of ideological approaches, united only by opposition to Indira Gandhi's Congress (I) Party. Although Jana Sangh members displayed party discipline and ideological unity, the Janata Party itself was riven by internal factions and power struggles, and ultimately split. In 1980, key members of the Jana Sangh joined to form today's BJP, the political party of contemporary Hindu nationalism today and a linear descendant, via the Jana Sangh, of the Hindu Mahasabha.

Women played some limited roles in the Jana Sangh. One woman, Shakuntala Nayar, served in the First Lok Sabha as a Hindu Mahasabha MP. Her husband was K. K. Nayar, who was known as "an outspoken Hindu communalist and a member of the RSS" (Gould 1969, 62). Shakuntala Nayar served in the Fourth and Fifth Lok Sabhas (general elections of 1967 and 1972, respectively) as a Jana Sangh MP; in between, in 1962 she was elected to the Uttar Pradesh state legislative assembly. K. K. Nayar served with her, also as a Jana Sangh MP, in the Fourth Lok Sabha. Craig Baxter, another important biographer of the Jana Sangh, chronicles some attempts to bring women into the party; but these were limited, halfhearted, and ultimately unsuccessful. The Working Committee, the most powerful body in the party, included no women in 1951 and 1954 (Graham 1990, 29, 61–62). The first woman on the Working Committee was Hirabai Iyer in 1958 (Baxter 1969, 186); that same year, a women's organization for the party, the Mahila Sammelan, was founded and became a regular part of annual Jana Sangh sessions. In a 1958 report, Deen Dayal Upadhyay noted that one-third of the party's rank-and-file members in Maharashtra were women, but the other provinces still had work to do. He called on the party to include one woman on every committee, but consistently failed to fulfill this resolve. In the end, "The Jana Sangh has been very much a men's organization [and] its record of enrollment of women contrasts poorly with the other major parties of India" (Baxter 1969, 186–87).

Ultimately, the Jana Sangh functioned as a "bridge" to what would become the most successful political party of Hindu nationalism, the BJP. Although its electoral performance was certainly better than the Hindu Mahasabha, the Jana Sangh carried forward many of the same contradictions that inhered in the Hindu Mahasabha. As Graham concluded, the party "failed to transcend the limitations of its origins" and always remained focused on issues primarily of interest in the northern states where it was based and failed to expand beyond them: advocating for Hindi as the primary language of the country; the status of postpartition refugees; and anti-Pakistani propaganda and agitation (1990, 253). The party's integration into the Janata Party in 1977 helped many of its key members gain governing experience at the national level as well as national name recognition and exposure; but these benefits redounded to the BJP. Ultimately, despite its improved electoral performance over the Mahasabha, the Jana Sangh remained a "relatively small and marginal" political party (Basu 2013, 81). Whereas the Hindu Mahasabha was the first national political party of Hindu nationalism, and the BJP its most successful, the Jana Sangh was a critical bridge between the two. For these reasons, the Jana Sangh has not been treated as a separate, stand-alone case in this study.

The Bharatiya Janata Party

As noted above, the Jana Sangh members formed the single largest constituency of the Janata Party. The Janata Party was not a coalition; rather, the Jana Sangh officially dissolved itself on April 30, 1977, and the Janata Party formally came into existence the next day, May 1, 1977 (Puri 1980, 248). Because the Janata Party was held together solely by its opposition to Indira Gandhi and her Congress Party, it fell apart within two years. Jana Sangh members were the most disciplined members of the new party, always voting together with each other. The brief stint in power both helped and hurt the Jana Sangh: while it raised the profile of several national leaders of the party, it also spread an image of the party as rigidly adhering to an extreme, chauvinistic, and intolerant Hindu nationalist ideology.

Accordingly, when the BJP was formed as a new party in 1980—with the exact same cast of characters as the Jana Sangh—it initially tried to position itself as the "true" successor of the Janata Party while simultaneously trying to distance itself from the Jana Sangh. Hence the name of the new party, the Bharatiya Janata Party, was a nod to the Janata Party itself. In a "bold attempt to depart from the chauvinistic Hindu nationalism of the Jana Sangh"

(Malik and Singh 1994, 37), the BJP adopted an official policy of Gandhian socialism. The party committed itself to uphold nationalism and national immigration, democracy, positive secularism, and value-based politics, with a focus on uplifting the poor, peasants, and Dalits. This approach was primarily advocated by those leaders from the Jana Sangh era who would come to be tagged as BJP moderates, in particular Atal Bihari Vajpayee.

Over its first decade contesting elections, however, in state- and national-level elections, the strategy of trying to distance itself from more hardline aspects of Hindu nationalist ideology fared poorly. It cost the BJP the support of Hindu nationalism's political base—urban middle classes and professionals in the northern Hindi-speaking states—and also left RSS cadres dispirited and RSS support for the party lukewarm. Prior to the 1989 elections, a VHP-led campaign to build a Ram temple at Ayodhya yielded better electoral results for the BJP (see Chapter 2); and between the 1989 and 1991 Lok Sabha elections, the BJP reverted to a Hindu nationalist ideology. This move entailed ceding ideological leadership of the party's agenda to those leaders from the Jana Sangh era who would come to be tagged as BJP hardliners, led by Lal Kishan Advani. Prior to the 1991 election, Advani launched a *rath yatra* (religious procession), building on the VHP's 1989 campaign. The procession wound about the country for weeks, gathering bricks for the temple as it proceeded toward Ayodhya.

This shift in ideology would come to be constructed as a return to the core aspects of Hindu nationalism, bringing electoral success, in contrast with electoral failures brought about by the party's dalliance with an ideology of Gandhian socialism. As Figure 1.1 shows, the BJP's electoral successes continued on a steady upward trajectory through 1991 as the party (re)turned to Hindutva[10] ideology. But the BJP and the other anti-Congress opposition parties could not break the dominance of the Congress Party without alliances with each other, and the BJP's growing electoral dominance in the northern and western states with its return to Hindutva ideology made it an indispensable part of any anti-Congress alliance.

The BJP's first stint in power at the national level was from 1999 to 2004, when it held power as the primary partner in the National Democratic Alliance (NDA) coalition.[11] This represented the first time since independence in 1947 that a non–Congress Party–led government completed a full five-year term of office. Indeed, BJP leaders considered their term of office so successful that they called elections early in 2004, expecting to win in a landslide. But instead they were ousted, and the Congress Party returned to power.

The accepted analysis of their time in office was that they were constrained from implementing Hindu nationalist agendas by their coalition partners (Adeney and Saez 2005; Chakrabarty 2006). In 2014, however, when the BJP returned to power after a decade in the opposition, it won absolute control of the Lok Sabha on its own. Although it took power with NDA coalition partners, it wasn't constrained by them as it was in 1999–2004. At the time, many observers and analysts argued that the BJP's upset win in 2014 did not necessarily signal widespread acceptance of Hindutva ideology by the Indian people. The party won only 31 percent of the popular vote, and the election results were largely a reflection of the personal popularity of the BJP's prime ministerial candidate, Narendra Modi. Modi himself campaigned less on the basis of his ideological Hindutva credentials than on a record of economic growth (Williams and Deo 2018). This record was premised on the economic success of the "Gujarat model" of development in the western state during his tenure as chief minister from 2001 until 2014.

The question after 2014 was whether the party would move aggressively to implement the agendas of Hindu nationalism. Modi's moves as prime minister suggested an increasing reliance on Hindutva ideology for his governing philosophy (Gettleman and Kumar 2018). During his first term in office, Modi undertook controversial and disruptive economic reforms that some hailed as painful yet necessary and good for the Indian economy in the long run. These included the sudden demonetization announced on November 8, 2016 that pulled all Rs. 500 and Rs. 1,000 notes—the most commonly used everyday notes and especially important for transactions of small businessman, the informal economy, and the poorest sectors of Indian society—out of circulation, ostensibly a measure to crack down on "black" money and thus corruption. This was followed quickly by a major revision of the tax structure in India and the implementation of a standardized Goods and Services Tax that came into effect on July 1, 2017. Other bumps in the Modi government's economic road included economic difficulties faced by farmers (well over 50 percent of India's population) and growing unemployment numbers. These were compounded by controversies over the calculation and release of accurate and reliable economic data by the government, which was publicly accused by over 100 prominent international economists of fudging and hiding economic data.

Based on such economic misadventures—when Modi's 2013 campaign was so focused on an economic agenda—it was anticipated that Modi and the BJP would likely win the 2019 election but perhaps with some reduced seat percentages compared to 2014. Instead, a February 2019 terror attack on Indian troops in the disputed region of Kashmir gave Modi an opportunity to run a campaign focused entirely on nationalism and security issues, which paid handsome dividends: the BJP actually increased its seat count in the Lok Sabha in 2019 (R. Jenkins 2019) (see Figure 1.1). The trumping, by underlying ideologies of Hindu nationalism, of a more secular ideology of Indian nationalism now seems a fait accompli. This shift is coincident with the expansion of India's middle classes, as the country transitions from a democracy focused on and driven by the needs of the poorest sectors of society to a middle-class democracy more akin to the developed democracies of the Western world.

The BJP's initial ascent to national power during the 1980s and 1990s, and its return to power in 2014, traced in Chapters 2 and 5 respectively, were deeply gendered. To lay the groundwork for that analysis, the remainder of this chapter examines patterns of women's involvement in Indian democratic politics, both as voters and as candidates and with a focus on putting the BJP into broader context with other political parties.

Women and Hindu Nationalist Parties: What Stories Do the Numbers Tell?

In this section I draw on primary and secondary data sources to answer two broad sets of questions. First, I consider the BJP's record with women as voters, asking: How has the BJP done with women voters over time—has it increased or decreased its levels of support from women voters, or held steady? And then, how has the BJP done with women voters compared to other parties—has it done better, worse, or the same as other parties? Have these trends changed over time, and if so, in which direction? Second, I consider the party's record with women as candidates. I ask: How has the BJP done running women candidates over time—has it increased or decreased the numbers of women it runs, or stayed the same? How has the win rate of women BJP candidates changed over time—has it increased, decreased, or stayed the same? How has the BJP done running women candidates compared to other parties—has it run them at similar, greater, or lesser rates? Have these trends changed over time, and if so, in which direction?

Praveen Rai categorizes women's political participation into four pyramidal categories: at the top, in the smallest group, are women as legislators (MPs and state-level members of state legislative assemblies); followed by women as candidates, party members, party officials, and party functionaries; then women as campaigners and party "torchbearers"; and the last, largest category, women as voters (2017, 60). She advocates for specific measurement of "women's inclusion in the electoral process . . . as party candidates and single interaction voters" (2017, 60). These are where the most reliable, continuous data are available, and this approach provides a quantitative foundation for subsequent qualitative and interpretive arguments tracing women's marginalization, mobilization, and incorporation in the BJP.

As early as the 1970s scholars argued that in India, "the presence of women at the highest political levels coexists with a generally low rate of overall participation in the political life of the country" (Desai and Bhagwati 1975, 165). If we compare the upper political levels (women as elected and party leaders) with women at the bottom of Rai's pyramid (women as voters), women's political participation has improved at both levels since the 1970s, but more so as voters at the bottom of the pyramid. Indian women's fight for suffrage started with the British partition of the eastern state of Bengal in 1905–8. The demand for women's suffrage was initially raised by the Women's Indian Association of Madras in 1917, and limited voting rights were first extended to select Indian women by the British colonial government between 1920 and 1929. In the 1935 election, gender quotas were instituted—over the objections of women's movement representatives—and 80 women were elected to the national Legislative Assembly. "At that point, India had the third highest number of women legislators in the world, after the United States and the Soviet Union" (Rai 2017, 62; Sinha 2000).

The biggest upsurge in women's turnout levels occurred over the decade of the 1990s. Yogendra Yadav argued that the 1990s was a decade of "governmental instability, rise of coalition politics, decline of the Congress and rise of the BJP." In this context,

> Although overall turnout figures have not increased dramatically, the social composition of those who vote . . . has undergone a major change. There is a participatory upsurge among the socially underprivileged, whether seen in terms of caste hierarchy, economic class, gender distinction or the rural-urban divide. (Yadav 2000, 120)

And within this overall rise was embedded a significant rise in women's voter turnout in Indian elections. Controlling for the fact that there are more men in the Indian electorate than women, Yadav still finds that "compared to men, there has indeed been a significant rise in the turnout among women" since the 1991 election (Yadav 2000, 127).

Subsequent analyses after the 2004 and 2009 elections confirmed these trends, measured in two ways: women's turnout as a percentage of registered women voters and as a percentage of total voters (Deshpande 2004, 5431). The percentage of women voters as a proportion of total voters grew from 42.9 percent in the 1991 election to 48.0 percent in 2004 (Deshpande 2004, 5432), while the gender gap in turnout (the difference between men's and women's turnout rates) dropped from 10.2 percentage points in 1991 to 4.4 percentage points in 2009 (Rai 2011, 51). Empirical analysis confirmed that the pattern of rising women's electoral participation in India from the 1990s on "is solely driven by the dramatic increase in women participation . . . since the 1990s, while men participation has remained unchanged" and "is not an outcome of any specific top-down policy intervention to raise voter turnout of women" (Kapoor and Ravi 2014, 63). Nor was the trend caused by more women registering to vote, but by more women actually casting ballots (Kapoor and Ravi 2014, 65). Thus analysts concluded unequivocally that "there has been a marked increase in voter turnout and election campaigning among women in India" (Rai 2011, 54) and, "Systematically the gender bias in voting is being reduced, over time and across all states of India. Voluntarily, more and more women electors are actually casting their votes" (Kapoor and Ravi 2014, 67).

The trend of rising women's voter turnout rates and the closing of the "gender gap" in turnout peaked in the 2014 election. Kumar and Gupta charted the turnout gender gap for each Lok Sabha election from 1957 to 2014 and found sharp drops through the elections of the 2000s, until by the 2014 election the gap was almost wiped out at a mere 1.46 percentage points (2015, 9) with the "highest female turnout ever, so far, in the 2014 Lok Sabha election" (Rai 2017, 58) at just over 65 percent (ECI 2017, 47).

Scholars spilled much ink trying to analyze the reasons underlying this trend. Kumar and Gupta considered women's self-empowerment (initially proposed in Kapoor and Ravi 2014), socioeconomic development, and interest in politics, ultimately concluding the data didn't provide conclusive support for any of these explanations and arguing for the need to see if the trend persists over time (2015, 17). Scholars also argued that gender alone was unlikely to be the sole factor driving the trend: breaking down women's votes by social group, Deshpande found voting patterns aligned more closely along social status lines than along gender or *across* social group lines, thus concluding that the "data suggests gender has a limited role in explaining women's voting behaviour" (2009, 84).

Within this context, to what extent has the BJP attracted women voters over time and compared to other parties? The prevailing understanding, and what the data have shown to this point, is that the BJP is not as strongly supported by women compared to other parties, and indeed has suffered from a gender disadvantage where women are just not as supportive of the party as men are, or as women are of other parties—in particular, the Congress Party. Beginning in the 1990s, when women's turnout rate first began increasing significantly, scholars concluded that "the Congress enjoys a definite advantage among women voters" (Deshpande 2004, 5433; Heath 1999; Yadav 2003). In 2009 again scholars found evidence for a gender gap in favor of Congress and the left parties (Communist Party of India [CPI] and Communist Party of India–Marxist [CPI-M]), and a gender disadvantage for the BJP among women voters. These studies relied on voting data, together with surveys that asked men and women about issues such as which is the most favored/disliked party; choice of prime minister; satisfaction with government performance; who's better for curbing corruption; should government get another chance. Across all such measures, the BJP faced a gender disadvantage versus the Congress Party (Deshpande 2004, 5433).

In trying to analyze women's support for different parties, analysts asked: of all the women who voted, which parties did they vote for? This has been the traditional definition of the gender gap in voting: "A gender gap is conventionally defined as the difference between the proportion of women and the proportion of men voting for any given candidate or party" (Deshpande 2009, 84). By this definition, the BJP has certainly suffered from a gender gap, especially as compared to the Congress and left parties. Building on Yadav (2003), Deshpande found that voting data over five national elections from 1996 to 2009 showed "a definite bias towards the Congress among women voters" (2009, 83). The gender gap between women versus men voting for the BJP peaked in 1998 at five percentage points (with 28 percent of men voting for the BJP and only 23 percent of women) but declined thereafter to just two percentage points in the 2009 election—with 20 percent of men and 18 percent of women voting for the BJP (Deshpande 2009, 83). However, data confirmed that the BJP's gender gap was not well explained by gender alone, but rather was operating in interaction with "other social indicators like caste, class, education, and locality" (Deshpande 2009, 87). Subsequent analyses

36 MARGINALIZED, MOBILIZED, INCORPORATED

have confirmed that the gender gaps for Congress and the BJP "are marginal if compared to gaps based on social identities like caste, religion and class" (Kumar and Gupta 2015, 13).

What happened to these trends in 2014? The key question for our purposes is whether the support of women voters made a difference for the BJP's victory in 2014. The BJP's losing campaigns in 2004 and 2009 featured declining support from women voters. But in 2014, there was a clear uptick in women's support for the party, and a virtual reversal of levels of support from women for Congress versus the BJP in particular. These trends can be seen in Figure 1.2.

The percentage of women who cast their vote for the BJP together with its allies was a plurality at almost 37 percent. The next largest vote getter among women was the Congress Party and its allies, with a large drop-off to 22.6 percent (CSDS 2017). Thus the BJP improved its own performance with women voters in 2014, compared to its previous performance, in a notable way (Deshpande 2014; Rai 2014).

Another way to measure varying gender support for different parties is to ask: of all the people who voted for a particular party (we can call them party voters), how many were men and how many were women? We can then calculate the gender difference among party voters by subtracting the percentage of women party voters from the percentage of men party voters.

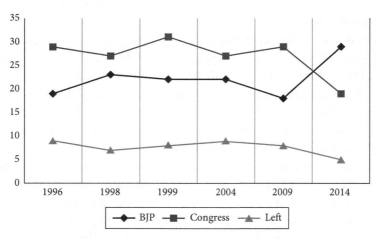

Figure 1.2 Percentage of women voters voting for BJP, Congress, and left parties (national elections 1996–2014)
Source: Data from Deshpande 2009; CSDS 2017.

Focusing on the 2014 election, we observe that of all the people who voted for the BJP, more were men than women: in 2014, about 56 percent of BJP voters were men. Yet this was true for almost all the political parties in 2014: that is, almost all the major parties had more men than women voting for them. The Congress Party, for example, drew its support from about 53 percent men and 47 percent women. Figure 1.3 shows that, defined in this way, the BJP's party voter gender difference was in double digits, at almost twice the party voter gender difference for the Congress Party (12 percentage points vs. six percentage points, respectively). The BJP thus fared worse than the all-India total, at 10 percentage points difference between men and women party voters, while Congress fared better. Yet two parties had an even greater party voter gender difference than the BJP: the Samajwadi Party (21 percentage points) and the Aam Aadmi Party (15 percentage points). In fact, only the left parties (CPI and CPI-M) bucked this trend and drew slightly more support from women than from men: of those voting for the left parties, about 49 percent were men and 51 percent women (CSDS 2017).

Defined either way, these numbers suggest two seemingly contradictory conclusions about women's support for the BJP: They suggest *both* that women have not historically voted for the BJP in overwhelming numbers, *and* that enough women did vote for the BJP in 2014 to have contributed substantially to the party's massive electoral victory that year.

Turning to the participation of women at the top of the pyramid—as candidates in elections, and as party officials—the rise in women's turnout

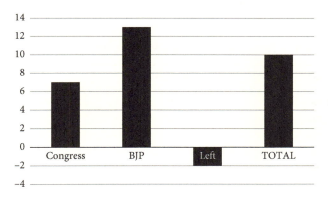

Figure 1.3 Party voter gender difference (men minus women voters for each party), BJP, Congress, and left parties (2014 election)
Source: Data from CSDS 2017.

from the 1990s on has led scholars more recently to argue that rising voter turnout by women is juxtaposed with "continued under-representation of women in legislative bodies and within the rank and file of political parties" (Rai 2017, 58). In the 1960s and 1970s, the representation of women at the highest level of Indian politics included the prime ministership of Indira Gandhi (1966–77, 1980–84) along with the participation of high-level women leaders of the independence movement such as Vijayalakshmi Pandit (Nehru's sister) and Sarojini Naidu. Yet such examples of women reaching the pinnacle of power in Indian politics, even then, did not translate at lower levels. India has long had the notoriety of having globally dismal rates of women's legislative representation at both national and state levels (Rai 2011). The percentage of women MPs in the Lok Sabha never even broke double digits until 2009—India's 15th national election. At the time of this writing, women globally constituted 25.1 percent of MPs,[12] putting India's representation of women MPs, at 14.4 percent after the 2019 election—itself a record in India (Radhakrishnan 2019)—still well below the global average. Table 1.1 shows the percentages of women in the Lok Sabha from 1996 through the 2019 elections.

At the time of independence, quotas based on religion, caste, and gender were debated by the Constituent Assembly, which ultimately decided only to institute quotas for the lowest castes and indigenous tribes. In 1974 came the publication of the *Towards Equality* report of the Commission on the Status of Women in India—which made clear, in numbers, how dismal the representation of women had been in Indian politics since independence. Thereafter, the "demand for greater representation of women in political

Table 1.1 Percentage of Women MPs in Lok Sabha, 1996–2014

Year	Percentage
1996	7.4
1998	7.9
1999	9.0
2004	8.3
2009	10.9
2014	11.4
2019	14.4

Source: Data from ECI Pocketbook 2017, 47; https://data.ipu.org/node/77/data-on-women?chamber_id=13418. Accessed November 3, 2020.

institutions in India was taken up seriously" (Rai 2017, 63; CSWI 1975, 285–305). Since then, Deshpande found that "in all surveys since 1996, people approve of women's reservations and their active participation in politics" (2004, 5435).

After four failed attempts, the Women's Reservation Bill (WRB) finally passed the Rajya Sabha (upper house of parliament) in 2010, but it was never passed in the Lok Sabha and has since lapsed. Praveen Rai argues that "India's failure to pass the Women's Reservation Bill is . . . the most telling testimony about lack of seriousness among political parties in taking better account of women's increasing electoral participation" (2017, 58). Despite popular support, resistance to quotas has come both from within and without the women's movements, with key concerns over how gender quotas would mesh with extant caste quotas, and the associated specter of only elite women being positioned to take advantage of gender quotas if they did exist (Randall 2006a; Rai 2017).

The general lack of support from the major national political parties for running women candidates has been noted by scholars for decades (Sirsikar 1979; Basu 1992; Kishwar 1996). These trends continued into the 2000s and 2010s (Rai 2011, 2017; Deshpande 2004), even in the face of rising women's voter turnout rates documented previously. Thus even if the WRB passed, without a pipeline of women leaders, Ravi and Sandhu argue, India's major national political parties would not be well positioned to take advantage of it, and "its impact would be dubious" (2014, 8). This suggests that the success of the WRB, if it were to pass, would be dependent on the critical role of parties as gatekeepers: if the WRB were passed as things currently stand, it might not make a large or immediate difference; and if parties would give a percentage of tickets to women candidates, then change could come about even without passage of the WRB (Ravi and Sandhu 2014, 13).

It is important to note that even when women run as candidates, they're often not running on a major party ticket. In 2009, just under a third of women candidates ran on a major national or state party ticket; a bit over a third each ran on a "Registered Unrecognized" party ticket or as independent candidates. Indeed, "Since 1989 . . . there have traditionally been more women who run as independents than those who run as part of a political party" (Ravi and Sandhu 2014, 5). My analysis of Election Commission of India data (see Figure 1.4) shows that major national political parties—including Congress, BJP, and left parties (CPI and CPI-M)—have hardly

40 MARGINALIZED, MOBILIZED, INCORPORATED

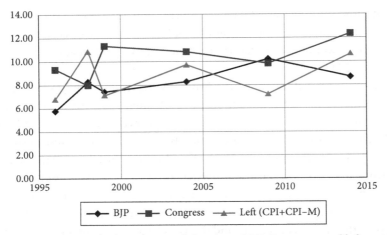

Figure 1.4 Percentage of women candidates run, BJP, Congress, and left parties (Communist Party of India, Communist Party of India–Marxist) (national elections, 1996–2014)
Source: Data from Election Commission of India.

moved out of the range of fielding around 10 percent of women candidates across six national elections from 1996 to 2014.

Ravi and Sandhu noted a significant increase in the absolute numbers of women candidates running on national party tickets in the 2014 election, finding that "nearly 60 percent of this increase is attributed to the BJP alone" (2014, 6). The BJP began to make up its lag behind Congress in fielding women candidates beginning in the 2009 election, when "the BJP fielded 50 percent more women than it did in 2004. This rapid increase by the BJP within two election cycles, helped it to catch up and overtake the Congress in the 15th Lok Sabha election." Yet it remains the case that "all parties are fielding significantly less than the benchmark of 33%" (Ravi and Sandhu 2014, 7).

Figure 1.5 shows the win rates of women candidates running on Congress, BJP, and left party tickets (along with the all-India win rate for women candidates) from 1996 to 2014. For most of this period, women's win rates for all the major national parties were better than the overall rate. Linking back to Ravi and Sandhu's (2014) finding that only about one-third of women candidates run on a major party ticket, this certainly suggests that women who run on a major national party ticket fare better than independents or smaller/unrecognized party candidates. In 2014 women BJP candidates

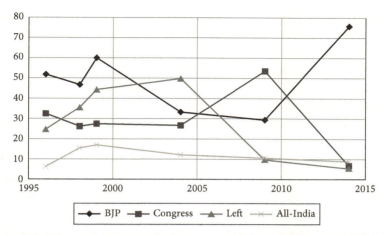

Figure 1.5 Win rate (percentage) of women candidates for Congress, BJP, left parties (Communist Party of India, Communist Party of India–Marxist), and all-India (national elections, 1996–2014)
Source: Data from Deshpande 2004; Rai 2011, 2017.

won at a remarkable rate of 76 percent (28 of 37) while Congress women candidates crashed to a win rate of just 7 percent (four of 57).

In the face of these trends and numbers, subsequent studies have emphasized the role of political parties as gatekeepers, posing obstacles to women candidates running for office rather than facilitating them. Rai, for example, argues that the prevalence of women leaders in internal party governance structures belies the extent of actual power they exercise within the party.

> Though women head a significant number of national and state level political parties as party leaders, their representation within the rank and file of prominent political parties is not in significant numbers. Women who have made their presence felt in inner party structures are also relegated to the second rung leadership and have failed to break the "glass ceiling." They rarely play any role in formulating policies and strategies in political parties and are assigned the job of keeping an eye on "women's issues" that could bring electoral benefits and dividends for the party in future hustings. (2011, 54)

Ravi and Sandhu concur that while many major parties provide for women's representation in their internal governance structures on paper, "these impressive constitutional rules are seldom followed" (2014, 9). On this count they argue that in 2014 the BJP was actually better than other parties. The BJP amended its constitution in 2007 to provide for 33 percent membership of women on all its governance committees, on the recommendation of a committee led by the prominent (late) party leader Sushma Swaraj (Ravi and Sandhu 2014, 10). It also lists the powers and forms of participation of the BJP women's wing, the Mahila Morcha (MM). These include the following:

- The president of the national MM is an ex officio member of the Central Election Committee, which makes the final selection of candidates at the national and state levels. The same is true for state MM presidents on the state election committees.
- The party meets its own benchmark on the National Executive Committee, which included 26 of 77 (33.7 percent) women. And "Women comprise 26% of BJP national office bearers, which is higher than all other political parties in India" (Ravi and Sandhu 2014, 10).

Nonetheless, women remain underrepresented on the Central Election Committee, on working groups, and on the Parliamentary Board—the most powerful decision-making body in the party. Furthermore, "Women are largely relegated to the Mahila Morcha, with no female representation on the Economic, Agriculture, Security, and Legal groups, and only marginal representation in other areas" (Ravi and Sandhu 2014, 10). Ravi and Sandhu conclude that "in general . . . most political parties in India flout the rules of their own constitutions. The absence of women in party leadership positions is indicative of an internal party infrastructure that is unsupportive of women's political participation" (2014, 12). Coming chapters analyze interpretively the participation of women in the internal governance structures of the BJP; these patterns were confirmed in my interviews (Chapter 5).

I also show in coming chapters that in the 2014 election, BJP leaders raised questions about women candidates' "winnability." The idea that women candidates are somehow inherently less likely to win elections has been undermined by the data since at least the 1970s. As early as the 1962 and 1967 national elections, Desai and Bhagwati found that while women's chances of getting a ticket are low, when they do run, they win at remarkable rates (1975, 174). Data from Thukral and Rahman (2014, 227; also ECI 2017, 47) show that over 15 national elections from 1957 to 2014, the average win rate for women Lok Sabha candidates was just over 22 percent, while for men candidates it was about 13.5 percent—and women candidates had a higher win rate than men in every single one of those 15 elections (see Table 1.2).

Rai notes that "political decisions of not allotting seats to women by political parties in national and state-level electoral competitions have been attributed to women's lack of 'winning ability.' . . . However, an analysis of victory ratings of women candidates in Indian general elections as compared with men reveals significantly higher female success rates in the last three general elections" (2017, 66).

Rai further notes that "women's under-representation in the Lower House and the trivialisation of women in political parties lead also to collateral effects when it comes to allotting cabinet berths in the central government" (2017, 66). The first cabinet in independent India included just one woman out of 20 members (5 percent). The BJP government in 2014 set the record with six women out of 23 ministers (26 percent) (Williams 2022b). Even this was a minor improvement that still fell far short of reflecting gender

Table 1.2 Win Rate (percentage) of Men and Women Candidates for Lok Sabha, National Elections, 1957–2014

	Men	Women
1957	32.02	48.89
1962	24.13	46.97
1967	21.33	43.28
1971	18.42	24.42
1977	22.08	27.14
1980	11.46	19.58
1984–5	9.4	25.15
1989	8.62	14.65
1991–2	5.89	11.52
1996	3.77	6.68
1998	11.17	15.69
1999	11.32	17.25
2004	9.8	12.68
2009	6.44	10.61
2014	6.36	9.13
Average	13.48	22.24

Source: Data from Thukral and Rahman 2014, 227.

demographics (Rai 2017, 66). There is also room for improvement in which portfolios are assigned to women:

> Indian women are mostly allotted ministries during cabinet formation which are termed as "feminine" portfolios, such as women and children, information and culture and social welfare, perceived as relatively less important, with fewer resources and reach among citizens. . . . Thus, women active in politics in India are relegated to the fringes in power sharing at the top level. (Rai 2017, 73; see also Kishwar 1996, 2870)

This is not to argue that the portfolios *are* less important; but scholars contend that they are perceived that way as more "feminine" areas and subjects.

Another way to assess the role of women in the BJP across different time periods, which I undertake in coming chapters, is to examine women's issues in party manifestos. Upon working out the intricacies of what exactly is included in the category of "women's issues," Rai argues that "promises by political parties in their manifestos on gender issues remain cliched and are conveniently forgotten after the hustings" (2017, 58). It is possible to trace the BJP's changing stance on issues concerning women by analyzing the party's election agendas across the 10 national elections it has participated in since its founding in 1980 through the most recent election of 2019. This analysis reveals several trends. The first notable trend is the increasing mentions of women and women's issues over time, from a few sentences to entire sections (including multiple sections) focusing on issues relating to women. In concert with increasing word counts, an increasing range of issues are mentioned. Early manifestos tended to focus primarily on implementing a uniform civil code; more recent ones expanded to include topics such as preventing violence against women, education, healthcare, and women as economic actors. There is also some evidence of a growing recognition of the need to have an intersectional approach to women's issues, addressing unique needs of women of disadvantaged and marginalized groups: those that receive explicit mention in more recent manifestos include women of lower castes, lower-income and rural women, and illiterate women (Williams 2019).

Another important trend is the appearance of one consistent issue across all agendas—the establishment of a uniform civil code—with one single exception: the 2014 manifesto. That year was unlike the others in multiple ways: the party "crowd-sourced" the manifesto, and it was not released until the day that voting started. The party stated that it was delayed in releasing the agenda because party leaders were busy campaigning, but there were reports that the delay was due to Modi's hand in shaping the agenda. Reports were that he wanted more emphasis on economic rather than cultural/Hindu nationalist wedge issues (of which the uniform civil code is a prime example), which if true, could account for the onetime disappearance of the issue from the party manifesto that year. When the uniform civil code reappeared in the 2019 manifesto, it had moved to "last place" in the agenda—it was literally the last item to be mentioned, and separated from the other sections of women's issues. It doesn't make sense to overinterpret this shift: it could mean declining importance of the issue to the party, or it could mean the issue remains important enough that the party wanted it to be the "last word" of the manifesto.

Holding an absolute majority in the Lok Sabha since 2014, the BJP has implemented some policies relating to women's issues.[13] But it has not pursued major policies that feminists support (such as gender quotas), or those that feminists oppose (such as the implementation of a uniform civil code)—despite itself having advocated both these policies consistently over time. The BJP has supported gender quotas in its election manifestos since 1984. Senior women BJP leaders I interviewed before the 2014 election averred that implementing gender quotas was a top priority for the party.[14] In 2014, and again in 2019, despite overwhelming majorities in the Lok Sabha, the party did not (re)introduce the WRB. Nor has the BJP done anything to implement a uniform civil code, which BJP election manifestoes have advocated consistently since 1991 (with the exception, as noted, of 2014).

* * *

The task of this chapter has been to lay the groundwork for the analyses to come through two basic frameworks: one historical and the other numerical. The historical section traced the relevant names, dates, and timeline of events that constitute the background to the origin and evolution of Hindu nationalist politics in India. This historical and genealogical analysis showed how Hindu nationalism changed, and continues to change, both within itself and with respect to the political context in which it operates. Begun as a movement in reaction to the founding of the Muslim League, Hindu nationalism has meant different things to its own constituencies and followers at different times and in different places. While the strands of the movement based in the northern and central parts of the country sought a broader vision of the scope of the movement—one more national, and nationalist, in its aspirations—those emanating from the western parts of the country were more focused on "sons of the soil" goals and agendas. Those who wanted to double down on re-establishing Hindu orthodoxies—including Brahmanical hierarchical social inequalities of the caste system—came from a different place than those with reformist tendencies. And when the more powerful, growing wing of the movement that sought to build a Hindu nation from the ground up, individual by individual and renouncing politics (the RSS), clashed with the organization that had a political set of agendas and connections from its inception (the Hindu Mahasabha), the former prevailed.

Before long, when even the RSS came to accept the necessity of political presence and influence, it founded the Jana Sangh, which eclipsed the Hindu Mahasabha and eventually morphed into today's BJP. But the RSS has not always been able to control the political party of the movement. Divergent incentive structures manifest between a political party that has to win votes in democratic elections, and at times also has to deal with coalition partners who have, and want to have, nothing to do with Hindutva ideology, and a social movement organization that needs to keep its base and membership motivated, engaged, and radicalized. The BJP and the RSS in particular have differed at key inflection points such as first NDA government in 1999 to 2004 (when the BJP's coalition partners restrained it from being able to implement the long-standing agenda items of Hindu nationalism that the RSS wanted to push harder on), and again when considerations of ideological purity versus electability seemed to be coming to the fore during the process of selecting the party's prime ministerial candidate in advance of 2014 election.

Numerical data on women voters as well as candidates, taken as a whole, indicate that the changing participation of women in Hindu nationalist politics is a critical lens for understanding its evolution and its role in the context of Indian democracy. The numbers showed both that BJP continues to suffer a gender gap between men's support and women's support, and that 2014 saw a large uptick in support from women voters that made it seem unlikely that the BJP could have won as big as it did without significant support from women. The numbers also showed that women's turnout, after making major gains in the 1990s that have persisted, shot up notably again in 2014, along with turnout numbers in general in that election. Despite the fact that the BJP did not run exceedingly high or low numbers of women candidates in 2014—remaining, like the Congress and left parties at least since 1996, in the range of 8–12 percent of candidates being women—women BJP candidates in 2014 saw a remarkable win rate of over 75 percent.

To begin to gauge the impact of women and gender on the political trajectory of the BJP and bring meaning to the history and the numbers, I argue, requires an interpretive approach to delve into what different forms of participation in Hindu nationalist politics have meant for women and for the party in different time periods. With basic historical and numerical data in hand, I undertake in the next chapter to delineate these meanings in the 1980s and 1990s, the period when the BJP rose to national political prominence through the gendered mobilization of women in three key political campaigns.

2
Women Mobilized

Three Controversies, Three Prongs of Gendered Mobilization, 1985–1992

As shown in the last chapter, the 1980s and 1990s comprised the foundational period of the BJP's initial rise to national political power, when the party ascended from marginality to viability on the Indian political scene. The participation of women was critical to that ascent. Examining women's participation in the BJP and Hindu nationalist politics in this period lays the groundwork for the analyses to come. Chapter 4 looks back to the early 1900s to gauge women's participation *before* Hindu nationalist politics attained political success. Chapter 5 looks to the 2010s to gauge women's participation *since* it attained political success. In this way the book eschews a simplistic chronological ordering. I start instead "in the middle" temporally, and politically in the "central" time frame when the party first rose to power. In this chapter I argue that the gendered mobilization of women sparked the BJP's initial ascent to national political power in the 1980s and 1990s. This chapter examines what gendered mobilization was, what it meant for the BJP in the 1980s and 1990s, and what it meant for women—both those who were mobilized and women more broadly.

Founded in 1980 from the remains of the Bharatiya Jana Sangh, in the aftermath of the dissolution of the Janata Party (see Chapter 1), the BJP began to increase its popular support from 1985 on. From the mid-1990s on, the BJP in coalition with other parties—some that espoused a Hindu nationalist ideology and some that did not—began winning national elections. In 1996, the BJP for the first time won a plurality of seats in the Lok Sabha (lower house of the Indian parliament). After a series of short-lived governments and multiple elections between 1996 and 1998, the BJP finally garnered enough support to head a coalition government (Malik and Singh 1994): from 1999 to 2004, the BJP-led National Democratic Alliance (NDA) became the first non–Congress Party–led government to complete a full five-year term in office since independence.[1]

There can ultimately be no one simplistic "cause and effect" type of explanation for the rise to national political prominence of a movement that had posted middling political success throughout the early twentieth century. But one key factor was what I call the BJP's *gendered mobilization* of women in this foundational period. Gendered mobilization comprised three analytically separable but practically inextricable prongs. One prong was to *deploy gendered discourses*. This entailed making gendered arguments about women's rights and women's issues; such discourses were deployed in party leaders' speeches and party documents. The second prong was to *challenge feminism*. Hindu nationalist women in this period challenged feminists both discursively—in speeches and in party documents—and physically, as they confronted feminists on the ground. The challenge to feminism entailed co-opting feminist agendas and undermining feminist claims to define women's rights and speak on behalf of Indian women. The third prong was to *rally women*. This entailed bringing (Hindu nationalist) women out of their homes and into the streets to participate in marches, protests, and demonstrations, as well as political violence against minority communities. At the rank-and-file level, women came into the streets, and at the leadership level, women rallied others into the streets. The three prongs of gendered mobilization are deeply imbricated with each other and difficult to disentangle in actual practice.

Between 1985 and 1992, the BJP's gendered mobilization of women manifested in three critical controversies. The first was a controversy over Islamic law and Indian Muslim women's rights to maintenance (alimony) after divorce. The second was a controversy over a modern-day case of sati—the (highly contested) practice of widow immolation on the funeral pyre of her husband. The third was the temple-mosque controversy that culminated in the destruction by Hindutva activists of a mosque in the northern Indian town of Ayodhya in December 1992. Each controversy was deeply gendered in its mobilization of women, and together they catapulted the BJP to national political prominence and into power at the national level.

This chapter analyzes each prong of gendered mobilization through these three controversies. My analyses demonstrate how all three controversies displayed, to varying degrees, each of the three prongs of gendered mobilization. But for conceptual clarity, I highlight one prong of gendered mobilization in each controversy (See Table 2.1.) First, I focus on the deployment of gendered discourses in the *Shah Bano* controversy over Islamic law. Then I focus on the physical and discursive challenge to feminism in the Roop

Table 2.1 Three Controversies, Three Prongs of a Gendered Mobilization Strategy

Controversy	Gendered Mobilization Prong
Shah Bano / Muslim personal law (1985–86)	Deploy gendered discourses
Roop Kanwar / sati (1987)	Challenge feminism
Ayodhya / Babri Masjid (1992)	Rally women into the streets

Kanwar controversy over sati. Finally, I focus on rallying women into the streets, both as leaders and rank-and-file participants, in the Ayodhya campaign to destroy the Babri Masjid ("mosque of Babur") and the communal rioting that followed in its wake.

My analysis is not meant to suggest that each controversy displayed only one prong of gendered mobilization; rather quite the opposite is true. I argue that this three-pronged gendered mobilization of women—deploying gendered discourses, challenging feminism, and rallying women—helped catapult the BJP to national power by the late 1990s. But it should not be mistaken for a strategy to benefit women. The gendered discourses of women's rights that the BJP deployed in the *Shah Bano* controversy were more accurately understood as majoritarian, antiminority—and especially anti-Muslim—discourses. Their challenges to Indian feminism paid dividends for Hindu nationalism by undermining feminist movements that question Hindu nationalist ideology as being beneficial to women, or Hindus, or the nation at large. Hindu nationalist women who rallied into the streets during the Ayodhya campaign and in the aftermath of the destruction of the mosque did not necessarily share in the spoils of the victory; some, indeed, were even expelled from the party.

In the wake of these controversies, feminist scholars and activists questioned whether gendered mobilization into Hindu nationalist politics could be seen as empowering for women (I expand on these debates in Chapter 3). My analysis in this book conceptualizes empowerment as a continuous rather than a dichotomous concept. Conceived in this way, gendered mobilization into Hindu nationalist politics meant increased access to the public sphere for (certain) women. In a society in which the public, political sphere is often strongly masculinized, this was no trivial matter.

Yet that access was circumscribed in multiple ways. It was only available to some women, for limited purposes: in support of Hindu nationalist ideology. At the leadership level, only women without family responsibilities in the private sphere gained access. For rank-and-file women, access was temporary: after coming out to march, protest, or demonstrate, they returned to domestic household responsibilities in the private sphere. Ultimately, the access to the public sphere that gendered mobilization enabled was not transformative for women in that it did nothing to undermine—and even reinforced—underlying patriarchal structures that continued to tether women to their social roles in the private sphere.

The remainder of this chapter proceeds as follows. The next section explores what women's gendered mobilization meant for the BJP by examining the three prongs in each controversy sequentially: the deployment of gendered discourses in the *Shah Bano* controversy, challenging feminism in the Roop Kanwar controversy, and rallying women into the streets in the Ayodhya controversy. The following section explores what gendered mobilization meant for women by expounding the gender ideology of the BJP in this period: it opened up some forms of access to the public sphere for women at the leadership and rank-and-file levels, but that access was constricted in multiple ways and ultimately reinforced rather than undermined the domestic and social roles that continued to tether women to the private sphere. I conclude by considering the patterns and implications underlying these three controversies and the three-pronged gendered mobilization of women into BJP politics in this foundational period.

Catapult, or What Mobilizing Women Meant for the BJP: Three Controversies, Three Prongs of Gendered Mobilization

Deploying Gendered Discourses: Shah Bano Begum and Muslim Women's Legal Rights, 1985–1986

The controversy over the *Shah Bano* Supreme Court judgment represented one of the first instances in which the BJP encountered the political power of gendered mobilization.[2] It brought the party to the forefront of the national political arena, and it displayed, in varying measure, all three prongs of the BJP's gendered mobilization of women beginning in 1985. The controversy rallied women into street demonstrations, marches, and protests, and the BJP challenged feminist claims to speak for women and co-opted feminist issues. Most clearly, this controversy showed the deployment of gendered discourses. In speeches and documents, party leaders made claims about enhancing women's rights and protecting women while seeking to eliminate or undermine multicultural legal protections for the minority Muslim community, thus pitting gender against religious rights. In this case, deploying gendered discourses worked to advance an antiminority agenda under the claim of advancing women's rights.

The controversy centered around the status of Muslim family law in India. Institutionalized under British colonial rule in the late 18th century, India's "personal laws" are a religious legal system in which laws relating to the family (such as marriage, divorce, inheritance, and adoption) are governed by an individual's religion.[3] Based in religion and customary practice, personal laws place women on an unequal legal and social footing with men. Common throughout much of postcolonial Asia, Africa, and the Caribbean, as well as the Middle East, personal laws have been frequently cited as a difficult test case for multicultural policies (Eisenberg 2009; Mahajan 2005; Benhabib 2002; Charrad 2001). In India, the major religious groups that have codified personal laws include the majority Hindu community as well as minority Muslim, Christian, Parsi (Zoroastrian), and Jewish communities. Of these, the most publicly debated and politically consequential have been Hindu and Muslim law (Williams 2006), although there have been issues around Christian law (Roy 1999; Subramanian 2014) as well as Parsi law (Sharafi 2014). At independence, the Indian Constituent Assembly debated whether to continue the system of religious personal laws or abolish them and establish a secular, uniform civil code of family laws for all Indians regardless of religion. Ultimately the uniform civil code was enshrined as an aspirational but nonjusticiable Directive Principle of the Indian Constitution (Article 44), and the religious personal laws were preserved as a form of multicultural protection for religious minorities.

The preservation of Muslim personal law in particular has remained contested by the forces of the Hindu Right (Williams 2006, Chapter 5). Following a couple of legal skirmishes in the 1970s, full-scale controversy broke out in 1985 over a maintenance petition filed by a deserted (and later divorced) Muslim woman, Shah Bano Begum.[4] Shah Bano was married to Mohammed Ahmed Khan in 1932. In 1975, Khan drove her out of their home and later divorced her. She filed a petition for maintenance, and Khan countered that he had already paid her what he owed her under Muslim personal law. The Supreme Court ultimately disagreed with Khan and upheld an award of maintenance to Shah Bano.[5]

The reaction of conservative Muslim leaders to the judgment was swift and negative: they argued that the grant of ongoing maintenance violated Muslim personal law as interpreted and practiced in India, which holds that a man is only required to support an ex-wife for a period of three months after a divorce. They organized meetings, demonstrations, and strikes against the judgment all over the country (Engineer 1987, 12). Initially, the Congress Party government under Prime Minister Rajiv Gandhi (the son of Indira Gandhi and grandson of Nehru) supported the Supreme Court judgment, along with progressive Muslims and women's rights advocates. But as the scale and frequency of conservative Muslim protest continued to grow, pressure on the government increased to find a way to reverse the judgment. By December 1985, the government decided to introduce an official bill that would effectively nullify the Supreme Court judgment by preventing similar judgments in the future. Accordingly, the government sponsored the Muslim Women (Protection of Rights on Divorce) Bill, which stated that in matters of maintenance for divorced Muslim women, the law of decision, when both parties were Muslim, would be Muslim personal law. The Muslim Women Bill was described by opponents and even some supporters as hastily drafted and flawed with respect to classical Islamic law.[6]

The government introduced the Muslim Women Bill, over numerous objections, in the Lok Sabha on February 25, 1986; it was debated in a marathon session on May 5, 1986. Prime Minister Gandhi had issued a whip instructing all members of the ruling Congress Party to vote for the bill, so there was no real question that it would pass, which it did by an overwhelming majority: 372 votes for, to only 54 against. In response to the controversy, public and elite opinion split. Groups that supported the Supreme Court judgment and opposed the Muslim Women Bill included progressive Muslims, feminist and women's rights organizations, and Hindu nationalists. Groups that opposed the Supreme Court judgment and supported the Muslim Women Bill included conservative Muslim leaders and Rajiv Gandhi's Congress Party government (though there was significant internal dissension over the position).

Thus both Hindu nationalists and progressive and feminist groups opposed the Muslim Women Bill, though for different reasons. The BJP argued that the Muslim Women Bill was a thinly veiled and ill-advised attempt to appease the forces of Muslim fundamentalism in India, and that the prime minister and the Congress Party government should uphold the Supreme Court judgment. Hindu nationalist organizations held demonstrations, protests, and meetings to support the judgment and oppose the Muslim Women Bill. High-ranking Hindu nationalist leaders were photographed burning copies of the Muslim Women Bill (Times of India 1986a, 1986c) and BJP leader L. K. Advani called for a Law Commission to be set up to draft a uniform civil code and open it to national debate (Times of India 1986b; Malik and Singh 1994, 111). The BJP called on Prime Minister Rajiv Gandhi to announce that the government would not yield to Muslim demands for separate laws (Engineer 1987, 238–39). In a context in which the Muslim community itself was already mobilized and divided, the BJP's interference in the controversy led directly to Hindu-Muslim conflict over the personal laws for the first time in Indian history (Williams 2006).

Feminist and other progressive organizations had long championed the reform of the personal laws and the establishment of a uniform civil code in order to enhance the legal rights and social status of women. Indeed, the demand for a uniform civil code was first made by the All India Women's Conference in 1937 (Menon 2014). But the elimination of the personal laws and the establishment of a uniform civil code have also constituted a central political plank of the Hindu Right since the 1950s, and BJP election manifestos have mentioned a uniform civil code, or reforming religious laws, consistently since 1991 (with the sole exception of 2014; see Chapter 1). The special target of the BJP's agenda was the minority Muslim community, whose personal laws Hindu nationalists constructed as a special privilege granted to fundamentalist, antinational Muslim extremists. The BJP's position during the *Shah Bano* controversy was widely understood as an antiminority and especially anti-Muslim stance cloaked under the rhetoric of advancing Muslim women's legal rights; their call for a uniform civil code was widely understood as a means to abolish Muslim personal law (Kishwar 1986). For example, K. R. Malkani, a key BJP leader, argued in an interview with me that the most important issue was for Muslims to first agree to give up their personal laws, and then the gender-equitable content of a uniform civil code could be considered (Williams 2006, 182). The BJP's arguments about protecting Muslim women (from Muslim men, and from Islamic law) replicated colonialist discourses of "white men saving brown women from brown men" (Spivak 1988, 296).

In the course of the controversy the Hindu Right wrested discursive control over the reform of the personal laws and the uniform civil code from Indian feminism. Today, progressive and women's rights organizations oppose the homogeneity implicit in the idea of uniformity. In response to the BJP's advocacy of a uniform civil code, feminist scholars and activists began to "move away from 'uniformity' and homogenization, and the statism implied by these terms" (Menon 2000, 92). These organizations now avoid the term "uniform," talking instead of a "common," "gender-just," or "egalitarian" civil code (Menon 2000, 90). And rather than the implementation of a compulsory uniform civil code, they now advocate a range of positions including reforms of the personal laws from within the communities; legislation on areas not covered by personal laws; an optional gender-just uniform civil code; or making the personal laws optionally applicable rather than mandatory (Menon 2000, 84–91).

In these ways, the BJP's deployment of gendered discourses—opposing personal laws and advocating a uniform civil code in the name of protecting women's rights—changed the language around this issue. The *Shah Bano* controversy highlighted this deployment of gendered discourses even as it rallied women into the streets and challenged feminist claims to represent the interests of Indian women. In the controversy over Roop Kanwar's sati, Hindu nationalist and BJP women's challenge to feminism extended to physical confrontations with feminist activists.

Challenging Feminism: Roop Kanwar's Sati, 1987

The controversy in 1987 followed quicky on the heels of the *Shah Bano* case and centered on the sati of a young newlywed in the western state of Rajasthan, in a midsize town called Deorala. Many of the very facts of Roop Kanwar's sati are contested. What is known and undisputed (Bombay Union of Journalists 1987) is that 19-year-old Roop Kanwar was married to Mal Singh in January 1987. In the early morning hours of September 4, 1987, Mal Singh died; later that day, his widow burned to death on his funeral pyre. We know the funeral pyre was lit by Mal Singh's younger brother, Pushpender Singh, a minor of 15 years. Thereafter, the facts and timeline become disputed. It was unclear whether Roop Kanwar ascended the funeral pyre before or after it was lit (Courtright and Goswami 2001, 201), and reports of how many people witnessed the event ranged from a dozen to thousands. It also remains unclear whether Kanwar's sati was voluntary or coerced—indeed the case pointed to the elision of any clear lines between what is voluntary and what is coerced.

By the time police arrived at 2:30 p.m., the sati was done. They later returned with reinforcements and registered a case under Section 306 (abetment to suicide) of the Indian Penal Code (IPC). In order to allow for religious rites to be completed, the police decided to do nothing further on the case until after September 16, although they did arrest Pushpender Singh on September 9. He was released on bail five days later. On September 16 a *chunri mahotsav* (veil festival) for Kanwar took place, despite a state high-court injunction against the event. Cremating a woman's veil after her death is a traditional practice common in the region, but feminists argued that the solemn practice, in a time of mourning, had never before been "celebrated" as a "festival" (Kumar 1997; Kishwar and Vanita 2007).

On October 1, 1987, the Rajasthan State Assembly passed the Commission of Sati (Prevention) Act; this was followed shortly by national legislation along the same lines. These legislative acts came under criticism from both pro- and anti-sati forces. Feminists argued that sufficient legislative provisions existed in the IPC to prosecute those involved with Roop Kanwar's sati—what was lacking instead was the will to enforce them. They also held that the 1987 legislation was actually worse for women than extant legislation, including the 1829 act passed by the British. While the new laws took the step of criminalizing any acts "glorifying" sati, they also criminalized the woman herself for attempting to commit sati (Dhagamwar 1988).

Two movements arose virtually simultaneously in response to Kanwar's sati, each in anticipation of the other. Anti-sati groups, led primarily by feminists, condemned the event and its glorification. Their mobilization and agitation preceded the passage of legislation at the state and then the national level prohibiting any act glorifying sati (the Sati Prevention Act, 1987). Sati had been banned by the British colonial government in 1829, but the new legislation sought explicitly to ban the promotion or glorification of the act. This was a central concern of feminists because in the region of Rajasthan, a woman committing the act of sati is widely revered as attaining divine status; indeed, the state has many temples dedicated to women who committed sati. Feminists did prevent the construction of a temple at the site of Kanwar's sati, but could not prevent the *chunri mahotsav*. A court order banning all "glorification" of the event was meant to include the veil festival, but no politicians or police appeared prepared to enforce the order (Bombay

Union of Journalists 1987). The Bombay Union of Journalists noted that the feminist mobilizations in response to the sati were never as well covered in the mainstream mass media—either English or vernacular—as were the sati itself and government officials' statements and responses to the event, which were often equivocal at best (Bombay Union of Journalists 1987).

The second critical response to Roop Kanwar's sati was that of a cluster of pro-sati groups, key among whom were Hindu nationalists at the state level led predominantly by Rajputs, the ruling caste of Rajasthan. Several scholars analyzed the role of the Hindu Right's intervention to conflagrate a regional/local matter and reconstruct it as a national issue, pitting women's rights against religious rights (as in the *Shah Bano* controversy) (Kumar 1997; Hawley 1994; Oldenburg 2007). The leaders of the pro-sati forces, they argued, were not local actors, suggesting that the pro-sati mobilization was not an organic, grassroots, or spontaneously emerging movement or sentiment. "The pro-sati campaign is not an indigenous product of Deorala. It is based in Jaipur [the state capital]. Its leaders are urban, educated men in their twenties and thirties . . . with contacts in New Delhi also. Thus, they constitute a powerful regional elite" (Kishwar and Vanita 2007, 360). Notably, in this controversy the national-level party apparatus ceded leadership on the issue to the state-level party in Rajasthan, supporting the latter's actions through silent acquiescence in them.

While feminist activists fought legal battles, Hindu nationalists sought victory in the streets: they rallied women and organized marches, protests, and demonstrations of Hindutva women in support of a woman's "right" to commit sati. They argued that when committed voluntarily, sati was a noble ideal of Hindu—especially Rajput—culture and tradition "that very few women have the courage to undertake" (V. Raje Scindia, quoted in Basu 2015, 269). They portrayed opposition to sati as the anti-Hindu response of westernized, city women seeking to suppress simple, ordinary, everyday devout Hindu women who sought simply to fulfill their traditional religious duties and attain salvation for themselves by committing this noble act of self-sacrifice, the ultimate sign of devotion to one's husband.

The Hindu Right's challenge to feminist anti-sati activism took both physical and discursive forms. Feminists and Hindu nationalist women came face to face with each other in the streets of Deorala, yelling and jostling each other. Many feminist activists expressed shock at encountering this rebuke from the very women whose rights they believed themselves to be fighting for and defending. One prominent feminist activist described her shock at being confronted by angry mobs of Hindu nationalist women who not only jeered at the idea that feminists were defending their rights, but argued that feminists were actually trampling on their rights. Another noted that in prior incidents surrounding sati in Delhi in 1983, feminists for the "first time ... had to confront a group of women in a hostile situation" who were advocating for a right to commit sati. For feminists, "Most distressing of all ... was the way in which the [Hindutva women] appropriated the language of rights [and] feminist slogans on women's militancy." This engendered "the humiliating sense of loss which accompanies the discovery that your own words can so readily be snatched and turned against you to serve an antithetical cause" (Kumar 1997, 174).

The literature on sati in general and on this event in particular is extensive. The feminist scholar Ania Loomba has perceptively divided the literature into three broad categories: work on colonial debates over the practice, culminating in the first major legislation passed by the British colonial state to ban it in 1829 (Mani 1998); the work of feminists in the Western academy (for example, Stein 1978; Mazumdar 1978); and "the spate of writings produced in India following the burning of ... Roop Kanwar" (Loomba 1993, 210). Across these literatures, a core theme was agency: did a particular woman "commit" sati or was she subjected to it? From this starting point flowed questions about good and bad satis, punishment and glorification of sati, and the role of the state in regulating sati. Ultimately, one very prominent analysis argued that all the debates over Kanwar's sati devolved into a series of (unproductive) binary oppositions: urban/rural, tradition/modernity, state/religious communities. Pro-sati forces were constructed as rural, traditional, spiritual, and religious; while anti-sati forces got constructed as modern, urban, and pro-state (Kumar 1997, 173).

One scholar has argued convincingly that the two cases of *Shah Bano* and Roop Kanwar, following closely on each other, were linked in multiple ways. Both cases highlighted "the subordinate and insecure status of women within all religious communities" (Qadeer 1988, 33). Both led to protracted legal and social battles and "disturbed the social, political and legal worlds around them" (Qadeer 1988, 31). In both cases, progressive forces waffled just enough in their stance on women's rights to enable an opening for religious, conservative, and right-wing forces to intervene. In the case of *Shah Bano*, the scholar Zoya Hasan argued that the secular Congress Party government shifted its stance—as it moved from supporting the Supreme Court judgment to advocating the Muslim Women Bill—from protecting women's rights, to deferring to the wishes of a minority religious community (Hasan 1998, 76–77). Likewise in the case of Roop Kanwar, scholars noted "how easily the focus shifted from the murder of a widow to the sanctity of tradition and the freedom to practice one's religion" (Bhasin and Menon 1988, 13). A critical difference was that the *Shah Bano* case concerned religious laws and practices of the minority Muslim community, while the Roop Kanwar case concerned a customary practice associated with some parts of the majority Hindu community. But above all, both cases indicated that "fundamentalist forces are capitalizing not upon an event or two but on a persistent feature of the social system: the position of women as second class citizens" (Qadeer 1988, 33), regardless of religion or majority or minority status. And my analysis points to another, critical link between these two controversies: they combined in the mid-1980s to position the Hindu Right to deploy gendered discourses and systematically challenge and delegitimize feminism in India by pitting religious freedom against women's rights.

The campaign around Roop Kanwar's sati, thus, threw into sharp relief the second prong of the BJP's gendered mobilization of women in the 1980s: challenging feminism's claims to speak for Indian women and define their rights, including physically confronting feminist activists. The tactic went far beyond advancing the trope of feminism as a "western import" (Narayan 1997): it proactively appropriated the issues and language of feminism, redefined them in retrogressive terms, and used them to undermine feminism. The Roop Kanwar case also showed the power of deploying gendered discourses and rallying women into the streets. This third prong of the BJP's gendered mobilization strategy in this period was highlighted in the BJP's campaign to destroy an ancient mosque and build a Hindu temple in its place.

Rallying Women into the Streets: Bringing Down the Babri Masjid, 1992

On December 6, 1992, in the town of Ayodhya in the northern state of Uttar Pradesh, thousands of Hindu nationalist *kar sevaks* ("volunteer workers") clambered onto the Babri Masjid, an ancient mosque built in 1527. In the course of several hours they reduced it to rubble, using crude tools like shovels, iron rods, and pickaxes, even tearing at the structure with their bare hands (Momin 2017; Gopal 1991). The destruction of the mosque sparked communal riots all over India in which 2,000 Muslims are estimated to have been killed; the worst violence occurred in Bombay. The BJP's campaign to tear down the mosque—a core plank of its political agendas since its founding[7]—extended over several years and rallied Hindu nationalist women into the streets at both the rank-and-file and leadership levels, including active participation in the religious rioting and violence that followed.

The site of the Babri mosque had been disputed long before Indian independence in 1947. Legend holds that a Hindu king built a temple to Lord Ram, one of the most widely revered of the Hindu deities, on the site of Ram's birthplace. Ayodhya was an important pilgrimage site for Hindus; during Mughal rule, even after the mosque was built on the site, Hindus would come to pray in the compound of the mosque. But the historical and archaeological record confirms only that in 1528, the Mughal emperor Babur built a mosque (the Babri Masjid) in Ayodhya, not that he tore down a temple to Ram to do so. When the British took over control of the territory that included Ayodhya, they put a fence around the site, forcing Hindus to pray on a raised platform just outside the fence. The controversy over the site began to flare up as an issue of Hindu-Muslim tension in 1949, shortly after independence. In that year an idol of Lord Ram appeared inside the mosque. No one has resolved the mystery of who placed it there, but many believers took it as a miraculous event. The incident led to serious Hindu-Muslim riots, which led the Nehru government to lock the compound and ban both communities from entering the mosque. The judiciary confirmed this status quo, which held until the 1980s.

In 1984, the Vishwa Hindu Parishad (VHP, "World Hindu Council"), one of the BJP's affiliated social movement organizations, began a campaign demanding access to the site for Hindus and organized an All Hindu Babri Masjid Action Committee (Malik and Singh 1994, 79–80). Pressure on Rajiv Gandhi's Congress Party government (itself just emerging from the *Shah Bano* controversy) grew, and in February 1986—on the orders of a district court judge—the site was unlocked and Hindus gained access to the compound.[8] Thereafter the VHP launched a campaign to tear down the mosque and build a temple to Ram, formulating a blueprint and a demand for a temple to be constructed on the site (Malik and Singh 1994, 80). In 1990, the BJP, led by then-president L. K. Advani, picked up the VHP campaign and launched a national procession—a *rath yatra*, or "chariot journey"—that began on September 25 in the western city of Somnath and wound its way around the country, to arrive in Ayodhya on October 30 (see Figure 2.1).

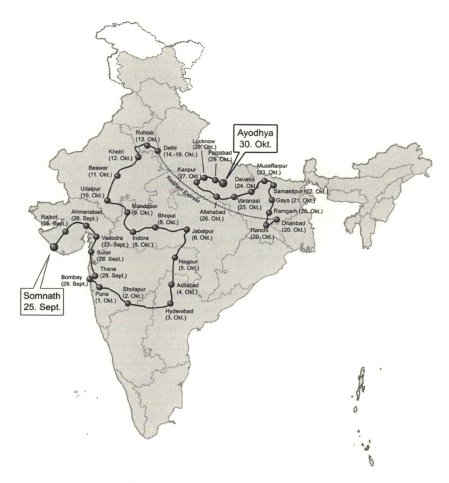

Figure 2.1 Route of Advani's *rath yatra*, September–October 1990
Source: Ludden 2002.

The 1990 procession was stalled by Advani's arrest on October 23, triggering mass protests and communal rioting all over the country. Hindu nationalist activists who had joined or accompanied the procession along its route—or were awaiting its arrival—converged on Ayodhya anyway. On October 30 they tried to storm the mosque, leading to 28 of them being killed (PTI 2019). After this the campaign subsided for a couple of years. Then the BJP won state elections in 1991 and formed the state government in Uttar Pradesh; shortly thereafter the party revived the campaign. On the morning of December 6, 1992, Hindu nationalist leaders and crowds convened at the mosque and by midday had reduced the structure to rubble. After the destruction of the mosque, communal rioting convulsed the country. The worst rioting took place in Bombay, in December 1992 and January 1993. Over 1,000 people were killed just in Bombay, most of whom were Muslims (Burns 1994).

Like the *Shah Bano* and Roop Kanwar controversies, the Ayodhya controversy also demonstrated all three prongs of gendered mobilization. Taped speeches of Hindu nationalist leaders—including women leaders—deployed gendered discourses urging Hindu men to violence against Muslims in order to defend the honor of Hindu women as well as Hindu religion; and the campaign to destroy the mosque as a whole challenged feminist as well as progressive commitments to secularism and the protection of minority rights. Most clearly, the Ayodhya controversy demonstrated the third prong: rallying women into the streets.

At the rank-and-file level, Hindu nationalist women rallied into the streets both before and after the destruction of the mosque. Beforehand, women came out to join, view, and participate in the *rath yatra* as it came through their towns and villages in its winding path around northern India. For Hindu women who were not regularly in the public sphere, "It was easy . . . to mobilize and gather on the roadside as a cortege went by or at the foot of the tribunes meeting after meeting" (Jaffrelot 2011, 336). Women performed religiously inflected dances alongside the procession as it passed through, and some women were seen offering their *mangalsutras* (a traditional necklace that the groom ties around the bride's neck in a Hindu wedding ceremony, signifying her status as a married woman) to Advani along the way. Documented evidence also shows that women were present at the destruction of the mosque as it was happening, though no women were seen physically climbing onto the mosque (Basu 1993b, 44; Sarkar 1993b, 24).

After the destruction of the mosque, in the communal violence that followed and spread throughout India, militant Hindu nationalist women's active participation in the bloodletting was well documented. In Bombay, the site of the worst violence, women were rallied into the streets in particular by the Mahila Aghadi, the women's wing of the Shiv Sena, the local Hindu nationalist party and a close political affiliate and longtime ally of the BJP.[9] Anthropologist Atreyee Sen has done extensive ethnographic fieldwork collecting oral histories of these women, including analysis of their participation in violence. Many of the women who participated in the post-Ayodhya riots were poor women from the slums of Bombay who rallied into the streets through their longtime affiliation with local Hindu nationalist organizations (Sen 2006; Banerjee 1996). Feminist activists and scholars documented that "in the 1993 Mumbai riots women actively took part in looting, assaults, and violent demonstrations" (Banerjee 1996, 1215). Hindu nationalist women attacked Muslim women, blocked emergency vehicles from accessing Muslim neighborhoods, and vandalized Muslim places of business (Banerjee 1996, 1214). In the aftermath of the riots, Sen documented the narratives of some of these women, including "a Hindu woman rioter attacking Muslims in Mumbai" (Sen and Jasani 2014, n.p.). This woman described feelings of "seething" and "anger" against Muslims and the encouragement of her compatriots in the Mahila Aghadi to have *himmat* ("courage").[10] In sum, women rioters in the aftermath of Ayodhya brought to the fore "poor women's contribution to communally charged public protests, street fights and open looting" (Sen and Jasani 2014, n.p.).

The Ayodhya campaign also rallied Hindu nationalist women at the leadership level; indeed, the controversy forged the rise to leadership of several women in the movement. The most prominent of these were Sadhvi Rithambara, Uma Bharati, and Vijaya Raje Scindia. Amrita Basu, the preeminent political scientist and scholar of women in Hindu nationalism, interviewed Bharati and Scindia in the early 1990s and outlined the leadership roles they took in the Ayodhya movement. The three women came from different backgrounds: Scindia, an older woman and a widow, came from a wealthy royal family and joined the BJP after many years as a Congress Party stalwart (for a detailed account of Scindia's political trajectory, see Chapter 4). Bharati and Rithambara, conversely, were both from rural, lower-caste, and poor backgrounds, and the Ayodhya controversy catapulted both of them to leadership roles in the BJP. Both were (and are) unmarried ascetic renunciants. Rithambara's voice is widely understood as "the single most powerful instrument for whipping up anti-Muslim violence" (Sarkar 1993a, 16) in the run-up to the demolition of the mosque. Cassette tapes of her virulent speeches were played at VHP temples and in public locations throughout north India in the months leading up the demolition. Uma Bharati was nominated to run as a BJP candidate in parliamentary elections, winning seats and serving in the Lok Sabha from 1989 onward. The Liberhan Commission (2009) indicted her for inciting the mob on that day; she admits she was there and does not apologize for her presence but denies the specific charge of inciting mobs. Thus evidence of the Ayodhya campaign at both the leadership and rank-and-file levels illustrates how women rallied into the streets—and rallied others, men and women alike, to join them—as a critical prong of the BJP's gendered mobilization of women in this period.

Tethered, or What Their Participation Meant for Women: Limited Access and Women Without Family Responsibilities

There is little doubt that the primary beneficiary of gendered mobilization in the 1980s and 1990s was the BJP itself. These three controversies, in which the BJP deployed gendered discourses, challenged feminism, and rallied women into the streets, were critical in catapulting the BJP to national prominence and to its first stint in power, from 1999 to 2004. What was the gender ideology underpinning the party's gendered mobilization in this era? The scholar Nandini Deo has argued convincingly that Hindu nationalism does not have a clear or consistent gender ideology, but reverts to whatever is politically expedient in a given context (Deo 2014). My analysis certainly supports this contention, and further specifies how the party's gender ideology looked different in each of the time periods I compare, to shed light on what women's participation in Hindu nationalist politics meant for them in different time periods.

In the 1980s and 1990s, the party's Hindu nationalist ideology stood in tension with the BJP's growing understanding that in order to be (or appear to be) a modern, competitive party in a competitive democracy, it needed the support of women. In the 1980s and 1990s, this tension was negotiated (though not resolved) as women claimed and gained access to the public sphere. Indeed I would argue that this was the primary benefit to women—and only to certain, Hindu nationalist women—of gendered mobilization in this period: greater access to the public sphere. Where the public sphere is still strongly masculine, this is not a trivial gain. Yet it is also not transformative, as their access was limited and remained tethered to women's social roles in the private sphere. For rank-and-file Hindu nationalist women, access was transitory: entry into the public sphere was followed by a return to everyday domestic duties and the strictures of the private sphere. For women at the leadership level, access was mediated by social structures (of widowhood and ascetic renunciation) that freed women from primary responsibilities in the private spheres of home and family. For these women, the movement and the Hindu nation became their surrogate family, to whom their duties and responsibilities became tethered. And these limited benefits accrued only or primarily to women who advocated Hindu nationalist ideology.

Access to the public sphere was constricted differently for Hindu nationalist women at the rank-and-file and leadership levels. For rank-and-file women, mobilization was not ongoing and continual. They could, and did, come out for rallies or processions or even participate in communal violence, and then returned into their homes to carry on day-to-day family responsibilities. This is not to say that their support for the party or for Hindu nationalist ideology was locational or sporadic, but rather that their actual active presence in the public sphere did not occur (and did not have to occur) continually.

At the leadership level, women's participation in the BJP in the 1980s and 1990s was limited to women who lacked any significant family responsibilities. Uma Bharti, Sadhvi Rithambara, and Vijayaraje Scindia were public, well-known, and identifiable faces of the movement through this period. The first two were celibate ascetic renunciants and the third was a widow. Amrita Basu argued that for these women, "their chastity heightens their iconic status for it is deeply associated in Hinduism with notions of spirituality, purity, and otherworldliness" (Basu 1993a, 27). The fact that these women were celibate had cultural resonance with renunciation as a moral and spiritual force in India, wherein an "ascetic lifestyle...connotes sacrifice, martyrdom, and selflessness" (Basu 1993a, 28).

Yet even women BJP leaders remained tethered to social roles in the private sphere. In the first place, it was their very *social* status of renunciation and widowhood that boosted their power and access to the public sphere. Basu notes two additional key characteristics, conjoined with celibacy, these three women shared: they were all financially independent of men, and relatedly, "None of their identities are defined by their roles as wives and mothers" (Basu 1993a, 30). It was precisely the absence of active roles as wives and mothers that underpinned the "the dazzling visibility of that triad of women" (Sarkar 1993a, 18) and the power of their voices in the public sphere and in the movement.

In the second place, for Hindu nationalist women, the nation itself, defined as Hindu, became their family or came to stand in as family. For example, Kamlabehn, a Hindu nationalist woman leader who was interviewed by the sociologist Paola Bacchetta, "has reduced her familial responsibilities to a minimum in order to devote more time" to the cause. Kamlabehn noted that her middle-class Hindu neighborhood is itself "like a family" (Bacchetta 1993, 42) and that she sees herself as married to the movement and to the nation. Bacchetta described this as "choosing independence through celibacy, dedication to other women . . . and an ideal (the Hindu nation) in place of dedication to an individual male" (Bacchetta 1993, 43). Bacchetta argued that Hindu nationalism provided a space for Hindu women's participation that allowed them to escape normal social constraints and to do so not only without sanction but even with approval—"as long as their demands are formulated not in terms of themselves, but rather in terms of self-sacrifice in the service of a higher cause, the Hindu nation" (Bacchetta 1993, 46).

This limited empowerment of women leaders in the BJP in particular is exemplified by the case of Uma Bharti. After her meteoric rise to power in the Ayodhya controversy, she was kicked out of the party, only to be rehabilitated and brought back in. Originally mentored and brought into politics by Vijayaraje Scindia in their home state of Madhya Pradesh, Bharti won election to the Lok Sabha on a BJP ticket in 1989. Then, as noted above, her role in the Ayodhya controversy launched her into the leadership ranks of the BJP. Her fiery speeches were noted for boosting the momentum of the controversy (Liberhan Commission 2009). Bharti's power in the party peaked in 2003, when she was the BJP's chief ministerial candidate for elections in Madhya Pradesh, where she led the party to a resounding victory and served as chief minister for a year. Thereafter, though, she increasingly clashed with BJP leadership and Advani in particular, for which she was suspended and then expelled from the party in 2004.

After the destruction of the mosque, the *Bulletin of Concerned Asian Scholars* (Basu 1993b), as part of a pathbreaking issue on the topic of women's participation in Hindu nationalism, reprinted a widely circulated photograph of Uma Bharti and L. K. Advani at the site of the mosque, along with an editorial arguing that women such as Bharti were being used by the movement for its own purposes, would not benefit from it, and would be cast aside as soon as their utility expired. It argued that women in the movement would only be given access to the "leftovers" of religious power, and that the status of women in the movement lasted only "as long as you remain a woman, a surrendered tool in the male order." The piece ended by asking of Bharti, "How long will you allow yourself to be used in this absurd, irrational blood bath?" (Basu 1993b, 52).

My analysis departs from an implication that women were "used" or "tools" without agency. But the editorial proved prescient in its suggestion that the party would eventually cast Bharti aside. Already at the time the article was published, Bharti had been involved in a flap with party leadership over the nature of her relationship with K. N. Govindacharya, at the time a rising star in the party. The 1993 *Bulletin* article mentions this, asking, "Have you forgotten, Uma, the Govind Acharya episode, when you were accused of having an affair with this leader of the Bharatiya Janata Party? Didn't they tell you that you were not a religious crusader, you were only a woman?" (Basu 1993b, 52). Bharti's expulsion from the BJP in 2004 made prescient some of the remarks in the article:

> Try one day to assert your independent will . . . against the wish, interest, and honor of the masters. . . . Then you will see where they will place you. One word of a man will tell you what your standing is, and you will find yourself out of the house. (Basu 1993b, 52)

Bharti's expulsion lasted seven years; the BJP brought her back in 2011, in time to help contest the 2014 election by reviving the party's fortunes in the key state of Uttar Pradesh and especially to facilitate outreach to upper and nonruling middle castes in the state (Economic Times 2011). After the BJP's national election victory in 2014 she served as a minister of state in Modi's government. After the party repeated and augmented its success in 2019, Bharti was appointed as a vice president of the party, then took a self-imposed three-year break from electoral politics (Noronha 2021). Her comings and goings in the party, whether imposed or voluntary, correspond precisely with its electoral successes and failures. Her rise to power coincided with the BJP's initial rise to national political power in the 1980s and 1990s; her expulsion overlapped precisely with the party's electoral collapses in 2004 and 2009; and her return presaged their electoral successes in 2014 and 2019. Accordingly, her case starkly illustrates the close correlation between mobilizing and incorporating women, and the BJP's electoral success, as well as how the marginalization of women coincides with the electoral failures of Hindu nationalist politics.

The scholar Amrita Basu (1998) has argued convincingly that religious communalism, unlike religious fundamentalism, opens some restricted spaces that can accommodate women's activism. Whereas religious fundamentalism tends to seek more traditional practices of keeping women in the home and consigning them to the roles of mother and wife, communalism—which more accurately captures Hindu nationalist ideology than religious fundamentalism per se—does make space for women's activism in the public, political sphere and within the movement. But ultimately, both communal and fundamentalist movements default to traditional conceptions of gender roles in society, and thus have limited emancipatory potential for women.

The spaces that Hindu nationalism creates for women's participation are restricted within patriarchal boundaries and limited to activism that supports the goals of the movement. Such restricted activism is not to be confused with emancipation of women or dismantling of patriarchal social structures, or the ceding of substantive decision-making power by an overwhelmingly male leadership within the movement. The anthropologist Saba Mahmood argued that Western feminism has conceived of women's empowerment and liberation solely in terms of resistance. In *Politics of Piety*, she studied a religious conservative women's movement to argue that in some forms, religious politics can be liberating for women. Yet Mahmood acknowledges that her argument focuses on a quietist movement, while Hindu nationalism is a more explicitly violent movement with very different roles and possible outcomes for women (Mahmood 2005, 37).

By deploying gendered discourses, challenging feminism, and rallying women into the streets, the BJP created spaces for women's activism that worked to support and advance Hindu nationalist ideology, rather than challenge or undermine it. Carving out such spaces did little to advance the emancipation of Indian women who did not subscribe to Hindu nationalist ideology. Even if we argue, as many plausibly have, that such campaigns enabled a certain type of empowerment among women who were otherwise confined to the home, non-Hindu women or Dalit women, for example, gained nothing tangible from these campaigns in terms of enhanced rights or increased access to the public sphere.

* * *

The events of the 1980s and 1990s constituted the "during" phase of the BJP's initial rise to power. This chapter specified the gendered mobilization of women as critical to that rise and broke it down into three analytically separable (but practically inextricable) constitutive prongs: deploying gendered discourses, challenging feminism, and rallying women into the streets. I traced these prongs through in-depth analysis of three major controversies that boosted the BJP to their first stint in power at the national level. These were the controversy over Muslim religious law and maintenance for a divorced and destitute Muslim woman, Shah Bano, in which gendered discourses about protecting Muslim women were deployed; the controversy over Roop Kanwar's sati, which challenged feminist activism by constructing sati as a woman's right; and the campaign to destroy the mosque at Ayodhya, and the subsequent political violence, in which Hindu nationalist women at both rank-and-file and leadership levels rallied into the streets.

My analysis of these three controversies also demonstrated how the three prongs were imbricated with each other: all three of them were present in each of the three controversies. Further, the three prongs of gendered mobilization encompassed both discursive and physical aspects that manifested in varying proportion in different cases. The *Shah Bano*, Roop Kanwar, and Ayodhya controversies followed chronologically on each other in an upward spiral of violence. They involved issues concerning both the minority Muslim community, in the case of *Shah Bano*; and also the majority Hindu community, in the case of Roop Kanwar. In the *Shah Bano* case, the BJP's deployment of gendered discourses changed feminist language and activism around legal reform for women's rights. The case of Roop Kanwar saw both discursive challenges to feminist claims to represent and advocate for Indian women and their rights, as well as physical confrontations with feminists on the ground. Finally, the Ayodhya campaign reached a crescendo of Hindu nationalist women's mobilization in antiminority and anti-Muslim violence: women leaders gave speeches goading men to violence before, during, and after the destruction of the mosque, and women at the rank-and-file level engaged in violence themselves.

The role of masculinity in all three cases is also noteworthy as part and parcel of gendered mobilization in this period. As argued above, in the *Shah Bano* controversy, the BJP's arguments about protecting Muslim women (from Muslim men and from Islamic law) replicated colonialist discourses of "white men saving brown women from brown men" (Spivak 1988). The Roop Kanwar case revived discourses of a Rajput community's "martial culture" of masculine warriors and women's sacrifice. And the destruction of the mosque at Ayodhya was catalyzed by speeches and discourses of women that "chide[d] and challenge[d]" Hindu men (Basu 1993a, 36) to protect the honor of Hindu women and Hindu religion, most especially from Islam's incursions.

The discourses and debate surrounding these controversies were highly "nationalized." That is to say, discussions around religion, gender, and rights as they manifested in these controversies almost exclusively referenced the Indian constitution. Article 14 provides for equality before the law for women, and Article 15 (1) bans discrimination on the basis of sex and religion, among other things. Articles 25–28 represent some of the strongest provisions in the world protecting freedom of religion, including Article 25 (1), which enshrines a fundamental right to "profess, practice, and propagate" religion (L. Jenkins 2019). Especially in the *Shah Bano* and Roop Kanwar cases, both feminist and progressive forces as well as conservative forces extensively debated the extent to which these two sets of constitutional provisions—nondiscrimination on the basis of gender and freedom of religion—were or might be in conflict with each other and how such a conflict could or should be resolved.

But absent from the debates around all of these controversies was any discussion of international law or international legal regimes. Virtually no part of the predominant debates or discussions, for example, referenced the Universal Declaration of Human Rights, adopted in 1948, or the Convention on the Elimination of All Forms of Discrimination against Women, which was adopted in 1979, signed by India in the 1980s, and ratified in 1993 (Mehra 2013). Debates were not framed in terms of universal or individual rights but rather in terms of religious freedom, minority protections, and nondiscrimination against women as specified in the Indian constitution.[11]

These controversies in the 1980s and 1990s also highlighted the presences and absences of the state, at multiple levels—local, state, national—as well as the dynamics of movement/party/government in interaction (Basu 2015). The *Shah Bano* controversy involved the minority Muslim community, and the BJP at the national level overtly interfered in this case (Williams 2006). Conversely, the Roop Kanwar case involved the majority Hindu community (with an "internal" debate over Rajput caste identity); in this case, the BJP at the national level took a stance of silent acquiescence to the party at the state level in Rajasthan, and in so doing signaled its support. The Ayodhya controversy was catalyzed to its final phase only after a BJP government was elected in Uttar Pradesh state in 1991.

In all these ways, the 1980s and 1990s were a foundational period for Hindu nationalism's initial political rise based on women's gendered mobilization. Scholars have argued that this phase of gendered mobilization and women's participation was an anomaly only for the Hindu Right—that other political movements in Indian history have always included women (Sarkar 1993b). Subsequent chapters find empirical support for this claim. But during this period, the gendered mobilization of women into Hindu nationalist politics by deploying gendered discourses, challenging feminism, and rallying women into the streets appeared as a novel and counterintuitive phenomenon that required explanation. In the next chapter I consider the scholarly, feminist, and activist responses to the events outlined in this chapter as well as my own positionality in conducting research on women's changing participation in Hindu nationalist politics.

3
Of Questions and Contexts

Feminist Responses, Scholarly Literatures, and Positionality

The events analyzed in the prior chapter—controversies over Islamic law, sati,[1] and the destruction of an ancient mosque at Ayodhya—highlighted the mobilization of women into Hindu nationalist politics and sparked a robust, interdisciplinary scholarly and activist literature. Over time, disciplinary studies of women, religion, and politics within political science have expanded as well. Yet these two bodies of literature—one interdisciplinary and the other disciplinary—have not been always, or fully, in conversation with each other. My analysis in this chapter suggests that the attenuated engagement stems from the different questions both literatures ask. A major aim of this book is to begin to bridge this gap by tracing the questions both literatures have asked, how they line up (or don't) with each other, and where my questions fit into and contribute to both. To set up the analyses to come in Chapters 4 and 5, in this chapter I thus examine the *questions* raised by the interdisciplinary literature on women in Hindu nationalism, followed by the disciplinary political science literature, including scholarship on women's political participation, religion and politics, and political parties. To complete the *context* of the research, I end the chapter by analyzing my own positionality in undertaking the fieldwork that underpinned the analyses of subsequent chapters.

On one hand, the interdisciplinary literature on women in Hindu nationalism has remained underpinned by a focus on two core questions: why women participate in Hindu nationalism and Hindu nationalist politics; and whether such participation can be empowering for women (Williams and Deo 2018). On the other hand, intersecting political science literatures on women, religion, and politics have focused on different kinds of questions: What are the micro and macro determinants of participation, and what are the barriers to women's political participation? How well, or poorly, do political organizations and institutions such as political parties—including those that are religiously oriented—represent women and women's interests? And how can, and do, women participate and carve out forms of agency for themselves within such organizations and institutions? Putting both literatures in conversation with each other, engaging the questions each has been asking separately, will enable a broader study of women's participation in Hindu nationalist politics while expanding disciplinary understandings of women, religion, and politics.

Accordingly, I begin this chapter by examining the interdisciplinary literature on women in Hindu nationalism, including feminist scholarly and activist voices, spurred by the events of the 1980s and 1990s that I examined in Chapter 2. This vibrant literature draws on religious studies, women's and gender studies, sociology, history, political science, and anthropology to focus on questions of women's participation in Hindu nationalism in India. I undertake close reading of secondary writing and contemporaneous accounts and analyses, particularly those of Indian feminist scholars and activists. Early scholarship viewed the participation of women in Hindu nationalism as both novel and counterintuitive, generating significant reflection and reassessment among South Asian feminists and within Indian women's rights movements. More recent scholarship has expanded to include additional scrutiny of masculinity and of gendered roles in the movement as well as longer-term, immersive ethnographic studies. As this interdisciplinary literature has evolved over time, it has continued to focus on two underlying questions: why women participate in Hindu nationalist politics; and whether or to what extent such participation could be empowering in feminist terms.

I then examine a series of disciplinary political science scholarships that ask related but different types of questions that bear on the topic of women's participation in Hindu nationalist politics. I first look at scholarship on political participation and, in particular, women's political participation. The former was inattentive to gender and based mostly on Global North democracies, shaped by questions of how much people participate, and what factors predict or explain participation. Across the scholarship on political participation, the forms of participation were derived initially and primarily from Western and Global North democracies (Whetstone and Williams 2019). Scholarship on women's political participation has largely been underpinned with a concern about why women don't participate and the barriers to women's participation, encompassing studies of representation and the gendered aspects of political institutions. A newly emerging area within women and politics scholarship explores how religious/conservative/

right-wing women represent women in politics and how they engage with feminism. These questions are related to, but different from, the questions that have long engaged the interdisciplinary literature on women in Hindu nationalism. My study shows how participation, through the lens of gender, looks different starting from a Global South democracy, and from the vantage point of Global South and conservative/religious women.

Shifting to the disciplinary scholarship on religion and politics, I find it has been dominated by questions of how religious beliefs and actors affect politics and motivate political action; questions about secularization and modernization; ideational versus institutional aspects of religion; and theoretical accounts of religious freedom and religious rights. Prevalent conceptions of religion in this scholarship tend to derive from, and accord with, what Western and Abrahamic religions (Judaism, Christianity, Islam) look like: congregational and textual. Historically, this scholarship was dominated by a focus on religion in American politics and positivist quantitative methods and studies; more recently, a good deal of energy in the subfield comes from mixed-method, comparative studies of a range of countries beyond the Western world. When the scholarship has engaged with issues of women and gender, it has been myopically focused on the status of women in just one religion—Islam. My study of Hindu nationalist women shows how religious politics looks from the starting point of a non-Abrahamic religion and provides an important corrective to an overfocus on women in Islam.

The third major body of disciplinary political science scholarship that impinges on this study concerns political parties, including Indian political parties and the BJP, as well as studies of women in/and political parties. This scholarship has broadly focused on the role and function of parties in democracy and democratization, how they originate, and whom they represent. But like other areas of disciplinary scholarship, studies of political parties began from an initial focus on European countries and Global North democracies, turning only later to consider developing countries and the extent to which arguments derived from the former apply to the latter (Randall 2006b). Scholarship on women in political parties has considered whether and how parties include women and represent (or don't represent) women's interests. A newly emerging body of work on women in Islamist parties helps decenter European countries and examines how women carve out different forms of agency in the context of religion and religiously oriented political parties.

Scholars of Indian political parties have examined the decline of Congress Party dominance and how the Indian party system has changed over time, while studies of the BJP have considered the causes and consequences of its rise and current dominance. But these works leave critical questions unanswered: they tend not to account for gender in the rise of BJP (that work is left largely to the interdisciplinary literature on women in Hindu nationalism), and they do not account for historical antecedents of the contemporary BJP—in particular, why Hindu nationalist political parties failed before they succeeded, even as the social movement wing of the party grew in a steady upward trajectory from the early 1900s on. My analysis answers both these questions together: I argue that before their initial rise, the marginalization of women was a major reason the Hindu Mahasabha—the first political party of Hindu nationalism and precursor of the BJP—failed (Chapter 4), and the lessons the BJP learned through mobilizing and incorporating women go far in accounting for their political successes since their initial rise (Chapter 5).

Virtually on repeat, the disciplinary political science literature starts out overfocused on Western and Global North countries and underfocused on gender, and then "adds in" consideration of non-Western / Global South cases and consideration of women and gender as the scholarship develops. But this has meant the conceptual templates—including the very questions being asked—were forged in Western / Global North contexts with insufficient initial attention to women and gender. My analysis inductively theorizes women's political participation, religion and politics, and political parties from the starting point of a non-Western democracy, a non-Abrahamic majority religion, and a religious nationalist political party—through the lens of gender—and thus yields different conceptions of what participation and religious politics mean. Rather than seeking to answer the long-standing and well-debated "why" and "empowerment" questions—which may well be ultimately unanswerable—in this study I seek to leverage the questions that different bodies of scholarship can bring to bear on understanding the participation of women in Hindu nationalist politics. I build on Charles Tilly's dictum that "how things happen is *why* they happen" (2006, 410)[2] to argue that we cannot understand why women participate in Hindu nationalist politics until we first understand *how* they participate, and how their participation has changed over time. And we cannot evaluate whether their participation can be empowering unless we understand what their participation *means*, for them, for the party, and ultimately for Indian democracy.

To the extent this study has been shaped by prior and extant disciplinary and interdisciplinary literatures, it has equally been shaped by the researcher. Thus I close the chapter by inserting the researcher—myself—into the research by assessing the context of my own positionality. Reflexivity is a critical aspect of both feminist and interpretive scholarship (Yanow and Schwartz-Shea 2014; Ackerly and True 2010). In analyzing my positionality, I try to move beyond cataloguing demographic characteristics, to consider how those characteristics—my own positionality—might have shaped the research as I undertook it. I reach two conclusions: first, my positionality—aspects such as caste, class, religion, national identity, and ethnicity—likely shaped access to research participants and implicitly set parameters around our conversations, including what was discussed and what was not. Second, my own background and status straddling the line between insider and outsider positioned me well to undertake the study, bridging the gap between disciplinary and interdisciplinary literatures and negotiating the space between being read as an overt ally or opponent of the movement.

Two Questions, Two "Phases": Interdisciplinary Scholarship(s) on Women in Hindu Nationalism

A well-developed interdisciplinary literature evolved in two phases over 20 years following (and based upon) the events of the 1980s and 1990s analyzed in Chapter 2: the campaigns over the Shah Bano case on Islamic law; the Roop Kanwar sati controversy, and the dramatic and visible role of Hindu nationalist women in the destruction of the mosque at Ayodhya and the subsequent communal violence (Basu 1998). One observer called the Ayodhya conflict a "turning point" in the role of women in the Hindutva movement.[3] In response to these events, a pathbreaking "first phase" of literature, driven by feminist scholarly and activist analysis, traced the rise to power of the contemporary BJP through a gendered lens (Basu 1993a, 1993b; Jeffery and Basu 1998; Sarkar and Butalia 1995; Sarkar 2001). Menon (2003) has argued that the extent of women's participation in militant Hindu nationalist politics may be overstated; but the overwhelming consensus has been that the BJP rose to power through what I analyzed in Chapter 2 as the gendered mobilization of women, comprising the deployment of gendered discourses about women's issues and women's rights, challenging feminism's claims to represent Indian women and define women's rights, and rallying women into the streets.

Similar to second-wave feminism in the United States, scholarship and activism have remained inextricably imbricated in the Indian feminist movement (Kumar 1997; Butalia 2001). Until the events of the 1980s and 1990s, South Asian feminist and women's rights movements operated, if implicitly, under fundamental assumptions of secularism, pluralism, democracy, and cultural autonomy (CSWI 1975; Kumar 1999; Gopalan 2001). The participation of women in Hindu nationalist politics challenged each of these fundamental assumptions.

An underlying sense of surprise and disbelief that women could or would participate in the forms of politics represented by Hindu nationalism is palpable throughout this early literature. Women's participation in Hindu nationalist politics seemed at once novel and counterintuitive: "The recent and very sizable entry of Hindutva women in violent campaigns, the leading roles of right-wing women in public politics is a new phenomenon that requires some explanation" (Sarkar 1998, 102). Indian feminists acknowledged having taken women as victims of violence rather than perpetrators and having taken women's public, political participation as a benefit (Sarkar and Butalia 1995, 3). A similar sense was evident in Pakistani feminists' initial responses to Islamist women in the same time period: one "describes the activities of right-wing women in Pakistan as 'disconcerting' and a 'new development'" (Jamal 2005, 64). There was almost a sense of stunned betrayal: "Indeed the very strata of middle- and lower-middle class women who had been subject to violence by their husbands and in-laws actively supported male-dominated movements directed against the minority population." Jeffery and Basu note clearly that despite long experience in the field, "neither of us had encountered women's complicity in violence, let alone violence against minorities" (1998, ix). Jamal argued that confronting political activism of conservative/religious women in South Asia "marks a conceptual crisis for feminism" (2005, 53), citing a "crisis in feminist scholarship, between acknowledging [conservative-religious] women as autonomous agents and rejecting their political contentions" (2005, 69).

In response to the events of the 1980s and 1990s, scholars and activists asked: "Why had so many women organized to support the destruction of the Babri Masjid in Ayodhya? What bearing did women's class backgrounds, religious beliefs, and gender identities have on their activism? Did the forms of women's activism that we encountered in India have parallels in other parts of South Asia?" (Jeffery and Basu 1998, x). They asked: "Had [we] been wrong in assuming that women were essentially non-violent and that they did not participate in violence and conflict? [H]ow were communal parties able to mobilize women so effectively and in such large numbers, particularly when their agenda where women were concerned was in all respects retrogressive?" (Butalia 2001, 108–9).

Underlying all these questions were two core concerns. First, why did women participate in such a political movement? And second, could women's participation in such a movement be seen as empowering? I call these the "why" and "empowerment" questions, and feminist scholars and activists quickly concluded that answers were not to be found in "the scholarly literature on women, religion, politics." These literatures instead focused on exegesis of theological texts and analysis of religious traditions rather than women's lived experience of religion, formal studies of religious laws and legal systems that did not analyze how women interpreted and used legislation, and feminist analyses that ignored women's activism on the religious right (Jeffery and Basu 1998, x).

The "why" question in turn raised several subsidiary questions. What is the universe of political movements that Hindu nationalist politics represents? Why was women's participation especially surprising? To whom was it especially surprising? The question touched on feminist assumptions about the peaceful nature of women, and a conception of women's interests that did not lie with a movement based in religion and nationalism, which assign women subordinate roles confined largely to the private sphere.

The "empowerment" question also raised knotty questions in its wake, touching on assumptions about what empowerment means, what kind(s) of empowerment feminism seeks for women, how such empowerment would look, and how we might know it's been achieved. In her pathbreaking book *Politics of Piety*, Saba Mahmood (2005) delinks agency from resistance, arguing that Western feminism has often assumed that women only exercise agency insofar as they subvert or resist patriarchy and specifically patriarchal religion. Through her study of women's religious networks in Egypt, she argues that feminism can, and indeed must, also (or alternately) understand women's agency in terms of their ethics and teleology as well as their intentions and bodily practices.

But the participation of women in Hindu nationalist politics carries very different political implications. Hindu nationalist women certainly have agency by Mahmood's definition, and are not undertaking overt resistance to dominant social or patriarchal structures (similar to Mahmood's research participants). The women in Mahmood's study were engaged in a quietist movement to reconfigure individuals' religious commitments and personhood from the "ground up." (Notably, the RSS says the same thing and works through its network of women's and other local organizations to achieve this.) But the BJP has no such pretensions: as a political party, they seek—and have since 2014 attained, virtually unchecked—the political power of state institutions to implement their agenda from the top down. Mahmood acknowledges that the Hindu nationalist movement in India is unlike the quietist, piety movement she studied in Egypt in that the latter "is neither a fascist nor militant movement, nor does it seek to gain control of the state" (2005, 37). The participation of women in Hindu nationalist politics thus raises different issues around agency and resistance. How were feminists to gauge women's participation and activism in a hegemonic, militant, violent, and intolerant movement rising, in the 1980s and 1990s, to political power?

Much to their credit, South Asian feminists, faced with the unsettling events of the period, reassessed many of their own core assumptions. After the *Shah Bano* case, women's rights advocates significantly reshaped their position on the personal laws, abandoning the call for a uniform civil code and shifting instead to calls for an "optional" or "gender-just" code of family laws (Menon 2014; Kumar 1997, Chapter 10; Hasan 1998). Women's participation in Hindu nationalist politics and violence raised issues of identity and representation: feminists could not afford to assume that a shared experience of womanhood superseded divisions of caste, class, religion, and community (Kumar 1997, 168). Because of the Hindu Right's "constant and skilful appropriation of the language, slogans, symbols and strategies of women activists" and feminism (Butalia 2001, 110; Williams 2022a), feminists could not take for granted their right to speak for or represent the interests of Indian women. They also analyzed the pitfalls of trying to achieve change through the institutions of the state—when often state representatives, such as police officers, were themselves implicated in the dangers women faced (Kishwar 2008), and as Hindu nationalism itself gained state power. Where women's agency, activism, and access to the public sphere had always been presumed to be beneficial, Indian feminists had to confront women's political activism that was, by their own measures, detrimental both to women and to society more broadly (Butalia 2001, 111; Sarkar 1999, 147).

The year 2004 was an important turning point, marking the end of the first BJP-led NDA government that held power at the center after the 1999 election. As I showed in Chapter 1, this period marked the "mainstreaming" or political acceptability of the party in Indian democracy. Prior to the

1999 government, the BJP was something of a marginal player on the Indian political scene, treated as a "pariah" by other parties, which steadfastly refused to enter into electoral alliances with the BJP (Malik and Singh 1994). Relatedly, after 2004 the ideological positioning of the BJP shifted from a more moderate to a more militant stance. After 2004, the BJP was an established political party that had become a viable alternative at the national level and was newly (re)committed to a more ideologically entrenched Hindu nationalism.

From about 2000 to 2004—during the period of the first BJP-led national government—a second phase of scholarship on women in Hindu nationalism emerged. This second phase began to look more explicitly at masculinity in the movement (Banerjee 2012; Anand 2007, 2011) and at the gendered conceptual roles for women that the movement constructs, such as "warrior woman" or "mother of the nation" (Banerjee 2005; Chowdhry 2000). These roles shape the empirical modes of participation—marginalization, mobilization, incorporation—I trace in this book. Later scholarship also came to encompass the insights provided by longer-term ethnographic studies (Menon 2010; Bedi 2016). Throughout both phases, the scholarship on women in Hindu nationalism has continued to be strongly interdisciplinary. Some studies look at the movement as a whole, while others have focused on particular organizations: the RSS and the Samiti (Bacchetta 2004), the VHP (Katju 2003), and the Shiv Sena (Sen 2007), as well as the BJP (Basu 2015). Nandini Deo's (2016) pathbreaking work compared Hindu nationalism and feminism as social movements and their effectiveness in advancing various religious and women's rights agendas. Importantly, the literature continues to evolve in significant ways (Sarkar and Basu, 2022).

Yet through this second phase, the "why" and "empowerment" questions have continued to undergird interdisciplinary scholarship on women in Hindu nationalism. Kalyani Devaki Menon, for example, writes that her book was "driven by a desire to understand what draws thousands upon thousands of women . . . to a movement that is xenophobic, exclusionary, and tremendously violent" (2010, 25). Tarini Bedi (2016) engages the "empowerment" question in unpacking how Shiv Sena women construct their own agency performatively and, in doing so, constitute a form of "political matronage" in which women are the agents and not just the recipients of what is traditionally studied as political patronage.

The persistence of the "why" and "empowerment" questions over time might suggest that we haven't found answers, or that we haven't been satisfied with the answers proposed—or that these questions might be ultimately unanswerable in the forms we have been asking them. As cited above, Charles Tilly, in arguing for the importance of immersive, interpretive studies such as this one to tease out even cause-and-effect relationships, argued that "how things happen is *why* they happen" (2006, 411). Building on this central insight, I argue that we cannot understand why women participate in Hindu nationalist politics until we first understand *how* they have participated, and how their participation has changed over time. And we cannot assess whether or how this form of women's participation constitutes empowerment without understanding what their participation *means* for women, for the party, and for Indian democracy. These reframed questions, I suggest, can shed different light and may help bridge the literature on women in Hindu nationalism with intersecting political science literatures on participation, religion, and political parties, to which I now turn.

Getting Disciplinary: Political Science Scholarship(s) on Women and Religion

As noted above, "the scholarly literature on women, religion, politics" (Jeffery and Basu 1998, x) offered little insight on the questions raised by Indian feminist scholars and activists in the 1980s and 1990s in the face of women's participation in Hindu nationalist politics. Three broad areas of scholarship in political science intersect with this topic: political participation (including women's political participation as well as religious-conservative women), religion and politics, and political parties (including religious-conservative parties and women in political parties). Across all these areas of political science scholarship, I find a repeating pattern: they begin with the study of Global North and Western democracies and tend to ignore the role of women and gender; then as each body of scholarship develops, it turns to consider how its conclusions apply (or don't) to Global South countries (as well as nondemocratic regimes), and how women and gender factor into the analyses. By starting from a non-Western context, and through the lens of gender, this study disrupts this pattern and contributes to refiguring what constitutes participation and religious politics from the ground up. In the following sections I briefly overview each of these bodies of scholarship, identifying both what they bring to bear on this study and what this study can bring to the literature.

Political Participation

Empirical studies of political participation grew from US electoral analyses using sample survey data (Salisbury 1975).[4] This scholarship began with a virtually exclusive focus on voting as the sole measure of participation, then slowly expanded its conceptual and empirical reach to include large-scale, cross-national studies of multiple countries with multiple measures of participation (Almond and Verba 1963; Barnes and Kaase 1979). Yet such studies either focused overwhelmingly on Western democracies or measured non-Western democracies against the standards defined by Western ones (Verba, Nie, and Kim 1978). It was not until after the mid-1990s that studies of political participation began to shift in notable ways away from a focus on wealthy and democratic countries (Uhlaner 2015). Mainstream indicators of political participation have included voting, donating to political causes, volunteering in political campaigns, running for office, making and/or signing petitions, and participating in civil society organizations as well as demonstrations and boycotts. At the macro level, both regime type and level of economic development are strongly correlated with these measures of political participation, with wealthier democracies evincing higher levels of participation. At the micro level as well, economic resources (including time) and higher levels of education are associated with greater political participation.

This scholarship on political participation did not fully account for women as political subjects through about the 1950s. Initial attempts to analyze women's political participation could be classified as an "add women and stir" approach: scholars began to research and study women's political participation using the same measures with which they had studied participation "generally," without fundamentally altering those measures. Thus scholarship did not start from the assumption that women might participate differently and then look for forms their participation might take; rather, it retained the same measures of participation it had been using and then checked to see whether and how much women engaged in them. Based on these measures, the scholarship became oriented to understanding why women participated "less" and where the barriers to women's participation lay. Early analyses resorted to individualistic explanations that seemed to blame women for their own lack of political participation (Lazarsfeld et al. 1944; Duverger 1955). Feminist political scientists soon turned to examine how political institutions themselves were gendered and thus shaped and limited women's political participation (Lovenduski 1998; Randall and Waylen 1998; Mackay,

Kenny, and Chappell 2010; Hern 2017; Krook 2014). Recent scholarship focuses on forms of representation and the importance of women's descriptive and substantive representation (Dovi 2015, 2018; Pitkin 1967).

Thus where the interdisciplinary literature on women in Hindu nationalism has been concerned with why women participate, the disciplinary scholarship on women's political participation has been concerned with why women don't participate. This book steps back from both these sets of questions to ask the prior question of how women participate. It shows that an increase in descriptive representation of women in Hindu nationalist political parties, from the 1900s to the 2010s, has not automatically translated to substantive representation of women's interests, and it expands our understanding of forms—marginalization mobilization, incorporation—that women's political participation, or exclusion from participation, has taken in an established Global South democracy. Indian democracy has long been an anomaly to the trend of wealth leading to higher levels of participation—measured primarily as voting—at both the macro and individual levels (Panda 2019). I bridge the gap between micro and macro levels of explanation by showing how women's participation helps drive high levels of participation in Indian democracy, documenting how the growing and changing participation of women in Hindu nationalist politics correlates with the movement's political success and consolidation.

With notable exceptions (Schreiber 2008), women and politics scholars have not extensively studied religious, conservative, and right-wing women. In the context of the explosion of right-wing populist movements globally—and especially in many of the established democracies—this is now beginning to change (Farris 2017; Och and Shames 2018; Celis and Childs 2012, 2018). Scholars are examining the role of conservative/religious women in political parties and legislatures, their impacts on policies, and how they represent (or don't) women and women's interests and issues in politics. Previous studies, focused on the United States and/or originating beyond the field of political science, have found that the participation of women works to normalize such movements and parties, making them more acceptable in mainstream politics (Blee and Deutsch 2012; Ferber 2004; Bacchetta and Power 2002). Comparative scholars have begun asking how conservative/religious women vote on or advocate for issues related to women, what kinds of candidates they support, how they respond to attacks on women, and how they co-opt the language and strategies of feminism (Och and Williams 2022). These questions intersect directly with the concerns of this study, which suggests that the increased participation of women has not moderated the radicalization of the party.

Religion and Politics

Arising in the 1980s, the subfield of religion and politics followed the same initial patterns as other bodies of disciplinary political science scholarship examined here: it started with Global North and Western countries and was inattentive to gender. Much early work was dominated by studies of the United States and was primarily (though not exclusively) quantitative and/or positivist in approach—even as scholars bemoaned insufficient "scienticity" in the early literature (Jelen 1998). The subfield has tended to wax and wane in alignment with external events that led scholars to question assumptions of secularization and the fading relevance of religion as a core component of modernization, arguing that such assumptions had led political science as a discipline to neglect the study of religion (Wald and Wilcox 2006).

The 1979 revolution in Iran led in its wake to a sharp increase in the study of "fundamentalisms" (Almond, Appleby, and Sivan 2003; Marty and Appleby 1991). A second "bump" in religion and politics scholarship came after the 9/11 terror attacks on the United States, as comparative political science research sought to understand how religion motivates political action. But scholarship in religion and politics has often tended to start from an Abrahamic and Western conception of religion, including major cross-national studies of religion and politics (Inglehart and Norris 2003; Norris and Inglehart 2011) or Samuel Huntington's civilizational model (2011). Western conceptions of religion often begin from a textual basis, assuming that knowledge of a founding text can reliably indicate the beliefs and behaviors of followers. Western religions also tend to be congregational, with believers gathering regularly in structured meetings presided over by a religious leader.

The case of Hinduism in India leads us to reconsider what constitutes religion and what its defining and politically relevant characteristics are. It lets us look at the "transition from religion as a set of practices that reproduce a belief system to religious ideology deployed as a tool of political mobilization and party politics" (Feldman 1998, 35) in a different way than starting from Western and Abrahamic religions does. In Hinduism, there is no single founding text nor a canon that gives rise to a unified creed or belief system.

Private worship, where much religious activity takes place within the home, and the absence of a congregation, mean that belief and behavior are conceived and implemented differently in the context of Hinduism. For example, Chhibber (2014) makes an important intervention by focusing on religious practice. He argues that as a community activity that is multiple, local, and frequent, religious practice in India bolsters citizens' political efficacy and positive sense of feeling represented, thus strengthening Indian democracy. Chhibber shows convincingly how starting from Hinduism leads us to think about religion and politics differently, a central insight this book builds on. My book expands on more recent trends of political science that examine core issues of religion and politics in comparative contexts, beyond the Western world, and use a range of methodological approaches (Smith 2019; McClendon and Riedl 2019; Kuru 2019; L. Jenkins 2019).

The distinction between ideational and institutional factors has been central to the study of religion and politics, though more recently scholars have begun to consider the ways ideational and institutional factors influence each other, thus starting to break down the distinction as an artificial dichotomy (Grzymala-Busse 2012). My study builds on this insight, engaging the micro level by examining the meanings and motivations of individual women—historically and contemporarily—who have participated in Hindu nationalist politics. It further seeks to trace the impacts of these individual women's participation on the institutional structures of Hindu nationalist political parties in Indian democracy, thereby revealing the interplay between ideational and institutional aspects of religion and politics.[5]

In general, studies of religion and politics that focus on gender have been sparse, with one notable exception: a focus on women in Islam (Fish 2002). Many scholars have been highly critical of Western scholarship's fascination with the "oppression" of Muslim women (Abu-Lughod 1998, 2013; Mahmood 2005; Mernissi 1987, 1992; Scott 2007; Moghadam 1994, 2003). Such an approach places undue emphasis on just one religion, constructing it as somehow especially oppressive of women. Focusing solely on women in Islam implies that there is something about Islam that is particularly corrosive of gender equality, or "shifts the blame" to Arab culture (Donno and Russett 2004). The potential political insinuations of such an approach risk undermining these analyses: is the purpose to study the role of women in religious politics, or is it to indict Islam as a gender-oppressive (hence "backward") religion? Such analyses can entirely miss the ways in which women/gender offer a lens into understanding a number of aspects around the politicization of all religions; my study of women in Hindu nationalist politics in India provides an important corrective.

Political Parties

As Montero and Gunther (2002) note, the study of political parties has been embedded within political science from its inception. It flourished from the 1950s to 1970s, then experienced a brief lull until the mid-1990s, when the journal *Party Politics* was launched. Key questions that have engaged scholars of political parties include their role in democracy: whether parties strengthen democracy—by connecting citizens with government—or weaken it, by promoting partiality and extremism (Schattschneider 1942). Scholars have debated their origins: do parties form institutionally, from the top down—starting as a means to organize legislatures, and then spreading out to the people (Duverger 1963, 1972)? Or sociologically, from the bottom up, reflecting social cleavages (Lipset and Rokkan 1967)?

Central insights of V. O. Key's ([1942] 1964) classic study of American political parties are deployed in this book. He separated out three faces or aspects of parties based on three core functions. The *party-in-government* "organizes the legislature and coordinates actions across the various institutions of national government, horizontally, and, for systems with vertical divisions of power, across the federal structures." The *party-in-the-electorate* comprised "the party of the campaign, the creation of the party's image and reputation in the public's mind, and the way the public used those sources as informational short-cuts and decision-making devices or aides." Finally, the *party-as-organization* included a party's "activists, resources, and campaign specialists . . . those who negotiate between the public and government" (Aldrich 2011, 197). These different faces of the party have shaped the areas in which I examine the changing participation of women in the Hindu Mahasabha and the BJP. In Chapters 4 and 5, I focus on the party as organization by examining the changing participation of women in internal party leadership structures, including the women's wing. I further trace changes in the party-in-the-electorate by examining women as candidates and women's issues in party platforms and how these changed between the early 1900s and the 2010s.

Initially, studies of political parties "were based exclusively on the historical experiences of surprisingly few West European democracies during the first six decades of the 20th century" (Montero and Gunther 2002, 14). Later, the study of political parties and party systems in the developing world was primarily concerned with processes of democratization (LaPalombara and Weiner 1966). An exemplary contribution in 2016 argued that established political parties—alongside and often growing out of social movements— were critical to securing the democratization process in less wealthy countries (Bermeo and Yashar 2016), an insight supported by the case of India (Tudor and Slater 2016).

Early studies of Indian parties and party systems focused on the dominance of the Congress Party (Kothari 1964). Yet as early as 1957, Myron Weiner presciently argued India was, or was becoming, a multiparty system (Weiner 1957). Yogendra Yadav's (1999) seminal work outlined three phases in India's party system prior to the rise of the BJP. In the first era, from 1947 to 1967, the Congress was dominant at both the center and in the states; in the second era, from 1967 to 1989, Congress continued to dominate at the center but declined in the states; and the third was an era of coalition politics from 1989 to 2014 (Chakrabarty 2014). The BJP's overwhelming victories in 2014 and 2019 have led scholars to herald the "dawn" of the fourth era in India's party system, in which the BJP is the hegemonic force—both electorally and ideologically (Vaishnav and Hintson 2019).

Comparative scholarship on Indian political parties has been centrally concerned with explaining the BJP's rise to dominance. Chhibber (1999, Chapter 7) has argued that it was most accurately attributed to the expanding middle class in India and the party's economic policy advocating less developmental state intervention than the Congress Party's pro-poor activism and policies. Subsequently, Chhibber and Verma (2018) demonstrated that the BJP's electoral success in 2014 was based on ideologies of statism and representation that had come to be more in line with those of the Indian public. Thachil (2014) has argued that the BJP was able to win Dalit and Adivasi votes in certain key regions, without losing votes from the elite classes whose interests it represents, by providing targeted social services such as education and health via local, grassroots affiliates. But such disciplinary analyses have accounted centrally neither for gender and the role of women in the BJP's rise—that task has fallen to the interdisciplinary literature on women in Hindu nationalism covered in the previous section—nor for the historical antecedents of the party's rise. That is, we cannot fully understand how the BJP succeeded without examining and comparing the periods when Hindu nationalist politics was flailing. This book addresses both these gaps simultaneously, providing a disciplinary account of the role of women and gender in the BJP's rise to political dominance by undertaking temporal comparison of women's participation before, during, and after the BJP's ascent to power.

With respect to women in political parties, two lacunae seem to reinforce each other: research in this area is sparse, and political parties themselves are sparse in their representation of women (Childs and Kittilson 2016; Brechenmacher and Hubbard 2020). Such conclusions certainly reflect those of Indian scholars vis-à-vis Indian political parties' marginalization of women (see Chapter 1). Some research has focused on women in left political parties (Banaszak, Beckwith, and Rucht 2003), arguing that parties of the Left have been more likely, and quicker, than parties of the Right to include women and integrate gender issues as part of their platform, at least in rhetoric. Other research has found that feminists tend to see Left parties as allies, while they see Right parties as strategic partners (Evans 2016)—a finding that accords with my analysis of the relationship of BJP women to Indian feminists (Williams 2022a). In Chapter 1 I showed that the two national-level left parties in India (CPI and CPI-M) are the only parties to draw a slight majority of their votes from women. Other studies find a pattern of women entering political parties primarily through a family link (Freeman 2000). The case of the BJP partly supports and partly refutes this model. On the surface, BJP leaders explicitly disavow "dynastic" politics, which they associate with the Congress Party under—and abjectly reliant on—the ongoing leadership of the Nehru-Gandhi lineage.[6] But as I elaborate in Chapter 5, while many BJP women did not come into the party through a family link, many others did—through the RSS and/or the involvement of their husbands and sons (Basu 2016). This book also bolsters recent scholarship on women's party organizations (i.e., women's wings). Chapters 4 and 5 focus on the women's wings of the Hindu Mahasabha and the BJP as a measure of women's marginalization or incorporation, respectively. My findings accord with initial findings on European parties that women's wings neither hinder nor necessarily boost women's representation in political parties (Childs and Kittilson 2016, 603–4).

As argued above, much of the disciplinary scholarship on political parties evinces a pattern of being underfocused on gender and overfocused on the Global North. One area that seems to diverge from these patterns is a growing literature on women in Islamist political parties in predominantly Muslim countries (Jamal and Langohr 2014; Clark and Schwedler 2003; Ben Shitrit

2016). Such studies follow Mahmood (2005) in posing a "direct challenge to a western hegemonic discourse of liberal feminism" by identifying "different modalities for 'feminist engagement' " and suggesting "that we cannot simply deem women's behaviors as instances of political subordination or marginalization, when in fact the sources of women's agency and empowerment are a complex and dynamic process" (Jamal and Langohr 2014, n.p.). My book, by focusing on women in a Hindu nationalist party, follows in this path while working to preempt any myopic focus only on women in Islam. This book also represents the kind of qualitative, contextual country study that scholarship on women in political parties argues the need for (Jamal and Langohr 2014; Evans and Kenny 2019).

Scholars of women and religion beyond the discipline of political science (including, but not limited to, scholars of women's and gender studies as well as religious studies, anthropologists, and sociologists) have tended to focus on questions of agency and how women can or do achieve it within the strictures of organized religion. A long feminist tradition critically examines the ways in which patriarchy has been supported by religious institutions and ideologies. This scholarly and activist tradition is being called into question by some feminist scholars considering a postsecular feminism (Deo 2018). In line with such scholarship, my study of Hindu nationalist women's political participation illuminates the idea of agency, or empowerment, in a more nuanced way: considering its collective aspects and lying along a spectrum, rather than seeing it in individualistic and dichotomous terms. The forms and types of women's participation in Hindu nationalist politics is precisely the subject this book tackles, showing how it has evolved over time from marginalization, through mobilization, to incorporation, while questioning whether such an evolution actually serves women's interests—and which women's interests such an evolution serves and does not serve.

Analyzing Positionality and Leveraging Liminality: Where I Stand Depends on Where I Sit

Both feminist and interpretive methodologies begin from the premise that research is framed not only by prior scholarship, but also by the positionality of the researcher. As noted earlier, reflexivity on the part of the researcher is a defining characteristic of both interpretive and feminist research (Yanow and Schwartz-Shea 2014; Ackerly and True 2010): both eschew a positivist "view from nowhere" that absents the researcher from the processes and the conclusions of the work. Accordingly, I close this chapter by considering my own positionality vis-à-vis this study. Rather than merely listing off my own demographic characteristics, though (and thus implicitly leaving the reader to intuit where the connections between research and researcher might lie), in this section I seek to theoretically analyze the connections between my own positionality and the ways it may have impacted the research of this book. Two key insights emerge: the ways in which aspects of my identity may have shaped my access to and interactions with research participants; and how a liminal status between insider and outsider positioned me well to undertake this research on women in Hindu nationalist politics in India.

In terms of access to and interactions with research participants, multiple aspects of my own identity became relevant to this research: these included my sex/gender, religion, caste status, and ethnic identity as a diasporic Indian. Being cisgender and woman-identified meant neither me nor my research subjects had to face issues of nonbinary or trans constructions of sex or gender, on which Hindu nationalism (as well as the literature on Hindu nationalism) has a spotty record (Shah 2015). I am also an upper-caste Hindu woman. This often meant neither I nor my informants had to confront issues of caste or religious minority bias in the party and the movement. It did lead, in one instance, to an assumption of my status as an insider: one informant felt comfortable going on in our interview complaining that the party, to court lower-caste votes, elevates lower-caste women and advances them ahead of (upper-caste) women who have been doing on-the-ground work for the party for much longer.[7]

During fieldwork I wore Indian *salwar kameez* (long tunic and loose pants), with a *dupatta* (scarf) usually wound around my neck and partially covering my chest. This was a fairly typical—neither overly "traditional" nor overly "modern"—form of presentation in my research sites. New Delhi and Lucknow are both large, sprawling urban capital cities where a range of presentations are more common and accepted, as compared to more rural areas. I generally wore a simple gold wedding band on my left hand and a single gold bangle on my right hand; other than these, I did not wear any of what is described in greater detail in Chapter 5 as the traditional markers of a married Hindu woman: I wore neither a sari, nor a bindi (the dot on the forehead), nor *sindoor* (red powder in the part of the hair). Overall, I would have been easily comprehensible as what I am: a married, diasporic, Hindu, upper-caste woman with some level of ties to India. Unlike other colleagues' experiences (Sehgal 2009; Behl 2017; Bedi 2016), no one commented on my dress or appearance during any of my fieldwork trips over the course of almost a decade.[8] Because I was conducting elite interviews, there was less of a power differential between me and research subjects (Schwartz-Shea and Yanow 2012, 60–63; Behl 2017), and I did present myself as being there to learn from them. No one tried to convince or convert me; and with just one exception (narrated in Chapter 5), I never sensed that research participants understood me explicitly either as an ally or as an opponent. This, I believe, was ultimately an advantage in positioning me to conduct this research.

In terms of my insider-outsider status, I came at the fieldwork as an Indian-born and US-raised researcher. I returned to study Indian politics with strong emotional and cultural ties to India and to my extended family there; but as a diasporic Indian, I work and research there as neither fully an insider nor fully an outsider.[9] I have been studying the BJP since the 1990s and have built up a virtually unprecedented level of access to top leaders of this political party, which tends to be suspicious of academics, especially Western academics. On one hand, my status as a diasporic, upper-caste, educated Hindu woman placed me squarely in the category of those who might be inclined to support the party and the movement. On the other hand, my status as a US academic potentially put me in the opposite camp. Had research subjects read me very clearly or explicitly as supporting or opposing the movement, in either case they would have been likely to respond to and engage with me quite differently.

Two particular incidents during my 2015–16 fieldwork help illustrate how my liminal status could have direct impacts on my research, particularly with regards to access to research subjects. In the first, an Indian colleague I had just met, upon hearing about my topic and that I was trying to gain access for elite interviews with BJP leaders, made a remark along these lines: "Oh well, you're American, so you'll get all kinds of access; they'll always easily talk to you." To which my immediate response constituted approximately "Um, no, I think you are confusing me with a white American!" Because of the "in between" nature of my own positionality, my access in a fieldwork setting in northern India was more complex than it might have appeared. If access for an Indian researcher is "hard," and access for a White Anglo or European researcher is "easy," as my colleague's remark was suggesting, then my own access fell somewhere in between. Rather than gaining the access that a full outsider might have had, I also did not have the same level of access that a full insider might have had. This is certainly one of many legacies of colonial subjugation, which scholars of postcoloniality have theorized thoroughly and insightfully (Nandy 1983; Guha 1997; Spivak 1999).

A second incident shed further light on the complexities of my insider-outsider status and access to research subjects. To get meetings with powerful politicians and public figures, I had first to deal with their personal assistants (PAs) by phone. Mostly I spoke to them in my fluent yet American-accented Hindi. Getting nowhere with one particular PA, I decided to try speaking in my 100 percent American-accented English, assuming that over the phone he would not be able to tell I was of Indian origin. Would I be able to gain access this way? I wasn't entirely sure if I wanted my impromptu experiment to succeed or fail. Success might mean gaining access to an important research subject, while failure, in my mind, would confirm differential access based on my (perceived) ethnic identity. In the event, my experiment turned out somewhere in the middle: the PA did blow me off again, and I still didn't get access to my research subject—but this time he blew me off more politely!

Feminist researchers of women in Hindu nationalism struggle with negotiating the tenuous and potentially risky space between being taken as an ally to the movement or an enemy of it. And doing interpretive research adds another layer of complexity. Engaging with questions of meaning, an important aim of this work is trying to understand what their participation means to Hindu nationalist women *in their own terms*. So it was not "just" or merely that my research subjects' ideologies and worldviews are unpalatable, incompatible, and even anathema to my own—which is a significant enough dilemma—but *also* that my research commitment was to try understand their participation in their own terms. How can I write empathetically, trying to understand them from their own worldview, about women participating in a hateful, violent, murderous movement? If I'm not outright condemning them, am I not myself complicit with them? And do I not risk giving further voice to their perspectives (Basu 2018; Blee 1993)?

I readily confess that I have not figured out clear or easy answers to such vexing questions. But I remain committed to the view that we must have some understanding of the movement and its participants in their own terms in order to have any hope of resisting it. I believe further that it is better for those of us with feminist commitments to try to study these issues rather than to ignore or avoid them or not have feminists engaging them at all. I also believe more generally that feminists must recognize and face down directly some of our own issues—including, for example, masculinity (Carver 2008) or religion (Mahmood 2005; Deo 2018). Ultimately, I would argue that a broad-based, inclusive, and deeply representative Indian feminism is critical to begin to combat the Hindu Right at the peak of its political power and ascendancy.

* * *

This chapter traced multiple ways that this book builds on and expands decades of disciplinary political science scholarship on women and religion, as well as critical, interdisciplinary scholarly and activist work in response to the mobilization of women into Hindu nationalist politics during the 1980s and 1990s. Broadly speaking, a first phase of interdisciplinary literature on women in Hindu nationalism, before 2004, concerned the BJP during its rise to national political power. Early scholarship in this first phase faced a political party still marked in important ways by the legacy of the Janata Party, the philosophy of Gandhian socialism, and the leadership of A. B. Vajpayee. In this early phase, the BJP was for the first time shedding its status as a political pariah and establishing itself as a contender for power, a potential ally for coalitions, and a viable alternative to the overwhelming and historical dominance of the Congress Party on the national scene. After 2004, the BJP was an established rather than aspiring national political force, and newly recommitted to hardline Hindu nationalist ideology. Even during ten years in opposition, the BJP's share of seats in the Lok Sabha never dipped below its performance in 1990. After 2004, a second phase of interdisciplinary literature built on longer-term immersion or engagement with women in the movement, such as ethnographic studies; and scholars also engaged more directly with the role of masculinity as well as gendered roles in Hindu nationalism.

Across both the early and later phases, interdisciplinary literature on women in Hindu nationalism continued to be underpinned by two core questions: why do women participate in the movement? And to what extent can, or should, or could such participation be (seen as) empowering for women? Decades of literature have shed considerable insight but offered no final answers to these questions. I suggest that as critical and constitutive as these questions are, they may not be amenable to such answers. Refocusing the "why" and "empowerment" questions, as this study does, can bring the insights of intersecting political science literatures to the interdisciplinary study of women in Hindu nationalism, and vice versa.

Disciplinary literatures in political science have asked different questions on the subjects of women, religion, and politics. Scholarship on women's political participation has been more concerned with why women *don't* participate than why they do. A nascent literature on religious/conservative women is focusing largely on questions of how such women represent all women or women's interests, or how they affect their parties or policies, whereas I start by examining what forms their participation takes and what it means. Scholars of religion and politics are beginning to grapple with the insights that the study of non-Abrahamic religion could bring, and my study of Hindu nationalism, through the lens of gender, thus adds two perspectives simultaneously that expand the reach of the scholarship. And disciplinary scholarship on political parties, Indian party systems, and comparative scholarship seeking to explain the BJP's rise to power has yet to fully undertake temporal comparison—looking at the party before, during, and since its rise to power—through the lens of women and gender, both of which this book does in one stroke.

Putting disciplinary and interdisciplinary literatures in conversation leads to my argument that in order to understand why women participate, it is first necessary to understand *how* they participate and how their participation has changed over time. And rather than asking whether their participation is empowering, it is first necessary to understand what their participation *means* for them, for the party, and for Indian democracy. Chapter 2 explored how women participated in the BJP *during* its rise to power its rise to power in the 1980s and 1990s. To place this participation in context requires examining how women participated, and continue to participate, in Hindu nationalist politics *before* and *since* the party's ascendance. The next two chapters thus look back from the 1980s and 1990s to trace the participation of women in Hindu nationalist politics when the movement was initially founded in the early 1900s (Chapter 4)—*before* Hindu nationalism attained political success—and then forward from the 1980s and 1990s to unravel the participation of women in the contemporary BJP during the 2010s (Chapter 5)—*since* the party's initial rise to power.

LOOKING BACK, LOOKING FORWARD

The prior chapters analyzed Hindu nationalist politics during the BJP's initial rise to power in the 1980s and 1990s. Chapter 1 excavated history and quantitative data to demonstrate that Hindu nationalism did not succeed politically as long as it continued to marginalize women. Chapter 2 developed a framework of gendered mobilization of women *during* the BJP's initial ascent to national political power in the 1980s and 1990s, which involved deploying gendered discourses, challenging feminism, and rallying women into the streets. Chapter 3 then analyzed the different questions underlying scholarly and activist analyses of women's participation in Hindu nationalist politics across disciplinary and interdisciplinary literatures, and finished by exploring the potential impacts of my own positionality in gathering the research that underpins the next two chapters.

Tracing a longer genealogy of women's participation in Hindu nationalism before and after the 1980s and 1990s, to place it into historical and comparative perspective, is the task of the next two chapters. Chapter 4 focuses on the All-India Hindu Mahasabha (or simply Hindu Mahasabha) from its establishment in 1915 until 1951, *before* the BJP's initial rise to power in the 1980s and 1990s. In this period the Hindu Mahasabha marginalized women from Hindu nationalist politics. This marginalization corresponded to a traditional gender ideology that saw women's place as being (literally and physically) in the home—even as other, contemporaneous political parties and social movements began to mobilize women albeit only in token ways. This failure to include women in even token ways paralleled the Hindu Mahasabha's electoral failures in this time period.

Chapter 5 then fast-forwards to the period around the 2014 election that returned the BJP to power after a decade in the opposition, to show how the BJP has incorporated women *since* its initial rise to power in the 1980s and 1990s. But the party has incorporated women while espousing a gender ideology of complementarity that continues to conceptually tether women to the private sphere through the trope of "family support" for women's political activities and the kin-like structures of the Rashtriya Swayamsevak Sangh ("National Volunteer Corps," or RSS).

Across both Chapters 4 and 5, I draw on insights of V. O. Key's ([1942] 1964) classic study to trace women's participation in Hindu nationalist politics. I trace women's participation in the party-as-organization by examining their roles in the leadership and governance structures of the party, including the women's wing; and I trace women's participation in the party-in-the-electorate by examining women as BJP candidates as well as excavating the role of women's issues party platforms.

4
Women Marginalized
The All-India Hindu Mahasabha, 1915–1951

This chapter historicizes the role of women in Hindu nationalist politics, before its initial rise to power, in its formative period in northern and western India at the turn of the twentieth century by focusing on the All-India Hindu Mahasabha (Hindu Mahasabha). The Hindu Mahasabha was the first political party of Hindu nationalism, and the predecessor, once removed, of today's Bharatiya Janata Party (BJP). In this period, women were marginalized by the Hindu Mahasabha from participating in any significant or ongoing ways. For women, marginalization manifested in a gender ideology that tethered women to the home and the private sphere literally and physically; while for the party, marginalization corresponded with political failure, the extent of which can be gauged in comparison to other political parties and Hindu nationalist organizations operating in the same time period. The historical record between 1915 and 1951 shows the persistent, unrealized efforts of one woman to be involved in the Hindu Mahasabha, and to get the party to do more to engage women on a larger scale. But the Hindu Mahasabha could not or would not balance its traditional gender ideology with its need to court women as voters as India moved toward independence and democracy.

Because of the trajectory of British political reforms in India, elections and suffrage slowly expanded prior to independence (Pearson 2004; Sinha 2000) and Indian political parties faced elections a decade before independence arrived. Insofar as women slowly joined the ranks of potential voters, this posed what I argue is a unique dilemma—or conflicting set of incentives—for the Hindu Mahasabha as a religious nationalist political party in a democracy. On the one hand, its traditional gender ideology confined women to the private sphere, constructing them as supporters *of* the nation rather than themselves constituting the nation. On the other hand, to win elections in a competitive democracy, a political party must win as many votes as it can get—and cutting out half the electorate is a crippling disadvantage. The poor electoral record of the Hindu Mahasabha—outlined in Chapter 1—coincides with its poor record including women and suggests that the party failed to find a way to negotiate these competing pulls.

In this chapter I employ interpretive empirical methods of close reading and discursive content analysis of primary and secondary sources based on archival research into Hindu Mahasabha party documents to reconstruct the parameters of women's marginalization in this period. During multiple fieldwork trips between 2010 and 2012, I examined complete folders of Hindu Mahasabha party papers; the papers of S. P. Mookerjee, a key leader of the party from 1939 to 1946; and microform copies of the *Hindu Outlook*, the party's main publication organ, all held at the Nehru Memorial Museum and Library in New Delhi. These documents included two folders of the papers of Jankibai Joshi of Pune in western India, who headed a women's wing of the Hindu Mahasabha from 1935 to 1950, working ceaselessly but ultimately unsuccessfully to convince men Hindu Mahasabha leaders to actively recruit Hindu women into the party. To my knowledge I am the first to analyze these papers.[1]

The marginalization of women from the Hindu Mahasabha was defined by the absence of consistent and structured attempts to bring women into the party. I trace women's marginalization in two ways. First, I examine the role of women internally, within the leadership and governance structures of the Hindu Mahasabha, including the women's wing. This corresponds to V. O. Key's "party-as-organization" ([1942] 1964). Internally, women were absent from the governance structures of the party; their participation was intermittent and dependent on individual personalities of men leaders and of women seeking to participate. Internal marginalization also manifested as lack of support for a women's wing of the party: even when one existed, its activities were minimal and sporadic rather than robust and ongoing, and dependent on the efforts of one woman acting without the support of—and often in the face of active resistance from—the exclusively male leadership of the party. Second, I examine the role of women in and through the party's electoral activities— what Key called the "party-in-the-electorate"—by focusing on women Hindu Mahasabha candidates as well as an in-depth analysis of the party's election manifestos. Electorally, there was no consistent, structured attempt to recruit women as candidates or give them tickets to contest elections for the party. Women candidates were usually relatives of a male party member—reflecting what has come to be called a "dynastic" approach to political parties in India, most often associated with the Congress Party. Women's issues in party platforms were not addressed qua women's issues: rather, they were secondary to other agendas such as social or religious reform.

It is useful here to briefly consider my use of the term "marginalization" to describe the role of women in the Hindu Mahasabha. The term, of course, implies deliberate, intentional forethought. Do I think men Hindu Mahasabha leaders deliberately marginalized women? I believe they did marginalize women deliberately in the sense that they knew what they were doing. As I will show, certain women were explicitly pushing them to include more women, but they did not take steps to do so. If women like Jankibai Joshi wanted to bring women into the party and seemed willing to try do so on their own, without any real help or support from the party structure, Hindu Mahasabha leaders (barely) tolerated such work, but they did nothing to actively support it. I will also show that Hindu nationalism was underpinned by ideological views that actually dictated against the role of women in the public, political sphere.

Accordingly, this chapter begins by demonstrating the Hindu Mahasabha's marginalization of women internally and electorally. I examine the role of women within the party, in its leadership and governance structures, including the struggles of one woman to establish a women's wing, the All-India Mahila [Woman] Sabha, and convince party leaders to include women in the party. Then I turn to women's marginalization in the party's electoral activities by examining women as candidates for the party and analyzing how women's issues were dealt with in party platforms. In the second section I lay out what marginalization of women meant for the party: in this period, it corresponded with almost total political failure for the Hindu Mahasabha. I elucidate this by comparing the Hindu Mahasabha to contemporaneous political parties and organizations. Finally, the third section examines what marginalization meant for women by laying out the ideological underpinnings and gendered discourses of Hindu nationalism that constrained the vision of women's possible roles in Hindu nationalist politics.

Women in the Hindu Mahasabha: Historical Marginalization

Internal Marginalization of Women: Governance Structures and the Women's Wing

Women did not hold any significant positions of leadership within the Hindu Mahasabha. Unlike the Congress Party, no woman ever served as Hindu

Mahasabha president. No woman's name was listed in all the lists of members of party committees that I examined. The clearest evidence of the marginalization of women from the party's governance structures can be gleaned from the papers and activities of one woman, Jankibai Joshi of Pune, Maharashtra, in western India, who worked tirelessly for the better part of almost two decades to convince Hindu Mahasabha leaders to actively recruit women. Figure 4.1 shows an image of one of her letters on Hindu Mahasabha letterhead. Joshi was convinced, and sought to convince male party leaders, that the Hindu Mahasabha needed to make special efforts to recruit women; she wrote, "My firm conviction is that it is for us, Hindusabhaites, to encourage women folk to interest themselves in Hindu Maha Sabha activities."[2]

Joshi's attempts to promote women's participation in the Hindu Mahasabha reflected her belief in the need for simple descriptive representation for women: "It is . . . fair that our Hindu Mahilas [women], who form about 50% of the total population of Hindus, should also have representation."[3] She argued that "the Mahasabha is the only representative organization competent to speak on behalf of the Hindus"[4] and thus was the only vehicle that could "genuinely" represent Hindu women. This reflected the general Hindu nationalist view that the Congress Party—as a party open to all communities—could not represent the specific interests of the Hindu community. Joshi further argued that the organization (the All-India Women's Conference [AIWC])[5] and the individual (Renuka Ray) whom British colonial officials had tapped to represent *Indian* women, could not adequately represent *Hindu* women. Joshi argued that the AIWC could not represent Hindu women precisely because it was open to *all* Indian women; and she argued that Ray could not represent Hindu women because Ray herself followed the Brahmo faith, a reform sect within Hinduism: "The All India Women's Conference cannot and does not represent us. Mrs. Renuka Ray . . . is not qualified to represent the Hindu women of India and . . . her representation will neither bind nor safeguard them."[6]

Joshi was also keenly pragmatic about the party's need to recruit Hindu women to be successful politically: Hindu women could provide a critical base of support for the party, in her view. As early as 1943, Joshi expressed concern that

> the principles of Hindu Maha Sabha have not as yet touched the minds of Hindu women. According to the 1935 [Government of India Act] Reforms

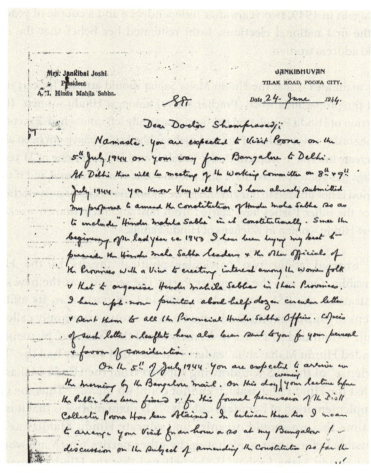

Figure 4.1 Letter from J. Joshi to S. P. Mookerjee, June 24, 1914
Source: Papers of S. P. Mookerjee (II-IV Inst), Sub. File-63, Nehru Memorial Museum and Library, New Delhi.

every literate Hindu woman of age is entitled to vote. After the War [World War II] political parties other than the Hindu Maha Sabha will exploit ignorance and apathetic condition of Hindu women and they will strengthen their position against Hindu Maha Sabha. It is therefore with a view to educate Hindu women, to remove apathy on their part and to make them Hindu-Sabha-minded that the Organisation like "Hindu Mahila Sabha" is necessary.[7]

Then again in 1949, two years after independence and a couple of years before the first national elections, Joshi reiterated her belief that the sabha should address women:

> My main idea is that the Hindu Maha Sabha should arrange for carrying out the propaganda work (Prachar Karya) amongst Hindu women. That portion of Hindu Population has been practically left untouched. Except in Maharashtra every where I noticed maha sabha leaders have not been able to create interest in women. Under "Adult Franchise" every one of 21 years of age has got a vote. We have still got one year at our disposal and if this period is not utilized to our advantage we should not think of next election. I see the other Parties have started from now and their women workers meet Hindu women in Kitchens of Hindu Families.[8]

Joshi worried about two particular political threats to the Hindu Mahasabha. One was the Congress Party. The second was the new social organization, the RSS, founded in 1925 and, in particular, its affiliated women's organization, the Rashtriya Sevika Samiti—commonly called the "Samiti"—founded in 1936.[9] Joshi mentioned the "Samitee" by name and reminded Hindu Mahasabha leaders that they had already had the "bitter experience" of the RSS withdrawing support from the Hindu Mahasabha and that the Hindu Mahasabha "cannot count on them."[10] Thus she urged the implementation of her ideas quickly: "My main motive is that it is now high time that we should organize and educate Hindu Mahilas as soon as possible before their exploitation by other parties which are working against Hindu Maha Sabhas."[11] She believed that the Hindu Mahasabha was well behind the curve in this aspect; she argued that the kinds of efforts she was still advocating in the 1940s should have been undertaken immediately after the 1935 Government of India Act was passed. Because the Hindu Mahasabha was lagging in its efforts, "Hindu women are likely to be persuaded and induced by other Political Parties which are mischievously working against Hindu Maha Sabha. They will thus add to their voting strength and this means danger to Hindu Maha Sabha."[12] On the eve of elections in 1950, she lamented, "I know . . . that the half the [sic] portion of the entire Hindu population was women and it was going under the influence of the Congress activities."[13] In fact, I show later in this chapter that Joshi was right: both the Congress Party and the RSS were far ahead of the Hindu Mahasabha in including women.

Another important woman leader in Hindu nationalist politics in this era was Vijaya Raje Scindia—often known as "Rajmata," or "Mother of the Nation." Born to a royal Indian family exiled to Nepal, in 1941 she was married to Jivajirao Scindia, the maharaja of Gwalior—one of the largest and wealthiest princely states of preindependence India. Gwalior was eventually merged into the state of Madhya Pradesh, and Scindia was inducted into electoral politics in 1957, when she was elected to the Lok Sabha on a Congress ticket, and reelected in 1962. After 1962, though, her autobiography traces a growing disillusionment with the Congress Party leadership; by the 1967 election she claims, "I had made up my mind to leave the Congress Party" (Scindia 1987, 195) and she ran for a seat in the Madhya Pradesh state legislative assembly on a Jana Sangh ticket and won that election, becoming the leader of the opposition and eventually the leader of the assembly (Scindia 1987, 195–203). When the Jana Sangh merged into the Janata Party that won the 1977 election, Scindia was appointed to a seat in the Rajya Sabha. Finally, when the Janata government fell in 1979 and the Jana Sangh reconstituted itself as the BJP in 1980, Scindia stayed with the party and became "its elected Vice-President" (Scindia 1987, 264) a position she held for almost 20 years, until she stepped down and left electoral politics in 1998.[14]

For the purposes of this study, what is perhaps most interesting about Vijaya Raje Scindia's political career is the total lack of evidence she was ever involved with the Hindu Mahasabha, despite two factors that would have portended such a connection. First, the princely states, and specifically Gwalior in central India, including what would become the state of Madhya Pradesh, were a key base of support for the Hindu Mahasabha, both geographically and demographically. Second, Scindia's ideological commitments to Hindu nationalism were evidenced by her long and strong post-1967 record of work with the Jana Sangh and BJP. Furthermore, as the Hindu Mahasabha originally functioned as a pressure group within the Congress Party (see Chapter 1), she could have belonged to both organizations simultaneously. I could find no evidence that the Hindu Mahasabha ever tried to recruit her or involve her with the organization; she is nowhere mentioned in any Hindu Mahasabha papers that I could find, including in the long lists of names that Jankibai Joshi forwarded and proposed at various times for committee and other Hindu Mahasabha memberships for women.

The marginalization of women within the Hindu Mahasabha can also be seen in the (failed) attempts to establish a women's wing for the party.

Joshi worked desperately to advance a national women's wing of the Hindu Mahasabha: the All-India Hindu Mahila Sabha. The earliest mention of a women's wing was in 1935, at the Hindu Mahasabha conference held in Pune. After 1935, Hindu Women's Conferences were held in conjunction with annual Hindu Mahasabha conferences in 1937 (at Ahmedabad), 1938 (at Nagpur), and 1939 (at Calcutta).[15]

Joshi focused significant efforts on trying to get the Hindu Mahasabha constitution amended to institutionalize the women's wing. She sought to have Mahila Sabhas established at the provincial levels, and to have annual meetings of the All-India Mahila Sabha coincide with party annual meetings. At the 1942 Hindu Mahasabha meeting in Kanpur, Resolution No. 5, to hold an All-India Hindu Women's Conference annually with the regular meeting of the Hindu Mahasabha, was accepted, but it was never implemented.[16] Two years later, constitutional amendments for a regular annual session and the establishment of provincial branches had still not passed, and Joshi remained concerned to have them considered.

> I am . . . really anxious to see this work taken up in the coming working committee meeting. I do not think it will occupy much time . . . if we set up for about 15 minutes we will be able to fix it up. There are a number of amendment [sic] lying in the office to be considered & for God's sake I do not wish my proposal for amending the Constitution should be kept hanging with these.[17]

She repeated the request again in 1946: "In order to spread the Hindu Maha Sabha principles amongst Hindu women and to make them Hindu-Maha-Sabha-minded the [All-India] Hindu Women's Conference should be arranged regularly with the [All-India] Hindu Maha Sabha sessions."[18] She was still repeating the request as late as 1950.[19]

Joshi also worked to try to build women's wings in the party at the provincial level. In 1943, the Working Committee in Delhi passed a resolution "insisting on Provincial Hindu-Sabhas to start the Hindu Mahila Sabha Organisation in their Provinces."[20] Joshi sent letters to the provincial Hindu Mahasabha presidents reminding them that "it is the duty of every Provincial Hindu Sabha to give special attention to the work amongst Hindu Women through such Hindu Mahila Sabhas and that in election to the Provincial Hindu Sabhas . . . due consideration should be given to the claims of representation of Hindu women."[21]

In these efforts, Joshi seemed to have received the most support from S. P. Mookerjee when he was president of the Hindu Mahasabha—but that support was primarily rhetorical. In his 1943 presidential address, Mookerjee made what must have been a reference to Joshi's work: "It is a matter [sic] for gratification that steps have been taken by some of our enlightened sisters from western India to consolidate Hindu women under the banner of Hindu Mahasabha. The Hindu Mahasabha must give this new venture the support that it undoubtedly deserves" (Mathur 1996, 202). One year later, with respect to Joshi's constitutional amendments, Mookerjee wrote emphatically to V. G. Deshpande that "the matter should be decided without any further delay. Kindly see that it is placed before the next meeting of the Working Committee."[22]

But nothing happened, and Joshi continued to encounter resistance, direct and indirect, at the central and provincial levels. Joshi named two central party leaders in particular that she feared were resistant to the work she was trying to urge the party to do: L. B. Bhopatkar (president of the Hindu Mahasabha in 1946) and Gokulchand Narang. With respect to the former, she expressed concern to Mookerjee regarding a subcommittee that had been charged with drafting proposed amendments, including those relating to women's participation. "I am still afraid because in the subcommittee Mr. Bhopatkar is one of the five members who is opposed to any such women's activities."[23] In a letter to Narang in 1944, Joshi referred to "difficulties" in getting her resolutions passed or even considered by the Subject Committee, which she said "threw out" her resolutions. She asked Narang if he opposed her proposals, and asked, if provincial sabhas submitted similar proposals to the Delhi office, would they be "rejected" by him and the subcommittee "for reasons you had already for throwing away my suggestions"?[24]

Then at the provincial level, Joshi noted that in response to central directives to establish provincial mahila sabhas, "some of them [provincial sabhas] raised technical difficulties and some were not attentive to carrying out the resolutions practically."[25] Specifically, they had been requested to include women among the representatives they were entitled to send to the central All India Committee of the party. But because they refused to do so, she found that "except myself there was no other Hindu Mahila duly elected on the All India Committee though the President and other members of the Committee were ready to elect one more Hindu Lady on the Working Committee."[26] She conveyed to the central party leaders that "some of the Provinces wish me to say that this work could be taken up when the Hindu Sabha Constitution would be suitably amended so as to include the Hindu Mahila Sabha in it."[27] Thus Joshi encountered what can only be called the runaround: provincial officials suggested they would do more for a women's wing if the central Hindu Mahasabha constitution was changed; but the central party leadership was sluggish about changing the constitutional provisions, and sought instead to slough the work off onto the provinces.

At the 1942 Kanpur session, Joshi was invited to serve as the sole female member of the Hindu Mahasabha Working Committee. But her appointment ended after five years, and she was never replaced by another woman member despite several requests and suggestions she made toward that end. Her papers betrayed her frustration at the obstacles she repeatedly encountered. Unable to garner support for a women's wing, by 1949 Joshi indicated that she felt "out of the loop" and cut off from the party.[28]

Electoral Marginalization of Women: Candidates and Platforms

In addition to their marginalization within the party-as-organization, the marginalization of women in this period can be traced in the party-in-the-electorate, through an examination of the role of women's issues in party platforms and women as candidates. As candidates, at the national level, women in the Hindu Mahasabha were notably absent. Only one woman, Shakuntala Nayar, served in the First Lok Sabha as a Hindu Mahasabha member of parliament. Her husband was K. K. Nayar, "an outspoken Hindu communalist and a member of the RSS" (Gould 1969, 62).[29] One party publication lauded another woman, Rajkumari Amrit Kaur, for her work as general secretary of the All India Women's Cow Protection Conference (Akhil Bharat Hindu Mahasabha 1942, 77)—a long and still-cherished platform of Hindu nationalism. However, Kaur was a lifelong Congress stalwart: she ran in the country's first elections as a Congress Party candidate and served in Nehru's government for many years (Rook-Koepsel 2015).

In their party platforms—including central and provincial branches—the Hindu Mahasabha did include many issues that affected women. As early as the 1920s, Hindu Mahasabha leaders stressed the need to "better the condition of Hindu women" (Weiner 1957, 166), called for greater attention to the education of girls, and denounced the dowry system (Mathur 1996). By the end of the 1930s, several of the party's platforms included the following points related to women: to encourage intermarriage by caste and sect, to protect those who intermarry from social repression, to encourage widow remarriage, to oppose child marriage and support raising the age of consent, and to reject the dowry system. Indeed several agenda points went even further: to remove purdah (veiling or seclusion), to promote the education of women and provide training for them to support their own livelihood, to provide physical training for women, and to encourage women to carry arms to defend their honor (Mathur 1996, 62–63).

At a glance, such agendas appear quite progressive. Of course, we will never know whether the Hindu Mahasabha might have enacted these agendas, since it never won power. But such issues were in the service of some other goal: most commonly, to reform Hindu socioreligious practices in ways that Hindu Mahasabha party leaders believed would strengthen Hindu society and religion. Accordingly, such calls were geared more toward improving women's status as a way to strengthen and unify the Hindu community as a whole, rather than reflecting a concern for the condition of women as an important issue in its own right. Hindu Mahasabha leaders believed that "the progress of women in all spheres of life and their emancipation from all bonds are indispensably needed for the regeneration of the Hindu society" (Mathur 1996, 63). For the Hindu Mahasabha, the emphasis on social reform related directly to the idea of the nation as a body, and social reform was necessary to strengthen that body. Mookerjee argued in 1943, "If the society is to be revitalized our mothers and sisters have to play their due part in the rebuilding of the Indian nation" (Mathur 1996, 202). This made, in the first instance, women's rights a means to an end rather than an end itself.[30]

What Marginalization Meant for the Party: The Hindu Mahasabha in Comparison

The Hindu Mahasabha's electoral failures stood in notable contrast to successor Hindu nationalist parties—the Jana Sangh and today's BJP (detailed in Chapter 1). Both before and after independence, the Hindu Mahasabha was unable to make headway in winning elections or getting its candidates elected to office. As detailed above, its second failure—to include women in even the most token ways—was equally notable. One might imagine this was a sign of the times rather than a particular failing of the Hindu Mahasabha; after all, the early 1900s in colonial India have hardly been marked as a period of great feminist consciousness. Globally, women in this period in the Western countries were still struggling for suffrage, property ownership, and the most basic political and economic rights. Indeed, political philosopher Carole Pateman has argued that the marginalization of women from the public, political sphere and their relegation to the private sphere was not just a sign of the times, but was actually the defining moment of the modern political era (Pateman 1988).

But there is an argument that the marginalization of women from nationalist projects was more a Western than a universal phenomenon. Jill Vickers agrees with Pateman that in the West, "women's loss of public, civic, and property rights was not an accidental feature of nation-state making and consolidation, but actually central to it" (Vickers 2008, 24). But in anti- and postcolonial nationalisms, women were involved and incorporated from the start: "In many post-colonial countries, women and men became citizens simultaneously . . . and women's participation in national movements often gained them civil and property rights in the new states" (Vickers 2008, 27). Indeed in India, universal adult suffrage came at the moment of independence in 1947. Regardless of the reasons, forms, or intentions, this made women and women's interests part of the national discourse (even if only in rhetoric) from its inception. But the Hindu Mahasabha failed to include women even in this minimal, rhetorical sense. And this failure cannot simply be chalked up to the time period. A brief overview of two contemporaneous political parties—the Indian National Congress and the Muslim League—shows the Hindu Mahasabha was behind the curve in including women.

These comparisons with a secular and a Muslim political party might suggest that Hindu nationalism itself was inhospitable to women's participation. But a final comparison demonstrates the opposite. I briefly examine the contemporaneous role of women in the RSS, a Hindu nationalist social movement organization founded in 1925—which quickly became the anchor organization of Hindu nationalism—to show how it also, despite initial resistance and with significant limitations, managed to involve women, albeit in a token and unequal way.

The Congress Party

Decades prior to independence, the Congress Party was more adept at fostering the participation of women in the fight for independence and in the public, political sphere more generally (Forbes 1996; Kumar 1997). Founded in 1885, within 40 years Congress had elected two women presidents: Annie Besant in 1917 and Sarojini Naidu in 1925.[31] After independence, Indira Gandhi was president in 1959 and again from 1978 1984. Sonia Gandhi held the position from 1998 to 2017. Thus, counting by years, the Congress Party has been presided over by women for 20 percent of its history. Ordinary women were also mobilized in the Congress Party's everyday activities at the local, village, and street levels (Thapar-Björkert 2006).

Women's involvement was not aimed primarily at their empowerment or liberation per se. India paralleled the experience of many anticolonial nationalisms in that it mobilized women in the quest for independence and relegated women's rights issues to be addressed after the primary goal of throwing off the colonial yoke had been attained. Many scholars have insightfully analyzed these vexed relations between women and the Indian national movement (Jayawardena 1986; Chadya 2003; Menon 2000; Thapar-Björkert 2006; Forbes 1981).

The first national women's associations were organized outside the purview of Congress. The Women's Indian Association, established in 1917, is generally cited as the first; the AIWC was established a decade later in 1927. Within the Congress, some regional women's organizations were established in the mid- to late 1930s,[32] followed finally by the official establishment of a Women's Department within the All India Congress Committee on July 20, 1940 (Franda 1962, 250). The tasks of the department were "to train and educate women workers and to encourage political awareness among them [and] mobilize support for the Congress" (Agnew 1979, 84). However, the department never really took off, in part because its creation was followed immediately by the launching of a major Congress agitation—the 1942 Quit India movement—which ended up landing most Congress leaders in jail; but also in part because of lukewarm support from Congress leaders who leaned to the conservative side of the political spectrum. By 1946, the department was essentially defunct (Basu 1995, 16).[33]

Much of the work of an active women's wing seems to have been carried out instead by the AIWC.[34] Founded in 1927 separately from the Congress Party, the AIWC has always maintained its status as a nonpartisan organization unaffiliated with any political party. Founded by European and Indian women together, it began as an organization focused on educational reform and access for Indian women, then expanded its scope to include issues of social and legal reform. Though never officially affiliated with the Congress

Party, the AIWC worked closely with Congress because of the personal connections and significant overlap between the leadership of the two organizations (Basu and Ray 1990). Over time, the AIWC came to be seen as a more reformist and even conservative organization. It continues to exist today with, as one author put it, "its headquarters in a huge building in Delhi, but . . . little connection with latter day feminist movements" (Kumar 1997, 69).

It is irrelevant to the argument of this book whether women's participation in Congress was merely symbolic; rather, the point is that the Hindu Mahasabha resisted even symbolic ways of involving women. The issue of having a woman member on the Working Committee, the apex decision-making body in both parties, perfectly captures the stark contrast between Congress and the Hindu Mahasabha. We saw above that Jankibai Joshi was the sole female member of the Hindu Mahasabha Working Committee between 1942 and 1947; after serving this one five-year term, she was rather unceremoniously removed from the committee and never replaced by another woman despite her persistent entreaties. The only person who seemed perturbed by the absence of a woman on the Hindu Mahasabha Working Committee was Joshi herself. The contrast with the Congress Party's Working Committee is revealing. Sarojini Naidu, a prominent woman Congress leader, had served on the Congress Working Committee for several years when in 1936, Jawaharlal Nehru, as president of the Congress, appointed a committee that excluded any women. The announcement of the committee without any women produced a large uproar and letter-writing campaigns in protest. In response, Nehru and Gandhi wrote back and forth, with the women leading the protest, variously dodging and assigning blame to each other until finally Nehru "issued a statement 'that he took full responsibility for the non-inclusion of women in the Congress Working Committee'" (Basu 1995, 11–12; see also Agnew 1979, 86–87). Again without arguing that the Congress's inclusion of women was ideal, it nonetheless represented an approach significantly different from that of the Hindu Mahasabha.

The Muslim League

One could reasonably posit that Congress, as a secular and center-left party, was more inclined to grant women a political voice and standing than a religious nationalist political party like the Hindu Mahasabha. Such an argument would accord with findings in the political science literature that progressive and left parties, broadly speaking, are more amenable to including women and women's issues than parties of the Right (Chapter 3). In this way, a case more comparable to the Hindu Mahasabha was the Muslim League. Like the Hindu Mahasabha, the Muslim League was a religious nationalist party: modern in its aspirations of establishing a state for the nation it claimed to represent, a nation defined by religious affiliation but in a political rather than a theocratic sense.

A brief examination of Muslim women's participation in the League brings a few key factors to light. The political participation of Muslim women in League politics is virtually impossible to disentangle from the movement for an independent state of Pakistan (Willmer 1996, 574), an idea that first arose in 1930 and then one decade later, in 1940, was articulated as an official demand of the League. Especially before 1940, the class profile of participation was largely limited to elite urban Muslim women, and especially those of the *ashraf* ("respectable") classes. There was also a large preponderance of women with family connections: many Muslim women who participated in League politics were wives, sisters, mothers, and daughters of key men League leaders. Women initially mobilized around issues of social reform, which came to turn centrally on the issue of purdah. There were debates about whether seclusion—the strictest form of purdah, in which women were physically confined to one part of the home—was Islamic or Hindu in origin; and as some Muslim women began mobilizing for the League, some came out unveiled, while others began to appear in public veiled (mostly in burkas).

As of 1937, the Muslim League Council (its apex decision-making body) included only one woman member—Jahan Ara Shah Nawaz, the daughter of League cofounder Mia Muhammad Shafi. When she pointed this out, the Council agreed, she claimed, that in future, provincial delegations should be asked to include two women each (Pirbhai 2014, 18). At the 1938 session of the League in Patna, Bihar, two key things happened with respect to the participation of women. First, a resolution was passed to increase the participation of women in League politics (Willmer 1996, 580). Second, the League established an All-India Muslim Women's Subcommittee, akin to a women's wing for the party. Its aim was "to coopt Muslim women to organize them for its [the League's] cause" by increasing women's membership numbers in the League, advising on social uplift issues for the Muslim community, organizing women at the provincial levels, and spreading propaganda and raising the political consciousness of Muslim women (Ali 2000, 198). Fatima Jinnah—the younger sister of Mohammad Ali Jinnah, the leader of the Muslim League and the first leader of independent Pakistan—was appointed as its convener (Pirbhai 2014, 18). One author argued that the subcommittee's work was critical for the League, even if the women serving on it were few in number and were mostly wives and sisters of male League leaders (Ali 2000, 260, 199).

In the 1940 Lahore Resolution, the Muslim League made an explicit turn toward a separatist agenda, when Jinnah formally articulated the two-nation theory and the demand for a separate Muslim homeland in the subcontinent. Available records indicate that the mobilization of Muslim women ramped up after this point. So a fairly small, elite, upper-class section of Muslim women mobilized for the vision of an independent Pakistan, where modernity could be achieved within the parameters of Islam—which, they held, could not happen in a united India (Willmer 1996, 583). As Jinnah argued at the time:

> I believe that it is absolutely essential for us to give every opportunity to our women to participate in our struggle of life and death. Women can do a great deal within their homes, even under purdah . . . if political consciousness is awakened amongst our women, remember your children will not have much to worry about. (Quoted in Pirzada 1970, 328)

That year, Muslim women began participating in marches and demonstrations and were arrested for the first time for such activities. Within a couple of years, "The participation of women in the Pakistan Movement were [sic] in full swing" and Jinnah was addressing large gatherings of Muslim women. This momentous upswing continued apace right up until independence: a Women's National Guard was formed, and younger, unmarried women were mobilized; a women's War Council ran an underground radio station (Ali 2000, 199–203); and by 1946–47, photographic evidence showed "the first . . . mass public mobilization of Muslim women anywhere in pre-independent India"—including women in burkas as well as unveiled women (Willmer 1996, 573).

Here again, as with the Congress Party, there is a debate about whether the mobilization of women by the Muslim League was predominantly a strategic maneuver to bolster support for the claim to an independent Pakistani state, rather than evidence of a primary concern for Muslim women's rights.

Many scholars have held that the League was mobilizing women for "political purposes" and "in the interests of its own nationalist agenda without actually formulating a definite agenda for women" (Willmer 1996, 584, 589). Many argued that women's interests, as in so many other anticolonial nationalist movements, were "backseated" once the goal of independence was achieved (Jalal 1991). Others, conversely, believe "the movement that freed the country also freed women from the bondage of the four walls of the house and they were accepted as members of society which so far had exclusively belonged to men" (Ali 2000, 200; see also Pirbhai 2014). But again, as with the Congress Party, the resolution of this debate is not the task of this chapter. Like the Congress Party and unlike the Hindu Mahasabha, the Muslim League seems to have grasped at least the symbolic or strategic role that women could play in the public, political sphere. A final brief comparison with the RSS shows that even another Hindu nationalist organization was able to figure this out.

The RSS

As noted above, the RSS was founded in Nagpur in 1925 by a physician, Dr. K. B. Hedgewar, and quickly became the anchor organization of the broader Hindu nationalist movement (Chapter 1). Since its founding, the RSS has been a men-only organization: even today, women cannot join it. Unlike the Hindu Mahasabha, however, the RSS, within about a decade of its founding, was able to find a way to include women. In 1936, a separate organization, the Rashtra Sevika Samiti (National Women's Service Committee, or "Samiti"), was established for women. Though it is closely affiliated with the RSS and is often referred to as the women's wing of the RSS, the Samiti is actually a separate and independent organization.

The founder of the Samiti was Lakshmibai Kelkar, who was introduced to the RSS through her sons (Figure 4.2). In 1936, she met Dr. Hedgewar and tried to persuade him to bring women into the RSS, arguing that women were critical to the advancement of the nation (Bacchetta 2004). Numerous Hindu nationalist websites attribute to her the following words: "Woman is the inspiring force for the family and for the nation. So long as this force is not awakened, society cannot progress."[35] She ultimately could not persuade Hedgewar to include women in the RSS itself, but he asked her to work with women separately from the men. Thus the Samiti was founded.

Figure 4.2 Lakshmibai Kelkar, founder of the Rashtra Sevika Samiti
Source: http://www.balagokulam.org/teach/biographies/mousi2.php. Accessed March 26, 2018.

Excellent studies have thoroughly documented the structure and organization of the RSS and the Samiti. The activities of both organizations begin at the local level, among individuals and families, and work up hierarchically through towns and villages. Both the RSS and the Samiti concentrate on inculcating what they see as core values of nationalism and patriotism: historically and today, they seek to build an Indian nation—defined always in Hindu terms—from the grassroots up, inculcating Hindu nationalist values in individual people, in families, in villages, and upward from there. This is done through daily meetings involving, among other things, physical exercises, drills, and training—led by the RSS for men, and by the Samiti for women. Kelkar died in November 1978, leaving behind a legacy of what is widely considered to be a highly successful women's wing of a highly successful Hindu nationalist organization, the RSS. Compared with the struggles Jankibai Joshi faced, the contrast with the Hindu Mahasabha is again stark.

Tethering: What Marginalization Meant for Women

If marginalization in this period spelled political failure for the Hindu Mahasabha, for women it meant being tethered to the home—literally and physically. Hindu Mahasabha leaders either could not or would not bring themselves to see women as active participants in the party. In its failure to include women, the Hindu Mahasabha seemed hostage to gendered ideologies of religion and nationalism. Religious movements tend to idealize a nuclear family model that arranges men's and women's roles hierarchically, with no specified limits on the man's/husband's authority over the woman/wife and children. Critically, women are consistently confined to the private sphere, and paid employment is constructed as incompatible with proper motherhood (Hardacre 1993, 132, 139). Nationalist ideologies work in similar ways. Nira Yuval-Davis argued that all nationalist projects implicated women and gender in multiple ways. The most critical areas for the purposes of this study were biological and cultural reproduction. Ethnic nationalism in particular constructed discourses of common origin (or kinship) in many nations, and nations had also to reproduce themselves physically. Women served as the main teachers of national cultures to children, and also often symbolically represented the nation itself as bearers of the collective identity and honor of the nation (Yuval-Davis 1997, Chapter 3; Day and Thompson 2004, Chapter 6).

The gendered ideologies of Hindu nationalism replicated several of these themes in ways that constrained how women could be imagined to participate in the public, political sphere. A close reading of key Hindu nationalist texts[36] shows that Hindu nationalist ideology constructed Hindu women as weak and in need of protection, and advocated social reform measures as a way to strengthen the Hindu community. The terms Hindu Mahasabha leaders most frequently used to describe the condition of Hindu society were "weak," "humiliated," and "impotent." Additional common terms were "divided" and "helpless." The traits that Hindus—most especially Hindu men—possessed were marked as feminized: weak, docile, submissive, passive, and, most explicitly, effete and effeminate. The weakness of Hindus was manifested, in an extremely common Hindu nationalist trope, by their inability to protect the honor of the Hindu religion or even the physical safety of Hindu women, children, widows, and orphans. In contrast, the Hindu Mahasabha sought to advocate a strong, eminently masculine approach. Hindus (men) needed to become "masters in their own house" and attain the ability to protect Hindu women and religion. A nation needed first to be physically strong and adequately armed, and only then could preach moral doctrines—which had to be backed up by a sword to be effective (Mathur 1996; Savarkar 1969).[37]

Women appeared almost invariably in Hindu nationalist ideology as supporters, caretakers, and nurturers *of* the nation, rather than themselves constituting the nation. The nation as people were always "he," "him," and "his." Women became primarily mothers and sisters, who "gave *us* the first suckle at *their* breast" (Savarkar 1984, 16; emphasis added). The nation as geography was sexed both male and female, constructed as both motherland and fatherland, even in the same sentence: "This land is the birth-place— the Matribhu (motherland) and the Pitribhu (fatherland)" (Savarkar 1969, 110). As motherland, "she" was nurturing and fertile, "the richly endowed daughter of God" (Savarkar 1969, 133). "She" served as nursery and cradle for the nation—Hindu men—and "wrapped *us* up in *her* mantle of love" (Prakash 1942, 56; emphasis added).

A key source of Hindu nationalist fear was related to demography. Yuval-Davis argued that women might be subjected to three possible demographic approaches in nationalist ideology: (a) a "people as power" discourse, which would encourage the growth and expansion of the nation and its members and thus ask women to increase the birth rate; (b) a eugenicist discourse that focused not on the size but on the health or quality of the national stock, and thus asked some women (those of the "right" stock) to reproduce more and others (of the "wrong" types) to reproduce less; or (c) a Malthusian discourse that feared overpopulation and thus sought to bring birth rates down (Yuval-Davis 1997, Chapter 2). The first two discourses were evident in the example of Nazi Germany, which called explicitly for (Aryan German) women to leave public employment and return to the home to bear and raise children, and structured incentives for this to happen (Williamson 2002, 57–9).

In the case of the Hindu Mahasabha, this reaction manifested as calls for broader reforms to restructure the Hindu social sphere to minimize losses by religious conversion to proselytizing religions—Christianity and especially Islam—and make it easier for Hindu women to stay within the fold.[38] Although Hindus never constituted less than an overwhelming majority in India (75 percent before 1947, and over 80 percent of the population throughout the postcolonial period), Hindu nationalism (re)creates itself by constructing Hinduism as perpetually under threat: from Congress-style secularism, westernization, and Islam. Despite the overwhelming Hindu advantage in numbers, Hindu Mahasabha leaders fed fear that Muslims would eventually outnumber them. They argued that Hindu sociocultural practices such as untouchability, the social bar against widow remarriage, and the lack of proselytization left Hindus vulnerable to other religions and gave Muslims fertile ground for conversion efforts (Savarkar 1984). Where Hindus were monogamous, Muslims, they suggested, could have multiple wives and (presumably therefore) much more copious progeny (Mathur 1996).

The upper-caste Hindu social bar against widow remarriage also contributed to the demographic problem of the Hindus, according to Hindu nationalist ideology. Here "the cause of Muslim proliferation" was read as "the desire of Hindu widows for Muslim males" (Datta 1993, 1307). That is, because some Hindu communities barred widow remarriage, Hindu nationalists feared that Hindu women would be attracted to the idea of converting to Islam in order to remarry. In this way, social, sexual, and economic explanations melded into each other, and the burden of demographic decline got shifted to Hindu women and their desires. None of these demographic fears were supported by data, now or historically. For example, current data show that the Muslim population growth rates in India are actually declining, and that polygamy is more prevalent among lower-caste Hindus than among Indian Muslims. But in such matters, the point is fear, not facts (Datta 1993; Jenkins and Williams 2021).

Hindu Mahasabha leaders had two solutions to these demographic fears. The first was to get Hindus organized. Underlying this obsession with organization was a conception of masses, castes, and hordes running rampant. Here they unwittingly acknowledged the political reality that despite an apparent overwhelming numerical advantage, Hindus hardly vote—or do anything else—as a bloc. Hindus are riven by divergences of caste, class, region, language, and local religious practices (Williams and Deo 2018). The second solution was to propose social reforms, which seemed in the first instance to make women important objects of Hindu nationalist political agendas, as outlined above. But these concerns were primarily socioreligious and only secondarily about women. For example, widow remarriage was advocated as a way to keep Hindu widows from converting to Islam in order to remarry— not because Hindu Mahasabha leaders were deeply concerned about the well-being of Hindu widows. Accordingly, Hindu Mahasabha agendas relating to women did not and perhaps could not make women important actors in Hindu nationalist politics. The underlying contradiction might be gleaned from a 1938 statement of Hindu Mahasabha leader Bhai Parmanand:

> There is a great campaign in progress in this country to safeguard the rights of women. In the opinion of those who champion this cause, they should be treated equally with men. It is urged that they should be accorded

representation in the Legislatures [sic], Municipalities and other public bodies. But I am absolutely opposed to this. The woman is the flower of the home. Her kingdom is the domestic sphere and her most important mission in life is to be the mother of the race. She has been made by nature to play her role in the home in the same way as a man's field is in the outside world.[39]

This ideological approach sheds light on what marginalization meant for women.

* * *

This chapter has shown multiple ways the Hindu Mahasabha marginalized women from Hindu nationalist politics in the first half of the 20th century both internally and electorally—in terms of governance and a women's wing; as candidates for election; and as subjects or objects of party platforms and political agendas. This record of marginalization contrasts starkly with the approach of successor parties to the Hindu Mahasabha in subsequent eras. I previously examined the BJP's gendered mobilization of women in the 1980s and 1990s as it catapulted to national political prominence (Chapter 2). Looking back from that period, to the Hindu Mahasabha, shows that women were not, in some way, "always already" active participants in Hindu nationalist politics; but neither did their participation appear suddenly and seemingly inexplicably during the 1980s and 1990s. Certainly a few women were active in Hindu nationalist politics before the 1980s and 1990s, such as the women discussed in this chapter––Jankibai Joshi, Vijaya Raje Scindia, Shakuntala Nayar––but they were exceptions that in many ways proved the rule: their participation was occasional and only inconsistently supported by the overwhelmingly male leadership of the Hindu Mahasabha.

The marginalization of women in the early, formative years of Hindu nationalist politics suggests that the participation of women in religious nationalist politics had to be constructed over time: it was not natural, or automatic, or inevitable. And this examination of the early 20th century also suggests that if the participation of women was not natural or inevitable, it seems to have been important. Following Jill Vickers's premise that anticolonial nationalism in the Global South *could* or *did* include women, the case of the Hindu Mahasabha suggests that they *had to* include women to succeed. In India, "Mass participation of women in the nationalist movement in the late 19th and early 20th century was unique. There were no contemporaneous western models" (Agnew 1979, x). This case of the Hindu Mahasabha shows that Indian political parties and movements could marginalize women as well as Western ones could; but it also suggests that doing so could cost them political success. Where the Congress and the Muslim League might have "used" women only symbolically, the Hindu Mahasabha didn't even give symbolic representation to women.

This was certainly a lesson the BJP seems to have learned by the 1980s: Chapter 2 showed how deeply its rise to national political prominence was gendered and marked by women's participation. After 10 years in the opposition, the BJP returned to power in 2014. Widely predicted and expected to win the election with its coalition partners in the National Democratic Alliance, the BJP instead won an absolute majority of seats in the Lok Sabha a landslide victory. But what has been the role of women since the BJP's initial rise to power in the 1980s and 1990s? Do approaches of marginalization or mobilization still prevail?

In the next chapter I show that the contemporary BJP has evolved a third form of women's participation in the party: what I call a model of *incorporation*. Through examination of party documents, in-depth interviews with party leaders, and ethnographic observation of party events in 2013 and again in 2015–16, I will show that the BJP has found ways to systematically incorporate women into the party--but that it has done so without significantly altering traditional gender ideologies. Its gender ideologies today are best captured by the notion of gender complementarity: the idea that men and women are equal, but have different roles to play in society. While incorporation allows for actual influence of important women leaders in the contemporary party, it also curtails the extent to which women's participation in the party might undermine broader patriarchal structures.

5
Women Incorporated
The Contemporary BJP, 2013–2016

In 2014, the Bharatiya Janata Party (BJP) returned to power at the center after a decade in the opposition. In 2004 and again in 2009 the Congress Party, leading the United Progressive Alliance, had swept to power. In 2014, a BJP victory was expected, due to multiple reasons: broad anti-incumbency sentiment (Varshney 2018); the personal popularity of their prime ministerial candidate, Narendra Modi; and the tepid if not dysfunctional state of the ruling Congress Party—its weak organization and lack of vision or viable leadership, a function of its now-total dependence on the dynastic succession of the Nehru-Gandhi line, and lingering auras of corruption scandals plaguing the Manmohan Singh government. What was unexpected in 2014 was for the BJP to win an absolute majority in the Lok Sabha (lower house of parliament). Although the party could therefore have formed a government on its own, it kept its commitment to its partners in the National Democratic Alliance (NDA) and formed a coalition government with them (Sridharan 2014; Kumar 2014).

Chapter 1 showed that each successive Hindu nationalist party has been more successful than its predecessor. This pattern continued in 2014, and the role of women in the BJP evolved accordingly. Today's BJP has evolved an approach very different approach from the Hindu Mahasabha's marginalization of women in the first half of the 20th century (Chapter 4), before its initial rise to power; and the gendered mobilization of the 1980s and 1990s (Chapter 2), during its initial rise to power. A key characteristic of the BJP in the current period has been its success in *incorporating* women. One author has argued that the extent of women's participation in militant Hindu nationalist politics may be overstated (Menon 2003); but the broader consensus is that the breadth and depth of women's participation in the movement is striking.[1]

Yet even as the BJP has incorporated women, the basic gendered ideological underpinnings of Hindu nationalism continue to conceptually tether women to the private sphere. Hindu nationalism today espouses a gender ideology of complementarity: the idea that men and women are equal but have different roles to play in society. Amrita Basu (1993a) has posited a critical distinction between fundamentalist and communalist movements (like Hindu nationalism), noting that the latter can create some restricted spaces for women's participation. It is these restricted spaces that I call incorporation. At its root is the idea of bringing women into existing power structures without fundamentally altering the structures themselves. This chapter explores what incorporation looks like for women in the BJP today and what it has meant for women and for the party.

The question of whether incorporation can empower or liberate women remains vexed: to deny it seems to deny women agency and rationality, but to support it remains anathema for many feminist scholars and activists (Butalia 2001). While incorporation might empower certain women in certain ways, that empowerment cannot be confused with dismantling broader patriarchal social structures that oppress not only women but other disadvantaged groups in society. But my intent is not to try to resolve this dilemma; with Mahmood (2005), I suggest that even to pose the question this way—to make women's liberation the way to measure the outcome of women's incorporation—relies on a constricted view of both. A secular feminist discomfort with the politics of women's participation in modern religious nationalist movements—which I share—has hampered our ability to uncover the meaning(s) of women's changing roles in such politics, both for the movements and for the women themselves. My purpose is to explore how the BJP has co-opted these tensions—between the pull of religion and nationalism for women into the private sphere, and the push of democratic politics for women outward into the political sphere—in order to understand what incorporation has meant both for the party and for women.

In this chapter I rely on entirely new materials, gathered during fieldwork between 2013 and 2016, to construct what women's incorporation in the contemporary BJP looks like. My analysis draws on 18 open-ended, in-depth interviews with BJP leaders, as well as journalists, at two sites over two and a half years: New Delhi, the national capital, and Lucknow, the capital of the northern state of Uttar Pradesh, which is the largest and most populous state in India and the heart of the Hindi-speaking "belt" of states that constitute the BJP's base of support. I conducted fieldwork in 2013—immediately before the 2014 election—and 2015–16, immediately after it. Interviews include three men and 13 women. I interviewed two of these women (one in

New Delhi, one in Lucknow) twice, once before and once after the election, to gauge their sense of the difference between pursuing power and holding it. Four interviews were with journalists (two in Lucknow and two in New Delhi) who had long been assigned specifically to covering the BJP. Two of the interviews were conducted by phone and one by email (Appendix A); all the rest were conducted in person by me in the combination of Hindi and English that characterizes upper-middle-class, urban discourse in India. I also attended the party's campaign kickoff rally in New Delhi in September 2013 and gathered visual images of campaign materials.

This chapter examines women's incorporation in the BJP along the same axes as the previous chapter. I first construct what incorporation looks like internally, within the party or in the "party-as-organization" (Key [1942] 1964) by examining the role of women in party leadership and governance structures, including the status of the Mahila Morcha, the women's wing of the party. Then I construct what incorporation looks like in the party's electoral activities—the "party-in-the-electorate"—by examining women as candidates, as well as analyzing the treatment and presentation of women's issues in the 2014 election platform. I further illustrate the parameters of incorporation through ethnographic and visual analysis of campaign events and materials. In the second section, I turn to consider what incorporation has meant for the party: incorporating women has been correlated with significant—and possibly lasting—political success for the party. Finally, I consider what incorporation has meant for women. I unpack the BJP's current gender ideology of complementarity to show how it continues to tether women to the private sphere through the tropes of "family support" and the kin-like structures of Hindu nationalist organizations that feed membership and women's recruitment into the party.

Incorporation: Women in the Contemporary BJP

Internal Incorporation of Women: Governance Structures and the Women's Wing

The BJP today prominently incorporates women in top leadership and governance positions within the party. I showed in Chapter 4 that Jankibai Joshi encountered persistent resistance to institutionalizing the regular participation and representation of women in the party's governing structures. In contrast, in 2006, then-BJP president Rajnath Singh, together with Sushma Swaraj, instituted a series of changes to the BJP's constitution to regularize and institutionalize the representation of women in the party's governing structures: the party pledged voluntarily to ensure that 33 percent of seats in all governing bodies within the party were held by women.[2] When I asked one interviewee whether this change was instituted with a view to winning elections, she responded that it was not an instrumental move in that way, but rather was meant to improve the representation of women within the party in a broader sense.[3] Indeed, even as the voluntary change was widely touted by party leaders as a sign of the BJP's commitment to gender equality—and it was in fact the first such step taken by any major Indian political party—it's unclear how such a move would have directly impacted electoral performance, the way a commitment to fielding certain percentages of women candidates might have. Indeed, one informant noted wryly that the party could give certain numbers of tickets to women to contest elections if they wanted to, even if it wasn't required by law.[4]

There were several limitations to this voluntary 33 percent commitment. In many cases, the size of a body or committee was expanded to accommodate additional (women) members without removing any existing members—men—from their positions on the committees. Another major limitation was that the changes did not apply to the Parliamentary Board, which is the real center of power and decision-making within the party. In 2014, the Parliamentary Board included only one woman—Sushma Swaraj—out of 12 members (Basu 2015, 65). Finally, multiple informants concurred that while Rajnath Singh had worked to ensure the 33 percent quotas were met while he was party president, these mandates have remained unfulfilled since Amit Shah became president in July 2014.[5]

Nevertheless, during the 2014 election campaign, the party worked hard to make women visible as party leaders in other ways. The BJP's team of national media spokespersons included two women: Nirmala Sitharaman and Meenakshi Lekhi. Media spokespersons "represent" the party in a literal sense: the faces of women appear in the media as the faces of the party, thus conveying the appearance that women hold an important place in the party—they literally "speak for" the party. During my fieldwork especially in 2013, anytime I mentioned my research in general terms to anyone as being on "women of the BJP," from taxi drivers to my relatives, people would respond by mentioning three names consistently as important examples of women leaders within the party: Sushma Swaraj, Meenakshi Lekhi, and

Nirmala Sitharaman. The latter two were media spokespersons during the campaign: constantly on TV, they conveyed an impression of the importance of women within the party to the general public. One of my interviewees claimed the BJP had 30–40 percent women as media spokespersons in the 2013 campaign, the maximum number of any political party.[6] But while media spokespersons certainly convey party positions publicly, that doesn't necessarily mean they play an important role in formulating them.

The BJP women's wing, the Mahila Morcha, is now a well-institutionalized if not necessarily powerful part of the party's organizational infrastructure. Five of my interviewees in 2015 and one in 2013 were or had been involved with the Mahila Morcha, including four in Lucknow and one in Delhi; and they included regional, state, and national leaders of the Mahila Morcha. Its primary function remains largely a social work and support organization for the party (Thachil 2014), with only a limited role as a launching pad for power in the central party organizations. Not all powerful women in the party came through the Mahila Morcha, nor do all the women who go through the Mahila Morcha reach upper positions in the party power structure. A prime example is Smriti Irani, a former model and actress who joined the party in 2003 and served in various roles, including as an executive member of the central committee, and party national secretary in 2010. That same year she served as national president of the Mahila Morcha. Despite this service, when Modi appointed her as minister of human resource development in his cabinet in 2014, several of my informants questioned what real work she had done for the party.[7] Conversely, a very active and committed former national vice president of the Mahila Morcha, whom others stated should have received a ticket to contest an election, did not. Thus work in the Mahila Morcha does not necessarily translate into powerful appointments within the party.

Women of the Mahila Morcha worked hard for the party in the 2014 elections, doing much of the door-to-door, face-to-face work of talking to people, recruiting them to the party, and convincing them to vote for the party. Two of my interviewees reiterated the idea propounded by Jankibai Joshi in the first half of the 20th century: that only women could go into homes and reach other women and family members for the party.[8] One interviewee explained that she sometimes even stayed with families for two to three days, talking with them about Modi's accomplishments and advancing their knowledge about the party, often to illiterate women.[9] Another described how during the campaign she was out all day, every day, visiting different neighborhoods in Lucknow, including some Muslim communities where women wouldn't come out of their homes.[10] A former national vice president of the Mahila Morcha confirmed that during the campaign, the Mahila Morcha was fully involved in door-to-door canvassing, seeking to recruit whole families to the party, not just the women. She stated that social work and helping women is a very important part of the Mahila Morcha's charge, but before the election, its primary purpose was to help the party win the election.[11]

Electoral Incorporation of Women: Candidates and Platforms

Virtually across the board, everyone I spoke with before and after 2014 agreed that the BJP needs to run more women as candidates. After the 2014 election, out of 280 BJP MPs in the Lok Sabha, a mere 31 (11 percent) were women.[12] The speaker of the Lok Sabha was a woman, BJP stalwart Sumitra Mahajan, who was elected to the post unanimously. In the Rajya Sabha, the BJP had three women out of 48 members—just 6 percent. These include three of the seven women who held ministerial appointments in Modi's government: Dr. Najmah Heptullah, cabinet minister for minority affairs; Smriti Irani, cabinet minister for human resource development; and Nirmala Sitharaman, minister of state for commerce and industry (independent charge) and finance/corporate affairs (Soni 2014).

Sushma Swaraj seemed to constitute a special case of the need to field more women as candidates. Described as a "universal" leader within the party,[13] Swaraj is a genuine political force, a skilled orator with an independent base of power who worked her way up through the party ranks. Swaraj was an official spokesperson for the BJP until the late 1990s, the first woman to serve in that capacity for any major Indian political party. When the BJP was out of power, she served as leader of the opposition in the Lok Sabha, the first BJP woman to do so (Shankar 2013, 222). In June 2013, the selection of Modi as prime ministerial candidate was controversial within the party. A "hard-line" faction argued the best way to win back power was to abandon moderation and return to Hindutva's core principles. But opponents feared Modi would be seen as too extreme and still tainted by his affiliation with the 2002 Gujarat riots, when he was chief minister of that state. His selection, pushed essentially by the RSS, prompted public objection and almost led to a defection from the party by L. K. Advani, a senior and longtime party leader and an RSS stalwart himself. The selection of Modi as the prime ministerial candidate was taken to represent the triumph of the hard-line faction and reinforced the idea that the moderate wing of the party was linked with failure (PTI 2013b; BBC News 2013).[14] Prior to Modi's nomination, speculation abounded that Swaraj could or would or should be the party's prime ministerial candidate in 2014. When she wasn't selected, I asked all my 2013 interviewees whether the fact that she was a woman might have put her at a disadvantage. One admitted that to a certain extent women were seen as representing the moderate face of the party,[15] where moderation had become linked with the political failures of 2004 and 2009. Yet they insisted that Swaraj being a woman had nothing to do with her nonselection, and that the PM candidate was selected solely on the basis of "winnability," or who was most likely to win the election regardless of gender.[16]

Of course, it doesn't take a great deal of sophisticated theorizing to recognize the discourse of "winnability" as a gendered one: men would virtually by definition be seen or assumed to be more likely to win elections. The idea was in any case empirically debunked in Chapter 1, where I showed that women's win rates are consistently and continually higher than men's throughout the postindependence period. More complexly, the association of women with the moderate face of the party was itself a gendered construction that may have disadvantaged Swaraj. More than one source described Swaraj as a "prime minister in waiting"; and one senior BJP leader sought to minimize the gendered aspect by pointing out that other men in the party, such as Advani, were also waiting.[17] Her skill and work were acknowledged by Modi in his appointment of Swaraj as cabinet minister for external affairs / overseas Indian affairs—an especially critical post for a prime minister who has forged such a strong support base in the diaspora, and a government that believes strongly that foreign relations are important.[18]

After the 2014 election victory, as discussed above, many other women leaders in the party received important appointments. Several of my interviewees—party leaders in Lucknow and journalists in Delhi—expressed concern that women were promoted based on name recognition rather than work done for the party, or that women who were "chasing" party leaders in hopes of receiving something from the party, now that it was in power, were being promoted rather than those who had worked for the party for years.[19]

Turning to the party platform, the BJP's 2014 national election manifesto was in significant part a product of social media and crowdsourcing.

Both the Congress and the BJP in 2014 set up Facebook pages and online websites to solicit popular input as they crafted their agendas. But they did not release the platform until May 7, 2014, the day that voting started—thus undercutting the idea that voters could use the agenda as a tool to weigh their decision.[20] The BJP's own explanation for the delay was that its manifesto committee members were themselves candidates and busily campaigning in their districts, such that they had not had a chance to convene and pull an agenda together. Observers speculated that the party was internally divided on key issues and could not resolve them adequately to get a manifesto out in a timely fashion (Mitra 2017, 137–38).

Once the manifesto was done, what did it have to say about women? The 2014 manifesto touched on violence against women, education, women as economic actors, healthcare, and property rights. This was a broader range of issues addressed as relating to or affecting women than previous manifestos. Overall, it conveyed a sense of women's important role in advancing society and the economy specifically, while needing to be physically protected. This came in tandem with a sense that women of disadvantaged and marginalized groups need additional levels of support and assistance. The full manifesto lists 23 separate bullet points under the category of things the BJP committed to doing for women (Appendix B). Ten of these referred broadly to topics including empowerment, welfare, and development; education; healthcare and hygiene; and women's legal and political rights—including the Women's Reservation Bill[21] and "property rights, marital rights and cohabitation rights" (Bharatiya Janata Party 2014, 22).

The remaining points focused either on violence against women (seven of 23) or women as economic actors (eight of 23). The latter included enhancing women's training and skills; facilitating banking, loans, and business and enterprise for women; and creating safe living and working spaces for working women. Measures related to violence against women included enforcing existing laws; aid and assistance for victims; and self-defense, IT, and police stations to be deployed or enhanced to create safe spaces for women. One broad statement promised measures to check a long list of practices that have been debated since colonial times, along with a few points of concern for modern Indian women's rights activists: "female foeticide, dowry, child marriage, trafficking, sexual harassment, rape and family violence" (Bharatiya Janata Party 2014, 22). The word "victims" is used three times, constructing and reinforcing the idea of women being in need of protection. The party "remains committed to give a high priority to Women's Empowerment and welfare" while also recognizing "the need for women's security *as a precondition to* women's empowerment" (Bharatiya Janata Party 2014, 21; emphasis added). On this point, one interviewee suggested that security for women has currently become a big issue, a "buzzword," perhaps to the extent of crowding out or overshadowing concepts of empowerment and equality.[22]

One notable absence in the 2014 manifesto was the lack of any mention of support for the Women's Reservation Bill (WRB). Previous attempts had been made to pass a constitutional amendment to reserve 33 percent of parliamentary seats for women in India. Such attempts had failed in 1993 (when it was presented as the 81st Amendment to the constitution), in 1998 (as the 84th Amendment), and again in 2000 (as the 85th Amendment). Most recently, it had failed to pass again in 2003, when the BJP-led NDA coalition government was in power.[23] Of the BJP leaders I interviewed, four (two in Delhi and two in Lucknow) mentioned the WRBin a positive light as something they and the party advocated.[24] Those who spoke to me about the WRB were passionate about it. One interviewee suggested that now that the BJP was in power rather than in the opposition, it would have to answer tough questions about what it would get done or not get done, mentioning the WRB as a specific example. But when I asked her whether the party would bring the bill forward now that it had outright control of the Lok Sabha, she hedged by responding that the WRB keeps "coming and going."[25] Another advocated for it in the following terms: if women are 50 percent of society, the party should bring at least 33 percent to parliament. If it can be done in the state legislatures and Panchayati Raj,[26] why not in the Lok Sabha? She specifically requested that her final statement in our interview be: this "Mahilaon ko bhi aage lao" ("Bring women forward also").[27] Another interviewee wished to be quoted directly: "Fighting an election in a women-reserved constituency is very tough because you're fighting against women from other parties. Then gender is no more an issue there." As someone in the BJP who focused on training women to campaign, she felt strongly that the WRB doesn't make it easier but actually harder for women to get elected. But she felt that was okay: fighting tough elections would heighten women's political skills, allowing them to be seen as more electable. She believed the WRB was being obstructed by men in fear of the idea that a third of the parliament could be women. Ultimately, though, she was convinced the WRB was important for women to get more tickets, especially in the strongest ("A-grade") constituencies. Even if the WRB faced "trouble and antagonism socially and politically" from male leaders, it would create the conditions for change over time, for seeing women as intrinsic leaders, as the Panchayati Raj reservations did: changes came, even if slowly, over a decade.[28] One interviewee claimed that passing the WRB was a dream of Vajpayee's, and now that the BJP controlled the Lok Sabha, BJP women were planning to ask Modi to bring the bill and pass it.[29] Another noted, more cynically, that everyone claims to support the bill but no one actually enacts it.[30]

The manifesto opens the section on women by noting that the "BJP recognizes the important role of women in development of the society and growth of the nation" (Bharatiya Janata Party 2014, 21). Three of my informants agreed that since the election, the party has not given as much attention to women's issues as it should.[31] Two interviewees are involved in implementing the "Beti Bachao, Beti Pardhao" ("Save Daughters, Educate Daughters") campaign promised in the manifesto.[32] But overall, the general consensus among my informants was that the party needs to do more.

The BJP's 2014 manifesto continues to convey belief in improving the status of women as a means to achieving something else, not unlike the Hindu Mahasabha of the early 1900s. This sense is betrayed in the title of the section on women: "Women—The Nation Builder." This seems hardly to have moved beyond historical conceptions, including colonial and early postindependence constructions of the role of women. In this context, one reference seems especially significant: the first statement on healthcare indicates there will be a special "focus . . . on domains of Nutrition and Pregnancy" (Bharatiya Janata Party 2014, 21). This declaration hearkens to Yuval-Davis's (1997) conception of women as physical reproducers of the nation's citizens; to Partha Chatterjee's (1993, Chapter 6) delineation of the independence movement's division of Indian society into the "home and the world" and its consignment of women to the former so that they can become present in the latter; and perhaps even farther back to Engels's ([1884] 2010) analysis of women as the means of reproduction of labor in capitalist economic systems.

Ethnographic Observation and Visual Analysis: What Incorporation Looks Like

Engagement with arts and the visual has been a critical part of the BJP's contemporary approach, and thus warrants some separate analysis. Globally, communication is becoming more visual (Howells and Negreiros 2012); in a country with high illiteracy rates, where women's literacy rates are even lower than men's, visual means of communication can become critically important and possibly even more so among women. The male literacy rate in India in 2014 stood at 80.9 percent, while the female literacy rate was 64.6 percent (Daily Mail 2013). Several women BJP leaders were quite involved with visual and artistic endeavors of the party. The Mahila Morcha coordinated with other wings of the party such as the youth wing and cultural cells to stage *nataks*: small traveling plays, in which a van of actors drives around with their set, stopping in markets and other crowded spots to stage short political plays for the elections and the party.[33] Two of the women I interviewed had backgrounds in the arts, and one very intentionally brought that commitment as her primary engagement with the party.[34]

Ethnographic and visual analysis shows incorporation has meant women are present but in limited and contested ways. Women's incorporation in the party is limited in terms of numbers, in the positions they hold, and in demographic representation. Not all Indian women are equally represented, but rather only a slice of Indian women: in particular, married, urban, educated Hindu women of upper-caste and upper-class status. Two important "texts" afford critical insight into the forms and limits of incorporation of women into the BJP today: the national campaign kickoff rally in New Delhi and a typical campaign poster I photographed at the rally. The rally took place just north of New Delhi in Rohini Park on September 29, 2013, an event that had been widely advertised in the media for weeks prior. By this time Narendra Modi had been selected as the prime ministerial candidate, so he was the main speaker, and all the party's major efforts were geared to making it as large and successful an event as possible.

I set off to attend the rally on a cloudy and overcast Sunday morning in a private taxi with Deep, the driver. As we drew closer to the venue, traffic became heavier, increasingly clogged with vehicles heading to the rally. In addition to a few taxis like mine and some private cars, we saw increasing numbers of larger vehicles like vans/minivans and buses transporting people to the rally. BJP flags and banners hung from these vehicles, and inside them I could see people of all ages heading raucously to the rally (see Figures 5.1, 5.2, 5.3). They were men by a vast majority, specifically younger men, looking in appearance to range from their teens to the thirties or so. There were also some women—looking to be slightly older than the men—as well as young children who looked to be of elementary school age.

WOMEN INCORPORATED 131

Figure 5.1 Drive to BJP campaign kickoff rally site, 2013
Source: Photograph by the author, September 29, 2013, New Delhi.

Deep and I arrived on one of the major roads leading into the park and plunged into a raucous crowd of hundreds of men marching toward the park. I did not see a single woman among the marchers, but the men seemed unperturbed by my presence in the crowd. We entered the park and ended up about 100 yards from the main platform and facing its right side (see Figures 5.4, 5.5, 5.6). Closer to the platform the crowding became suffocatingly dense. The crowd was overwhelmingly male; a few women were either clustered in groups of six to eight or walking around on their own. Men and women alike were all, without exception, visibly identifiable through their grooming and dress as lower or working class.

Though it can be hard to tell for certain, most of the crowd appeared to belong to the majority Hindu community. The Hindu nationalist movement in India has built its reputation on antiminority rhetoric, targeting Muslims in particular (although over time, the targeting of Christians and lower-caste Hindus and Dalits has expanded as well), and it would have been surprising to see Muslims in any large numbers. During the campaign, accounts of Muslim women being invited or asked to attend BJP rallies—or just as likely, rounded

132 MARGINALIZED, MOBILIZED, INCORPORATED

Figure 5.2 Drive to BJP campaign kickoff rally site, 2013
Source: Photograph by the author, September 29, 2013, New Delhi.

up by politicians and deposited at the rallies—accompanied reports that the women were asked specifically to come wearing burkas to demonstrate both female and Muslim support for Modi and the BJP. A great deal of uncertainty surrounded such reports (Haider 2013a, 2013b; Poornima 2013; PTI 2013a). At the rally I saw one group of Muslim men marching behind a pro-Modi banner, but no (groups of) Muslim women in burkas were visible to me.

A typical poster for the rally (Figure 5.7) similarly illustrates women's incorporation in the BJP today as present but limited and contested in numbers, position, and demographic representation.

The poster is typical of campaign posters in India in that it is colorful and features faces of key party leaders as well as sponsorship by a local, private business—in this case, "Chaska Restaurant & Party Hall," as in the banner across the bottom of the poster. The main text of the poster translates as follows:

>   New Thinking—New Hope
>   Let's Go to Japanese Park, Rohini

WOMEN INCORPORATED   133

Figure 5.3 Drive to BJP campaign kickoff rally site, 2013
Source: Photograph by the author, September 29, 2013, New Delhi.

> [to hear] Brother Narendra Modi Sir's
> Lion's Roar
> Sunday, 29 September, Morning 10 o'clock

The largest face in the most prominent position, in the upper left of the poster, is Narendra Modi's. The white background of the poster, together with the white Nehru-collar kurta (tunic) he is wearing, serve to encircle his face in a halo of white—an effect further compounded by his white hair and beard. The next place the eye is drawn to is down slightly and to the right, to the second-largest face on the poster, a woman—Rekha Gupta, as her name is written in red beneath the image of her face. Gupta has been a party leader in Delhi, including the Mahila Morcha, having become active in BJP politics through the student wing in her college years.[35] Modi clearly doesn't need to be identified in the same way; he is the subject of the poster itself; his name referenced in much larger blue lettering, preceded and followed by honorifics "Brother" and "Sir." The symbol of the party—the saffron-hued lotus flower—is also displayed near Gupta's image. As noted above, visuals

134 MARGINALIZED, MOBILIZED, INCORPORATED

Figure 5.4 BJP campaign kickoff rally site, 2013
Source: Photograph by the author, September 29, 2013, New Delhi.

matter in a country with high rates of illiteracy: in India, every party is associated with a visual symbol that is included on every ballot for unlettered voters.

The other notable visual feature of the poster is the string of 10 additional faces across the top—all BJP leaders. Of these, three are immediately recognizable to me: Atal Bihari Vajpayee on the leftmost end, L. K. Advani next to him, and then after one more face, Sushma Swaraj in the fourth position from the left. One might have thought that Swaraj's image would be bigger than Gupta's, since the former is much higher in the party hierarchy; however, as I saw traveling around northern and western India during 2013, most political and campaign posters in India retain a local flavor by featuring a prominent local or regional leader together with a/the major national one. The net count, then, is two women out of 12 total faces on the poster.

Both the women—Swaraj and Gupta—share notable visual features on the poster that illustrate the limited representation of Indian women in the party.

Figure 5.5 BJP campaign kickoff rally site, 2013
Source: Photograph by the author, September 29, 2013, New Delhi.

Both are identifiably Hindu: a primary marker for both is the bindi, or red dot on the forehead. The bindi is technically only makeup, without any specified meaning (unlike *sindoor*, the red powder placed in the parting of the hair that specifically signifies a Hindu woman's married status). Nevertheless, only married Hindu women customarily wear the bindi—a Hindu widow would be extremely unlikely to wear one, as would any non-Hindu woman. Both women have their hair pulled back in the same style, and both seem very clearly to be wearing saris—the form of Indian dress most commonly associated with married, Hindu women in India. One author has argued that Swaraj has "fashioned herself as the quintessential traditional Hindu *nari* (woman), with the large *bindi* on her forehead and *sindoor* in the parting of her hair" (Shankar 2013, 222). This same visual demeanor is conveyed in Gupta's image.

The caste and class makeup of women incorporated in the contemporary BJP is bifurcated. The women portrayed on the poster were upper class and likely to be educated and upper-caste women. During the campaign rally,

Figure 5.6 BJP campaign kickoff rally site, 2013
Source: Photograph by the author, September 29, 2013, New Delhi.

women on the dais were predominantly of upper caste and class status, as part of the party leadership, while those in the crowd were predominantly lower caste and lower or working class. In these ways, incorporation of women in the BJP today remains constrained by the "politics of respectability" (Forbes 1988), with space for "respectable" women at leadership levels while women of lower-caste/lower-class status remain relegated to the lower ranks. Similar patterns appeared across many campaign posters throughout 2013, though of course women did not always appear on posters (see Figures 5.8, 5.9).

In sum, campaign materials visually reinforced the "present but limited and contested" incorporation of women in the party. The poster analyzed featured two women leaders of the party sharing visual space with male leaders. However, the space is not shared equally—again, Gupta's image is slightly smaller, lower, and off to the right. And Gupta and Swaraj are the only two women in the midst of 10 men. They have a space on the poster, undisputedly, but it is not the same space, or as much space, as the men.

Figure 5.7 BJP campaign poster, 2013
Source: Photograph by the author, November 13, 2013, New Delhi.

What Has Incorporation Meant for the Party?

As discussed in Chapter 3, a scholarly consensus has emerged on the role of women's participation in normalizing radical movements and organizations in mainstream politics (Blee and Deutsch 2012; Ferber 2004; Bacchetta and Power 2002). The BJP seems to have heeded these lessons in the run-up to the 2014 election. Incorporation certainly corresponded with great political success for the BJP in 2014. Party leaders worked to bolster the visible position of women prior to 2014, and the Mahila Morcha played an important role helping the party to success in 2014.

What has incorporation meant for the BJP and for religious nationalist politics within the broader context of Indian democracy? In order to unpack this question it is first necessary to grasp the scale and scope of the BJP's 2014 electoral victory. Seasoned observers of Indian politics have called it "a major realignment of Indian politics" (Mitra 2017, 158). A single party winning an absolute majority in the Lok Sabha has only happened once

Figure 5.8 BJP campaign poster, 2013
Source: Photograph by the author, September 15, 2013, New Delhi.

before in independent India, in 1984. The political context of that sweeping 1984 Congress Party victory was this assassination of Prime Minister Indira Gandhi and the outpouring of a massive sympathy vote for the Congress and her previously apolitical son, Rajiv Gandhi, running as the party's "reluctant" prime ministerial candidate. Even in all its decades as the center of gravity of Indian democracy—most especially in the two decades after independence, under Nehru, when the Congress dominated at both the national and state levels—1984 was the only time even the Congress Party won an outright majority in the Lok Sabha.

Perhaps even more significant than the scale of the BJP's 2014 victory was the substance of it. The party expanded its vote share in two politically significant ways. Regionally, the party expanded its presence into regions and states where it had long had difficulty making significant inroads. These included several states in western, north central, and northwestern India. The party also made small but important and symbolic gains in southern and

Figure 5.9 BJP campaign posters, 2013
Source: Photograph by the author, November 2, 2013, New Delhi.

northeastern states where it previously had no presence at all. Analysts of Indian politics have long held that as long as the BJP could not expand very far beyond its traditional base in northern and western India, it would remain limited in how far it could go as a truly national political party. In 2014, the BJP seemed finally to have crossed those previous boundaries.

The second significant way in which the BJP expanded its votes in 2014 was on the basis of caste and class. The "traditional" BJP voter, the party's core base of support, has long been urban, upper and middle classes, and upper castes. In addition to its regional limitations, this limited demographic base of support has been the other factor leading analysts to suggest the BJP could not become a truly national party until it could bridge these gaps. Indeed, in important and not just symbolic ways, the issue of caste divisions struck at the very foundation of the BJP's constitutive vision: the construction of a politically unified Hindu community. Caste was—and in many ways remains—the primary threat to this idea, the primary proof that no such thing as a (politically) "unified Hindu community" does or can exist, the primary obstacle to the BJP's self-conception and reason for existence. Indeed, I would argue that caste can be seen as the "original sin" of Indian politics in much the same way that race can be seen as the original sin of US politics.

But in 2014, the BJP "managed to dramatically increase its appeal among the lower classes, the poor, the Other Backward Castes, Scheduled Castes and Tribes—key constituents of the Congress party's traditional social base" (Mitra 2017, 135). Thus the two ways that the BJP expanded its vote share in 2014 were critically important not merely in terms of the numbers of votes and seats it won, but symbolically in overcoming the final barriers to its ascension as a truly national Indian political party.

So overwhelming was the 2014 victory, numerically and symbolically, that scholars began to contemplate whether the BJP may be in a position to replace the Congress Party as the center of gravity of Indian democracy. Chhibber and Verma (2018) argue that the base ideology of the average Indian voter—with ideology defined along two axes of statism and recognition—has shifted such that the BJP's ideology along these two axes is more in touch with them than the Congress Party now is. The politics of *recognition* concerns the extent to which the state should work to "accommodate the needs of various marginalized groups and protect minority rights from assertive majoritarian tendencies," while the politics of *statism* concerns the extent to which "the state should dominate society, regulate social norms, and redistribute private property" (Chhibber and Verma 2018, 2). Chhibber and Verma hold that the BJP's ideology opposes both statism and recognition, while the Congress Party's ideology (insofar as it currently has a coherent one) tends to support both. The average Indian voter, they convincingly demonstrate, has moved from high to low levels of statism, and from high to low levels of recognition. This constitutes a shift away from core Congress ideologies and closer to the BJP's position. This is displayed visually in Figure 5.5.

I argue that this shift that Chhibber and Verma identify represents the "middle-classification" of Indian democracy—a shift from an orientation and a rhetoric of representing, addressing, and prioritizing the needs of the poor and marginalized (Varshney 2013, Chapter 1) to representing, addressing, and prioritizing the needs of the (growing) middle class in India. For better or worse, this shift brings Indian democracy more in line with those of the advanced industrial Western democracies, including the United States.

Along the way, the BJP seems finally to have grasped the lessons of anticolonial nationalism that other movements and organizations sensed much earlier: where nationalism in the Western world was built on the exclusion of women, the story of anticolonial nationalism in India suggests that it actually *had to* include women in order to succeed. The inclusion of women may have been, and arguably was, merely rhetorical, strategic, and/or symbolic. But anticolonial nationalist movements that did not include women in these minimal kinds of ways (like the Hindu Mahasabha in the early 1900s) did not succeed politically and electorally, while those that found ways to include women, even imperfectly—like the Congress Party and even the Muslim League—did. The lesson of the inclusion of women in anticolonial nationalism was analyzed by historians studying the colonial origins of Indian nationalism (Chatterjee 1993, Chapter 6). In the modern era, the BJP seems now to have grasped that regardless of its regressive gender ideologies rooted in religion and nationalism, it cannot appear to be a modern political party in a competitive democracy without incorporating women.

The arrival of the BJP as a mainstream player in—if not the actual new center of gravity of—Indian democracy is constitutive of all these shifts. Thus I suggest that the BJP and its religious nationalist politics have become incorporated in the texture of Indian democracy, just as this chapter demonstrates how women have become incorporated in the BJP itself. Religious politics was marginalized as an illegitimate facet of Indian democracy in the early years after independence under a Nehruvian concept of secular nationalism—just as women were marginalized from religious politics under the Hindu Mahasabha. In the 1980s, religious politics were mobilized into Indian democracy under the Congress rule of Prime Minister Indira Gandhi and her son Rajiv Gandhi—just as women began to be mobilized into religious politics by the BJP.

To be sure, my argument is not meant to suggest that the incorporation of religious politics in the texture of Indian democracy has been smooth or uncontested. Significant resistance to the mainstreaming of Hindutva politics manifests in multiple ways, for example as opposition to beef bans (Sathyamala 2018) and caste-based conflict (Bennett 2017). One author observes that the "greatest challenge for the BJP in the upcoming years will be to deliver economic results combined with social harmony and political unity" (Mitra 2017, 159), to fulfill Modi's campaign promises (Williams and Deo 2018). Nonetheless, many seasoned observers agree with Chhibber and Verma (2018) that a significant, substantive, long-term if not permanent realignment has taken or is taking place in Indian democracy, a prediction that seemed to be borne out by the results of the 2019 election (Ganguly 2019; Vaishnav and Hinston 2019). I suggest that the incorporation of women in the BJP is a potent lens through which to understand the meaning of these changes. To reiterate, I am not making a causal claim in a narrow positivist sense. I am not arguing that women's incorporation "caused" these shifts; rather, I am suggesting that the changing role of women in the BJP's religious nationalist politics is a way to understand the changing role of religious politics itself in Indian democracy.

What Has Incorporation Meant for Women?

To unpack what incorporation has meant for women requires understanding both what has changed from prior periods and what has not. What has not changed is the tethering of women to their roles in the family and society as the source of their voice and power in the public sphere. What has changed is the form or nature of that tethering. Under the Hindu Mahasabha, tethering was literal and physical: party leaders believed women didn't really need to be in the public sphere or involved in politics at all. As "flowers of the home," and as carers and nurturers of the nation, women were constructed as political subjects only indirectly if at all and virtually in absentia.

Under the BJP, women have been important political actors. In the 1980s and 1990s they were fiery orators or demure and dignified widows, themselves rallied into street politics and rallying men with gendered discourses. But women leaders in this period were largely desexualized: most prominent women leaders were either widows, or celibate, or otherwise without pressing familial responsibilities (Basu 1993a). Today, women are incorporated as important leaders in the upper echelons of party governance structures, candidates and parliamentarians, spokespersons, as active members of an institutionalized women's wing, and even in notable numbers as cabinet-level ministers. But unlike the 1980s, women leaders in the BJP today have or have had active heteronormative family lives, especially marriage and children. All the party leaders I interviewed, men and women alike, identified as cisgender and heterosexual in their familial relationships. One woman was a widow, one had never married, and one had a husband who worked abroad. All the rest were married, and most had at least one child.[36]

The BJP's contemporary gender ideology is best captured by the concept of complementarity: the idea that men and women are equal but have different roles to play in society. The idea of complementarity is widely traced to sociologist Talcott Parsons's work in the middle of the 20th century on socialization and differentiation of functions within the nuclear family (Parsons

1964, Chapter 3). Complementarity constructs women as essentially different from men, whether on the basis of biology or socialization. This view was manifested in various ways in my fieldwork: for example, in the idea that politics is a "dirty" business, and not really a place for women and certainly not for respectable women; and its mirror image, the belief that women work with honesty and integrity and will improve politics by becoming involved in it.[37] It underpins the idea—and the actual fact—that women party workers can access the insides of homes and families that men cannot.

This "different but equal" gender ideology was expressed in various forms throughout my interviews. One interviewee argued that women have an "intrinsic need" to nurture and care, though this is often mistaken for a biological need.[38] Another party leader argued that society could be imagined like a *channa* (chickpea), and men and women were like the two halves of that whole. She argued that the position of women could not be isolated to women alone: women were all part of society, with the family as the central unit. Women's position within the family constituted the backbone of Indian society, and the role of women in society comes from their place in the family. Given this approach, she argued, Indian women do not need or desire *equality* in a Western sense but rather would fight for *unity* of the sexes making up the whole of society.[39] Another senior leader trotted out the well-worn postcolonial view that sex/gender differences were never part of Indian culture but came from "outside" in different forms (Narayan 1997). He argued that Indian culture has worshiped women, unlike Europe—and that India would be unable to become an open society like Europe but still is, mistakenly, trying to do so.[40]

Complementarity represents a significant shift from denying women any role at all in the public sphere, to acknowledging that women have a role to play in the political sphere even if their role is essentially different from men's. But ultimately complementarity continues to tether women to the private sphere—not physically as in the early 1900s, but now more conceptually. This conceptual tethering manifested in two ways that emerged from my fieldwork: in the trope of "family support" for women's political work, and in the kin-like structures of the RSS.

One thing was almost universal among the women I interviewed: the assertion that for a woman in India to become active in politics, she had to have her family's support. All but two women mentioned this explicitly as a necessary factor, without my prompting. I came to understand "family support" as standing in for patriarchal (men's or familial) permission for women to engage in political activity. The trope of "family support" played a similar role in the contemporary BJP that the trope of "adjustment" played for women leaders of the Shiv Sena in Mumbai (Bedi 2016): that is, it is the discourse that enables women party members to balance public, political careers with family life and commitments. It signals that women have permission from family patriarchs (husbands, fathers, fathers-in-law) and their children to do political work. More than one informant argued explicitly that without family support, if a woman insisted on being politically active anyway, it would "break the family." The BJP has thus shifted from a place where women were or had to be desexualized to a place where "family support" has become the trope for a woman's permission to enter the political sphere.

Conceptual tethering of women to the private spheres of home and family also manifests in the kin-like structure of the RSS. BJP leaders I spoke with drew a sharp contrast with the dynastic politics of the Congress Party, in particular their view that women entered and advanced in the Congress Party based on familial connections with men.[41] Yet the "family lineage" of the RSS plays a similar function of bringing women into the contemporary BJP through the involvement of male relatives. Husbands and sons who are involved in the RSS in turn encourage and support their wives' and mothers' involvement. This buttresses the RSS's construction of itself as building the entire (Hindu/Indian) nation as a family, and in turn, the RSS itself becomes one big family.

Based on my fieldwork, this latter dynamic was more prevalent in Lucknow than in Delhi. Four informants—all from Lucknow—were involved with the RSS before joining the BJP, all through their husbands and sons. In fact, none of my Delhi interviewees came into the BJP via the RSS, and they made a point to emphasize this. Two informants (one in Delhi and one in Lucknow) were in the BJP's student wing and got involved in party politics as university students. And three (two in Lucknow, one in Delhi) explicitly mentioned they were first drawn into the party in the 1990s under the leadership of Atal Bihari Vajpayee, whom they admired greatly, and with whom they had a personal connection.[42] So family and family-like connections via the RSS are an important, though certainly not the only, route for women into the BJP—especially outside the central leadership in New Delhi. Such connections seem more akin to dynastic politics than BJP leaders may see them as.

* * *

In this chapter I constructed incorporation as bringing women into political party structures without fundamentally altering the gendered aspects of those structures or their patriarchal underpinnings: incorporation doesn't disturb underlying gendered power structures, it just brings women into them. I argued that incorporation entails the public, political presence of women in limited and contested ways, demonstrated by examining women as BJP candidates and leaders in party governance structures, the Mahila Morcha, and the role of women's issues in the 2014 party platform. Ethnographic analysis of the BJP's 2013 campaign kickoff rally and visual analysis of a typical campaign poster further illustrated the role of women as "present but limited and contested" in the party. Women's presence is limited in numbers, in the positions they hold, and in demographic representation: women who are incorporated represented predominantly urban, educated, cisgender, married, Hindu women of upper-caste and upper-class status.

I then demonstrated what incorporation of women has meant for the BJP in this contemporary period. As literatures on conservative women more broadly have argued, the presence of women serves to "soften" and normalize radical and even violent movements and organizations, and this dynamic can be seen in the incorporation of women in Hindu nationalist politics and the BJP. This is evidenced in the deliberate steps taken by BJP leaders prior to the 2014 election to incorporate women and the association of women leaders with the "moderate" face of the party; and the significant work done by the Mahila Morcha to assist the party in its sweeping electoral victory in 2014. But the incorporation of women has not translated into actual moderation of the BJP's agendas—a point I expand in the next chapter.

Finally, I considered what incorporation has meant for the women of the party themselves, showing what has changed and what has not compared to prior periods. The key aspect that has not changed across time periods is the tethering of women to their roles in the home and the family as the source of their power, position, and voice in the public, political arena. What has changed is the form that tethering takes. In the early 1900s, the gender ideology of the Hindu Mahasabha tethered women to the home literally and physically: women were marginalized, seen as having no place in politics. By the 1980s the BJP began mobilizing women into politics in conjunction with a gender ideology that primarily brought desexed women (as widows or celibate renunciants) into the political arena. Women with husbands, children (particularly young children), and concomitant family responsibilities thus remained confined to the home.

In today's BJP, women are incorporated in the party—even in limited and contested ways—and continue to carry out and have heteronormative family responsibilities. Instead of physical tethering or desexualization, women in the party today are *conceptually* tethered to home and family. This conceptual tethering manifests in the trope of "family support" for a woman's political activities and in the kin-like structures of the RSS, with husbands and sons bringing wives and mothers into the party and the RSS modeling its conception of the nation as a family unit.

The gender ideology of complementarity blurs the lines between family and society, as families become the basic unit of society and society itself gets modeled on the basis of, and as, one big family. The family, in turn, remains under patriarchal control. This underlying aspect of Hindu nationalist ideology does not change over time and underpins my argument that the participation of women—whether through mobilization or incorporation—has not changed and probably cannot fundamentally change underlying patriarchal structures. To do so would require undermining the very tethering on which all the various forms of women's participation—marginalization, mobilization, incorporation—have been built.

In the 1990s, leading scholars such as Amrita Basu studied the mobilization of women by the forces of Hindu nationalism and concluded that in contradistinction to religious fundamentalism, ideologies and movements of communalism such as Hindu nationalism in India could create and accommodate some limited spaces for women's activism in the political sphere. In this it seems accurate to infer that the Hindu Mahasabha was closer to a fundamentalist political movement than a modern (communal) Hindu nationalism whose politics are represented by the BJP. Such a conclusion is supported by the outright and emphatic denial by several of my interviewees of linkages, ideological or otherwise, between the Hindu Mahasabha and the BJP.[43] Incorporation and conceptual tethering are the logical evolution of the mobilization and desexualization of the 1980s and 1990s, so insightfully theorized by prior scholars. In the final, concluding chapter I explore the implications of my analysis for women's political participation and Indian democracy.

6
Denouement

"The Condition of Its Women": Women's Political Participation and Indian Democracy

You can judge a nation, and how successful it will be, based on how it treats its women and its girls.
—US president Barack Obama[1]

"The status of a civilization can be judged by the condition of its women." Though the source of this phrase remains historically uncertain, the sentiment underlying both these quotes, so far removed in time and political context, was foundational to British colonial rule in India: Indians (Indian men) were unfit to rule themselves, as evidenced by the degraded status of (their) Indian women (Sinha 1995; Mani 1998; Spivak 1988). Across "civilization" and state, British colonial rule in India was a deeply sexed and gendered enterprise. I have argued elsewhere that being (or appearing to be) progressive on women's rights was a critical narrative legitimizing British colonial rule as well as Indians' right to rule themselves in the independence movement (Williams 2013a). This book is built on the premise that "the condition of women" continues to be a driving narrative of Indian politics today.

In this context, it is productive to examine the extent to which being (or appearing to be) progressive on women's rights continues to be a critical narrative of legitimation for the Indian state under the BJP. What is the "condition" of Indian women today, and what does it tell us about the "status" of the Indian state today? These questions lie at the core of the argument this book has sought to build. A cursory glance might suggest the current condition of Indian women is not that good. In a case that shook India, a 23-year-old student was gang raped on a bus in South Delhi in December 2019; her male companion was beaten. She subsequently died of her injuries. The incident led to massive protests and demonstrations across the country. Of the six men who committed the heinous crime, four were convicted and hanged on March 19, 2020 (Gettleman, Kumar, and Venugopal 2020).[2] The incident haunted narratives of progress or even complacency and re-energized feminist activism on women's rights. This re-energization made clear, though, that any assessment of the "condition of Indian women" cannot be a uniformly positive or negative narrative, but rather complex and multilayered assemblages of meanings and effects.

Indians are rightly proud of their democracy: as seen in Chapter 3, even with its imperfections it is one of only a few countries in the developing world with as long a record of democratic succession, basic civil rights and freedoms, and high levels of political engagement, efficacy, and participation. Taken as a whole since independence, it is a record that stands with those of wealthy, industrialized Western democracies; and it is widely understood as the most significant anomaly in prevalent theories that find widespread societal wealth, education, and literacy—none of which India has—to be key predictors of democratic stability. Indian women fought alongside Indian men for independence and alongside British suffragettes for the vote (Sinha 2000), and India granted universal adult suffrage at the moment of independence in 1947.

Perhaps based on such historical precedents, women's political participation has long been assumed as an unalloyed good both by Indian feminists and by scholars of participation and democratic theory. This study doesn't seek to negate this assumption, but it does complexify it and ask for nuanced evaluation. To more deeply assess the parameters, and the meanings, of women's political participation, it asks us to specify: which women? which politics? and which (forms of) participation?

Which Women?

I showed in Chapter 1, and have argued in greater depth elsewhere (Williams 2022a), that Hindu nationalist women are deeply unrepresentative of Indian women more broadly. Though precise membership numbers are difficult to obtain, BJP women tend to be overwhelmingly Hindu, upper caste, middle to upper class, urban, educated, Hindi-speaking, and from the party's regional bases in northern and western India.[3] Surveys and voting data have consistently shown that women's support for the BJP comes overwhelmingly from wealthy and upper-caste women (Deshpande 2004, 2009). This unrepresentativeness has important consequences in terms of understanding which women participate, and who gains what kinds of benefits from participation.

I have argued that across all the time periods studied, the primary (potential) benefit of women's participation in Hindu nationalist politics has been increased access to the public sphere. Yet that access was restricted in different ways before, during, and since Hindu nationalism initially rose to political power in the 1980s and 1990s. Before that period, in the early 1900s under the Hindu Mahasabha, Hindu nationalist women were denied access, and even their right or need to gain access was questioned: this was what marginalization meant for women. In the 1980s and 1990s, during the BJP's initial rise to power, through gendered mobilization the party deployed gendered discourses, challenged feminism, and rallied women into the street at both the leadership and rank-and-file levels. BJP women leaders in this period were widows or celibate renunciants: their access to the public sphere was mediated by social structures that desexed and marked them as free from primary domestic responsibilities in the home. For rank-and-file women, their access to the public sphere was transitory: after coming out for demonstrations, marches, or protests, they returned to primary domestic responsibilities in the home. Finally, in the 2010s, since the BJP's initial rise to national political power, women were incorporated in the party's structures and activities in a more institutionalized way, and Hindu nationalist women accessed the public sphere with patriarchal permission manifested in the form of "family support" for political activism and the kin-like structures of the RSS. As such, the party's gender ideologies never untethered women from their social roles in the private sphere, and in fact reinforced those ties.

Clearly, Hindu nationalist women's participation was aimed at advancing the party's Hindu nationalist agendas rather than undermining or questioning them. Indian women who do not advocate Hindu nationalism gained little or nothing from Hindu nationalist women's mobilization or incorporation—not even restricted access to the public sphere. (This does not mean that non-Hindu nationalist women had no access to the public sphere; but rather that Hindu nationalist women's mobilization and incorporation did not give or expand access for non-Hindu nationalist women.) Indeed, there was much for non-Hindu nationalist women to lose from the mobilization and incorporation of Hindu nationalist women: they were often the targets of gendered mobilization and incorporation, facing the "othering" rhetoric of exclusion as well as physical violence at the hands of BJP women leaders or those they mobilized. Nor have Hindu nationalist women's mobilization and incorporation advanced women's issues or women's interests at large. Despite some rhetorical support and initiatives for women, since taking power the BJP has not advanced any major proposals relating to women that it has claimed to advocate over time: neither those that feminists support (such as legislative gender quotas), nor those that feminists have come to oppose (such as the implementation of a uniform civil code of family laws).

Literature on right-wing women has broadly argued that the participation of women can soften the image of a radical movement, lending it a more mainstream legitimacy (Blee and Deutsch 2012; Ferber 2004). While such an argument would be difficult to test, the case of BJP women complicates this idea. The party has long evinced splits between extremist and moderate factions. Extremist elements combine a more strident Hindu nationalist ideology (often affiliated with the RSS) and a willingness to work outside the bounds of institutional politics. Generally, moderate elements represent some combination of less strident Hindu nationalist ideology and a greater propensity to work within the framework of institutional politics. The dividing line between extremists and moderates is shifting, blurred, and inexact to be sure; but in the 1980s and 1990s, A. B. Vajpayee was seen as a moderate while L. K. Advani was seen as extremist. And more extremist women have coexisted with more moderate women across time periods within the party. In the same period as Vajpayee and Advani, Uma Bharti and Sadhvi Rithambara represented a more extremist element of the BJP, while Vijaya Raje Scindia represented a more moderate element. In the contemporary period, Pragya Thakur represents a more extremist element in the party, while the late Sushma Swaraj could be seen to represent a more moderate element. One party leader suggested that women in general tend to be seen as more moderate;[4] but the continuing presence and power of more extremist women in the party aligns poorly with the idea of presenting a "softer" image of the party. If anything, mobilization and incorporation of Hindu nationalist women have tended to correspond with, and signify, the ascendance of a more extremist politics.

Which Politics?

I have argued throughout this book that the BJP's politics are majoritarian and Hindu supremacist. The core of Hindu nationalist ideology since its inception and first articulation in the 1920s by V. D. "Veer" Savarkar has virtually equated being Indian with being Hindu. Insofar as minority religious communities exist in the nation, they (can) do so only as fundamentally second-class citizens by accepting Hinduism as their culture, as innately superior to other cultures, and as the predominant culture of the nation.

Multiple studies have analyzed what the case of the BJP can tell us about the inclusion-moderation hypothesis: the argument that the inclusion of radical/religious political parties in democratic processes works to moderate the agendas of such parties (Brocker and Kunkler 2013). Scholars have rightly concluded that the BJP does not provide support for the hypothesis (Ruparelia 2006; Jaffrelot 2013; Basu 2015; Flåten 2019). I would go one step further and suggest that the case of the BJP has the potential to turn the inclusion-moderation hypothesis on its head: inclusion of the BJP has undermined Indian democracy rather than democracy undercutting the party's extremist ideology. The BJP has participated in Indian democratic politics since its founding, but its increasing political success over time has done nothing to water down its radical agenda to tear down an Indian nationalism built on a foundation (however faltering and imperfect) of secularism and minority rights, and rebuild it on a foundation of Hindu supremacy. Some moderation of the BJP's radicalism was partially realized from 1999 to 2004 during its first stint in power at the national level leading a coalition government. At the time, its coalition partners forced the BJP to refrain from implementing its more radical core policy goals: abolishing Article 370, which established the special status of the Muslim-majority state of Jammu and Kashmir, building a Ram temple at Ayodhya, and eliminating the religious family laws. (The latter two of these goals were detailed in Chapter 2; all three are covered in more detail below.) This "forced moderation" resulted in some tension between the party and its more radical social movement support base in the RSS (Adeney and Saez 2005; Chakrabarty 2006, 2014).

Since 2014, the case of the BJP raises significant questions about how the inclusion-moderation hypothesis should be specified. Jaffrelot (2013) argued that the Hindu nationalist parties, rather than becoming more moderate over time, have tended to oscillate between ideological retrenchment and strategic pragmatism with respect to their more radical policy goals. It now seems accurate to argue that even the strategy of oscillation is gone (Flåten 2019), as the BJP's inclusion has led not to moderation but to electoral dominance followed by an increasing turn to political authoritarianism (Tepe

2019; Varshney 2021). Thus if anything, over the long term, the inclusion of the BJP has undermined Indian democracy, rather than democracy undercutting the radical agendas of the party as the inclusion-moderation hypothesis would posit.

Extremist politics in the party, I would argue, have evolved in phases over time. And the incorporation of women has aligned with the expansion of extremism, and the undermining of more moderate forces, in the party. From the 1980s through 2004—the period of gendered mobilization of women—the moderate and extremist factions within the party were in conflict with each other, and the former was generally politically ascendant. This was evidenced in the prime ministership of A. B. Vajpayee, and the ways in which coalition rule forced the BJP to curtail its more radical agendas. After its victory in the 2014 election, unencumbered by coalition partners, the party evinced notable silent acquiescence in the face of extremist Hindu nationalist violence committed at subnational levels, outside the formal frameworks of national and institutional politics, by actors not always directly affiliated with the BJP. The BJP under Modi did as much damage to secular norms and civil rights by its silences as by any direct actions. Politicization of institutions and organizations by government officials accompanied censorship and violence against religious minorities and journalists, and policing of youth, women, and sexuality by nonofficial actors created what came to be called a chilling atmosphere of intolerance in the country. In response to particular acts, each time something happened, Modi and high-ranking BJP officials hemmed and hawed and delayed in silence. What they did not do is immediately and strongly condemn mob actions or make it clear that such attacks would not be tolerated and would be dealt with most severely. Such silences and absences embolden potential future perpetrators of such acts, while voices of resistance become more vulnerable, and fewer and farther between.

Since 2019, I would argue, the BJP has accelerated more direct, explicit, and overt attacks on the pillars of Indian secularism, protections of minority rights, and civil rights and freedoms. These attacks can be seen in three key policy agendas the BJP has advocated since 1980 as central to advancing Hindu nationalist ideology:

(a) The abrogation of Article 370 of the Constitution, which granted special autonomous status and powers to Jammu and Kashmir, India's only Muslim-majority state

(b) Building a temple to the Hindu god Ram at the contested site of Ayodhya, where the existing mosque, the Babri Masjid, was torn down by Hindu nationalist *kar sevaks* (volunteers) in December 1992

(c) The abrogation of the system of religious personal laws founded by the British in the late 1700s and the establishment of a uniform civil code applicable to all Indians regardless of religion

It is not coincidental that these have also been three key pillars, however imperfect, of Indian secularism and multicultural protection of minority rights since independence (Williams and Jenkins 2015). At the time of this writing, the BJP has made significant headway on attaining the first two goals. On August 5, 2019, the party announced in parliament its unilateral decision to split up the state of Jammu and Kashmir and to abrogate Article 370 by rescinding many of its key provisions, such as one that prevented nonresident Kashmiris from purchasing and owning property in the state. Presented under the guise of advancing economic development in the state, the expected outcome of its elimination is for the historically Muslim-majority status of the state to be swamped and ultimately diluted. At the same time, the state of Kashmir was placed under a complete lockdown—cut off from communication with the outside world—which continues virtually unabated today.

The second constitutive pillar of the BJP's agenda has been the construction of a Ram temple at the contested site of Ayodhya, after the 1992 destruction of the ancient mosque that stood on the site (covered in detail in Chapter 2). The case regarding the construction of a temple languished in the courts for several decades; then on November 9, 2019, the Indian Supreme Court declared that the temple could be built on the contested site, and granted an adjacent site for a Muslim mosque to be rebuilt to replace the historical Babri mosque. The judgment was widely and correctly interpreted as a significant triumph for the BJP (Gettleman and Kumar [2020] 2021).

These developments leave the third pillar—elimination of the religious personal laws and the establishment of uniform civil code—as the last unattained target of the BJP's core agendas. It is also the most obviously gendered pillar, directly affecting the lives of Indian women across religious affiliation. Since the establishment of the personal laws in the late 1700s by the British, and certainly since the landmark *Shah Bano* case of 1985–86 (covered in detail in Chapter 2), women's legal and social rights have been inextricably bound up with the personal laws. The validity of Muslim law has been incrementally chipped away under BJP rule: in 2017 the Supreme Court declared the practice of "instant divorce" (triple *talaq*) unconstitutional (*Shayara Bano v. Union of India* (2017) 9 SCC 1 (SC)), and in July 2019 the Lok Sabha (the lower house of the Indian parliament) criminalized the practice (BBC News 2019). If this third and final pillar falls, the effects for Indian women will be momentous and unprecedented; it is not at all clear what such a change would look like or what the public response might be, even to those of us who have studied the issue for decades.

To assess what the rise of the BJP through the mobilization and incorporation of women has meant for Indian democracy requires thinking through what democracy itself could, should, or does mean and how to define it. Scholars have long debated minimalist versus more robust definitions of democracy (Whetstone 2020). The minimalist school, which can trace its roots to the work of Joseph Schumpeter ([1942] 1987), holds that democracy can be measured by the presence of competitive elections. These theorists do not see low levels of participation in elections—or the absence of robust political participation beyond elections—as a detriment to democracy. Instead, low or moderated levels of participation are actually good for democracy. This is because, they argue, most average voters are poorly informed and have low information levels, and democratic systems and structures are not well set up to handle high levels of popular participation. Indeed, "too much" participation, on this view, can damage or even destroy democracy itself (Lazarsfeld et al. 1944).

Against such minimalist definitions, more robust definitions of democracy include protection of civil and political rights such as freedom of assembly, freedom of the press, and even minority protections and freedom of religion. It is this more robust meaning of democracy that the rise of Hindu nationalist politics has threatened.[5] India's democratic status has been downgraded by all the major organizations that track these developments globally: Freedom House (freedomhouse.org), V-Dem (v-dem.net), and the Economist Intelligence Unit (eiu.com).

At the same time, India continues to score highly on the presence of competitive elections across all these platforms. But the corrosive effects of years of BJP rule on a more robust democracy are already apparent. Freedom of the press has been severely stressed as major media outlets fall in line to support government edicts. Some do so voluntarily, in actual agreement with BJP policies, while others do so facing the certainty of official pressure and popular backlash if they don't (Baker 2021). Journalists and reporters who oppose the BJP get constructed as enemies of India and pay with their lives (Yasir et al. 2018; Raj and Schultz 2018). Whether vigilantes patrolling Indian society in the name of Hindu nationalism—attacking interfaith couples, censoring books, and persecuting critics—are or are not actual members of the BJP, they remain assured that they will face only recalcitrant silence from the ruling party for their actions.

In this sense, then, the mobilization and incorporation of Hindu nationalist women has accompanied the hollowing out of a more robust democracy. This argument does not require assuming that Indian democracy prior to the rise of the BJP was ideal. But it does capture movement in the wrong direction. This leads to the third set of complexities around women's political participation that I argue the case of Hindu nationalist women leads us to question: the forms that women's participation takes.

Which (Forms of) Participation?

This study has elucidated gendered mobilization and incorporation as key forms or types of women's political participation. Marginalization is harder to conceptualize as a form of participation, as it is actually the absence of women's political participation. In the 1900s, before the BJP's initial rise to power, the Hindu Mahasabha did have a women's wing, the Hindu Mahila Sabha, built primarily on the efforts of one woman—Jankibai Joshi of Pune in western India—to convince the party's (male) leadership to engage and involve Hindu women in order for Hindu nationalism to be a competitive political force in the coming context of Indian independence and democracy. Her appeals were ignored, and her concerns proved prescient as the marginalization of women corresponded with electoral failure for the Hindu Mahasabha. In the 1980s and 1990s, during the BJP's initial rise to power, the party's gendered mobilization of women comprised three conceptually distinct (but practically inseparable) prongs: deploying gendered discourses, challenging feminism, and rallying women into the streets. Each prong was evident in three major political controversies between 1985 and 1992: the *Shah Bano* case on Muslim family law, the Roop Kanwar sati. and the destruction of the Babri mosque at Ayodhya. Since the BJP's initial rise to power, the shift to a more routine politics of incorporation began in 2004, with then party president Rajnath Singh's mandate to increase women's descriptive representation in the party's internal governance structures and committees. After 10 years in opposition, the BJP's return to power in 2014 came with the incorporation of women internally and electorally.

Each form of participation—marginalization, mobilization, incorporation—meant something different for women and corresponded with different gender ideologies. For the Hindu Mahasabha in the early 1900s, the marginalization of women entailed literally and physically tethering women to the private spheres of home and family and denying them both the right of, and the need for, access to the public, political sphere. In the 1980s and early 1990s, the party resolved its need to gain the support of women by mediating women's access to the public sphere. At the leadership level, women BJP leaders lacked significant family responsibilities in the domestic sphere through their social status as celibate renunciates or widows. At the rank-and-file level, women rallied into the streets in support of the BJP's big campaigns and controversies; but after participating, these women returned to their everyday familial activities and responsibilities. Incorporation was underpinned by a shift to a gender ideology of complementarity: the idea that men and women are equal but just have different roles to play in society. In this period the trope of "family support" for women's political activities came to stand in for patriarchal permission for women to engage in routine political participation for the party along with the kin-like structures of the RSS. Overall, the forms of women's participation in the BJP over time demonstrate what has changed and what has not in the limited spaces for women's activism that communal politics allows (Basu 1998).

Marginalization, mobilization, and incorporation stand in a complex interrelationship with more traditional or mainstream ways that political participation is measured (Chapter 3): voting, campaigning, petitioning, demonstrating, or running for or holding office. Women's political participation, I would argue, must be assessed contextually, in particular times and places. I believe marginalization, mobilization, and incorporation provide a broader context within which to assess the meaning of women's participation as more conventionally measured. In the case of BJP women, gendered mobilization and incorporation have intersected and overlapped with more traditional measures that they may encompass at different times and in different ways. For example, incorporation as studied here clearly included women running for and holding elected office; they also did so under mobilization and even marginalization, though to lesser extents. And in each case the meaning of women's officeholding was very different. Under marginalization, a woman holding elected office was an "exception that proved the rule" that women's place was primarily in the home. Under mobilization, women's officeholding became a way to advance the party's electoral success without untethering women from their social roles in the domestic sphere. And under incorporation, women's officeholding signaled the more institutionalized status of the party in power.

My analyses of marginalization, mobilization, and incorporation bring questions of women's descriptive and substantive representation to the fore. The movement from marginalization to mobilization and incorporation can be seen to represent an increase in women's descriptive representation: women are present in the party in growing numbers, and in that narrow sense the party can claim to have become "more representative." But Hindu nationalist women are unrepresentative of Indian women more broadly on a number of bases: religion, caste, class, language, region/geography, and education at a minimum. This, in turn, points to the question of substantive representation: has expanded descriptive representation of Hindu nationalist women translated into expanded substantive representation of Indian women's interests? I argue it has not. The BJP has made no notable policy advances on women's issues that it claims to support: neither those that feminists also support (such as legislative gender quotas) nor those that feminists have come to oppose (such as a uniform civil code). In the end, the party and the movement have benefited more from increasing women's participation over time than women have: marginalizing women left the Hindu Mahasabha out of power; mobilizing women brought the BJP initially to power; and incorporating women returned the BJP to power.

* * *

What, in the end, is left to conclude about the changing forms of Hindu nationalist women's political participation and what they have meant for Indian democracy? Has Hindu nationalist women's political participation been good or bad for women, and has it been good or bad for democracy? In some ways this is the obverse of the question some feminist analysts have asked about whether democracy is good for women (Walsh 2011). If "women's political participation" cannot be taken as an undifferentiated whole, but must be broken down analytically into constitutive questions—which women? which politics? and which participation?—then what remains are not simplistic or one-dimensional assessments of good and bad, but rather nuanced and complex fields of consequences and meanings.

I shall try, then, to return to the question posed at the start of this chapter: what does the "condition" of Indian women today tell us about the "status" of the Indian state under the BJP? To what extent has being (or appearing to be) progressive on women's rights continued to be a critical narrative of legitimation for the Indian state under the BJP? Examining the broad sweep of Hindu nationalist political parties from the Hindu Mahasabha in the early 1900s to the BJP today shows clearly that marginalizing women (a lack of participation) corresponded to electoral failure for the Hindu Mahasabha, while mobilizing and incorporating women corresponded with electoral success for the BJP. But mobilizing or incorporating women (increasing their descriptive representation) has not, in turn, meant the BJP has done much to substantively advance women's issues or women's rights in India (increasing their substantive representation).

Unlike the Hindu Mahasabha, the BJP has hewed more closely to the path of previous regimes by expanding women's political participation and claiming to care about making progress on women's issues such as gender quotas or a uniform civil code. The question of whether these or other particular measures would actually be "good for" women remains both debatable and ultimately irrelevant to what the party gains from such claims-making. For the BJP, women's expanded participation, from marginalization to mobilization to incorporation, has meant a steep ascent and full consolidation of political power. Meanwhile for women, expanded participation in Hindu nationalist politics has meant restricted access to the public sphere while continuing to keep them tethered, in various ways, to social roles in the domestic sphere of home and family. This does not constitute a meaningless change, but nor does it rise to the level of being transformative.

As someone whose intellectual beliefs and political commitments skew away from Hindu nationalist ideology but toward expanded women's political participation, I have struggled with how to end the book on a note that is not pessimistic. At the time of this writing, India is buried under a devastating second wave of Covid-19; and Modi's BJP suffered losses in multiple state elections in May 2021 (most prominently, the crushing loss in West Bengal to Mamta Bannerjee's All-India Trinamool Congress Party). At this point, it seems the electoral losses in West Bengal resulted from a unique confluence of particular circumstances rather than being scalable. To this point, Modi's BJP at the national level has seemed impervious to any effects of policy or state-level electoral failures. Yet it was difficult not to notice that the defeat in West Bengal came at the hands of one of India's most formidable woman political leaders. If the mobilization and incorporation of Hindu nationalist women has accelerated the rise of a movement that is undermining democracy, then it may be reasonable to posit that a medley of women's voices and activism, in the form of a robust feminism, is needed to counter that rise—in India and perhaps globally as well.

APPENDIX A
Interviews

Interviews with BJP leaders were conducted at two sites in both 2013 and again in 2015–16: New Delhi and Lucknow, the capital of Uttar Pradesh—India's largest state and a key base of support for the BJP. I have also drawn on two earlier interviews, conducted in 1994 for my dissertation research. Interviews were conducted primarily in English interspersed with some Hindi; all translations from Hindi are mine. All were conducted by me in person unless indicated otherwise. For the reasons outlined so thoroughly by Kalyani Devaki Menon (2010, 23), I did not make audio recordings of my interviews, but took handwritten notes of the discussions.

1994

Name	Position	Site	Date
Sikander Bakht	BJP Leader of the opposition in the Rajya Sabha	New Delhi	May 1994
K. R. Malkani	Vice President, BJP	New Delhi	May 1994

2013

Name	Position	Site	Date
Nirmala Sitharaman	National spokesperson	New Delhi	10/3/13
*Pinky Anand	Member, BJP National Executive Council	New Delhi	10/28/13
Lalji Tandon	MP	Lucknow	11/9/13
*Sanyukta Bhatia	National VP, Mahila Morcha	Lucknow	Nov. 2013
Sunita Aron	Journalist (*Hindustan Times*)	Lucknow	11/6/13
Manish Pandey	Journalist (*Hindustan Times*)	Lucknow	Nov. 2013

2015–16

Name	Position	Site	Date
Pushpa Singh Chauhan	Regional President, Mahila Morcha	Lucknow	12/16/15
Sunita Bhansal	State President, Mahila Morcha	Lucknow	12/17/15
Ranjana Dwivedi	State President, Mahila Morcha	Lucknow	12/18/15
Reeti Singh		Lucknow (Phone)	12/20/15
Anita Agarwal		Lucknow	12/19/15
*Sanyukta Bhatia	National VP, Mahila Morcha	Lucknow	12/21/15
Kusum Rai	MP	New Delhi	12/24/15
*Pinky Anand	Additional Solicitor General	New Delhi	1/5/16
Vani Tripathi Tikoo	MP	New Delhi	1/12/16
R. Balashankar	Chief, Intellectual Cell; director, National Training Program	New Delhi	Jan. 2016
Mohua Chatterjee	Journalist (*Times of India*)	New Delhi (Phone)	Jan. 2016
Radhika Ramshesan	Journalist (*Telegraph*)	New Delhi (Email)	Jan. 2016
Deep Singh	Driver	New Delhi	9/28/16

* Interviewed twice, before and after the 2014 election.

APPENDIX B

2014 Manifesto Items on Women, Coded

Coding Key

EC	Economic
ED	Education
V	Violence against women
• S	• Safety/security
• GC	• Girl child
PL	Political/legal rights
G	General
I	Intersectional
H	Healthcare/hygiene

Code-1	Code-2	Item
PL	G	Women's welfare and development will be accorded a high priority at all levels within the government, and BJP is committed to 33 percent reservation in parliamentary and state assemblies through a constitutional amendment.
GC	ED	Launch a national campaign for saving the girl child and educating her: Beti Bachao–Beti Padhao.
GC		Structure a comprehensive scheme, incorporating best practices from past successes like Balika Samruddhi, Ladli Laxmi, and Chiranjeevi Yojana to encourage positive attitude among families toward the girl child.
H	I	Program for women's healthcare in a mission mode, especially focusing on domains of nutrition and pregnancy—with emphasis on rural, Scheduled Castes, Scheduled Tribes, and Other Backward Castes.
EC		Enable women with training and skills—setting up dedicated women Industrial Technical Institutes (ITIs), women wings in other ITIs.
V		Strict implementation of laws related to women, particularly those related to rape.

V		Fund for relief and rehabilitation of rape victims lies unused at the Centre as the government has not worked out the modalities of dispensation. BJP will clear this on priority.
V		Government will create an acid attack victims welfare fund to take care of the medical costs related to treatment and cosmetic reconstructive surgeries of such victims.
V		Make police stations women friendly and increase the number of women in police at different levels.
V		Introduce self-defense as a part of the school curriculum.
V		Use information technology for women's safety.
EC		Set up an All Women Mobile Bank to cater to women.
EC	S	Special skills training and business incubator park for women.
EC	S	Set up special business facilitation center for women.
EC	S	Expand and improve upon the network of women / working women hostels.
EC		Set up a dedicated women small and medium enterprises cluster in every district.
EC		Review the working conditions and enhance the remuneration of Anganwadi workers.
PL		Remove any remaining gender disparities in property rights, marital rights, and cohabitation rights.
ED	I	Start special adult literacy initiative for women with focus on Scheduled Castes, Scheduled Tribes, Other Backward Castes, and slum residents.
EC		Ensure that the loans to Women Self Help Groups are available at low interest rates.
G	I	Special programs aimed at girls below poverty line, tribals, and indigent women.
V		Take appropriate measures to check female feticide, dowry, child marriage, trafficking, sexual harassment, rape, and family violence.
H	I	Transform the quality of life of women in rural India by providing electricity, tapped water, cleaner fuel, and toilets in every home.

Notes

Introduction

1. My dissertation examined the relationship between India's religious laws and Hindu-Muslim conflict over time and was published as Williams 2006.
2. Sikhism, Jainism, and Buddhism began as reform movements within Hinduism. Though they are considered separate religions today, forces of Hindu nationalism—as well as more secular forces at different times—tend to subsume these three religions under a broader umbrella of Hinduism. See Williams 2013a.
3. Between the Hindu Mahasabha and the BJP, another party—the Bharatiya Jana Sangh, or Jana Sangh—was the primary political party of Hindu nationalism. I briefly consider the Jana Sangh and the role of women in that party in Chapter 1, but I do not analyze it as a separate case. This is because the Jana Sangh, in retrospect and due to political events, became primarily a "bridge" between the Hindu Mahasabha—the original political party of Hindu nationalism—and the BJP—its contemporary and most politically successful standard-bearer.
4. In 2014 the BJP won absolute control of the Lok Sabha—the lower house of the Indian parliament—surprising even the most seasoned observers of Indian politics and signaling what many believe is the steep decline of the secular, center-left Congress Party that led India's independence movement and dominated the politics of independent India. See Chhibber and Verma 2018.
5. I am grateful to Annulla Linders for pointing me to this argument.
6. The BJP is not the only Hindu nationalist political party in India, but it is the primary national party that serves as the political wing of the Hindu nationalist movement. Some have studied the Shiv Sena, an avowedly Hindu nationalist political party that has contested for and held power in the western state of Maharashtra—including the role of women in the party—but it is a regional rather than a national party, and in fact recent studies have illuminated points of divergence between regional parties like the Shiv Sena and the national-level Hindutva movement (Sen 2007; Bedi 2016).
7. Abrahamic religions share a belief in a monotheistic deity whose follower, Abraham, features in the origin stories of the religions as a man whose faith is directly tested by God, who asks him to sacrifice his son as a show of devotion. For an argument against the use of the phrase, see Hughes 2012.
8. http://www.dictionary.com/browse/incorporate?s=t. Accessed October 7, 2017.
9. The (highly contested) Hindu practice of widow immolation on the funeral pyre of her husband.

166 NOTES

10. Of course, these are not the only ways to measure women's participation in the party, but I found them to be the most comparable across very different time periods, hence a particularly effective set of measures for comparison over time.

Chapter 1

1. Other Hindu nationalist parties grew from and were based in explicitly regional agendas. Most notably, the Shiv Sena in the western state of Maharashtra advocated what was essentially a "sons of the soil" movement. See Sen 2007.
2. I use the term "communal" as it is commonly used among scholars of India, to denote a (presumed or constructed) commitment to one's religious community as one's primary identity. In this context it also implies intolerance toward religious communities other than one's own.
3. Several outstanding studies of the RSS, as well as its women's wing, the Rashtra Sevika Samiti, include Andersen and Damle 1987; Sarkar 1993a, 1993b; Hansen 1999; Bacchetta 2004.
4. Interview with the author, Lucknow, India, November 9, 2013.
5. Eventually Mookerjee resigned from the government as well, as differences escalated over the treatment of migrant populations in the aftermath of partition.
6. After independence this became the state of UP, or Uttar Pradesh, the most populous state in India and still a crucial support base for Hindu nationalism.
7. Bihar Provincial Hindu Sabha, Patna, Resolutions n/d. 1946 Gorakhpur Session, *Papers of the All-India Hindu Mahasabha*, Nehru Memorial Museum and Library, New Delhi (hereafter PAIHM) File No. C-132 Pt. I, p. 107.
8. See its website at http://www.abhm.org.in.
9. See, for example, https://www.bjp.org/en/integralhumanism. Last accessed May 24, 2019.
10. Hindutva translates roughly to "Hindu-ness" and is used interchangeably with "Hindu nationalist" both in this book and in common usage.
11. The NDA included political parties covering a broad range of the political spectrum, including regional parties, caste-based parties, and Congress splinter parties. Other than the BJP, the NDA included only one other avowedly Hindu nationalist party, the Shiv Sena, whose strength is regionally concentrated in the western state of Maharashtra. According to the BJP website, the NDA coalition included the following member parties in 1998: Bharatiya Janata Party; All-India Anna Dravida Munnetra Kazhagam (AIA-DMK); Samata Party; Biju Janata Dal; Shiromani Akali Dal; Trinamool Congress; Shiv Sena; Marumalarchi Deravida Munnetra Kazhagam (MDMK); Pattali Makkal Katchi; Lok Shakti; Haryana Vikas Party; Tamizhaga Rajiv Congress; Janata Party. http://www.bjp.org/manifes/manifes99.htm#aa.
12. https://www.ipu.org/our-impact/gender-equality. Accessed November 3, 2020.
13. Some examples are listed here: https://wcd.nic.in/schemes-listing/2405. Accessed January 8, 2021.
14. Pinky Anand, interview with the author, New Delhi, October 28, 2013.

Chapter 2

1. Technically, the NDA did not complete the *full* five-year term; so confident were they that they would win again in 2004 that they called elections a few months early—and lost badly. But there is little doubt that, had they not called elections early, the government would have completed the full term.
2. This section draws on Williams 2006, Chapter 5.
3. There are optional/secular codes of family laws for interreligious marriages, but these remain very rarely used in India, as indeed interreligious marriages themselves remain rare in India.
4. *Mohd. Ahmed Khan v. Shah Bano Begum*, AIR 1985 Supreme Court 945.
5. Khan paid Shah Bano the Rs. 3000 as *mahr* (or dower), and argued that this was all he owed her under Muslim personal law. The Supreme Court judgment, however, argued that *mahr* was actually a sum payable in Muslim marriages in consideration of marriage. The amount is often fixed at the time of the marriage, but the actual payment of this sum can be deferred till such time as the marriage is dissolved by death or divorce (which was what happened in Shah Bano's case). But since *mahr* was a sum payable in consideration of *marriage*, it could not be a sum payable in consideration of *divorce*. Therefore, the Court concluded "Mahr is not a sum which, under the Muslim Personal Law, is payable on divorce." As such, the amount of *mahr* could not be considered in lieu of maintenance for the woman. *Shah Bano*, 954. As for Shah Bano herself, she recanted the maintenance award she had won after local religious leaders "explained" to her that the award contradicted Islamic law (Nussbaum 2000, 382–83; Pathak and Sunder Rajan 1989, 565). She died in 1992;her ex-husband passed away in 2006 (Khan 2011; OneIndia News 2006).
6. Tahir Mahmood, interview with the author, New Delhi, May 1994; Engineer 1987, 14–15.
7. The other two main planks of the BJP's agenda toward religious minorities included the elimination of Article 370 of the constitution (which granted special status to Jammu and Kashmir state, the only Muslim-majority state in India); and the elimination of religion-based personal laws and the establishment of a uniform civil code—which was at issue in the *Shah Bano* controversy. See Chapter 6.
8. Several scholars and analysts argued that Rajiv Gandhi's decision to open the mosque compound to Hindus constituted in effect—and by one allegation, an explicit deal—a "tit-for-tat" action to appease the Hindu Right after having appeased Muslim conservatives by passing the Muslim Women Bill. See Hasan 1993, 13–14.
9. Although the Shiv Sena predated the BJP and began as a "sons of the soil" nativist movement, the parties have been allied since 1984, when the Sena adopted strident Hindu nationalist and anti-Muslim platform to shore up its waning base. The alliance was never perfect, however, and as of November 2019 it seemed to have frayed. See Biswas 2019; Dutta 2019. Women also participated in post-Ayodhya rioting in other parts of the country, such as the town of Surat (Basu 1993a, 32).
10. Women's reasons or justifications for participation in the Ayodhya and post-Ayodhya violence seemed quite localized. At the site of the demolition, one scholar noted that

"interviews with women demonstrators at Ayodhya convinced us that their affirmation of the ... issue was no mindless gesture but a highly informed conviction" (Sarkar 1993a, 24). But in the oral histories Sen gathered in Bombay, one woman rioter specified, "I don't care much about Babri Masjid" (Sen and Jasani 2014, n.p.).
11. As noted above, however, scholars have frequently referenced the *Shah Bano* case as an example of the perils of multiculturalism for women and placed it in a comparative context with other cases and countries (Eisenberg 2009; Mahajan 2005; Benhabib 2002; Charrad 2001).

Chapter 3

1. The (highly contested) practice of widow immolation on the funeral pyre of her husband.
2. I am grateful to Annulla Linders for pointing me to this argument.
3. Sunita Aron, Editor, *Hindustan Times*, interview with the author, Lucknow, November 2013.
4. This section draws on Whetstone and Williams 2019.
5. I explore the ideational underpinnings of women's participation in Hindu nationalist politics in greater detail in Williams and Deo 2018.
6. Chandra (2016) has argued that political parties' weak organizational structures contribute to dynastic politics in India.
7. Reeti Singh, interview with the author, Lucknow, December 20, 2015.
8. For a detailed analysis of how aspects of my positionality in researching BJP women changed between the early 1990s and the 2010s, see Williams, 2022b.
9. A childhood story captures this dynamic. The Hindu myth of Trishanku (which varied slightly in some details in my parents' telling) held that he was a "mythological king, an ancestor of Lord Rama" who sought to ascend to heaven in his own mortal body, which was not allowed. Nevertheless, he convinced one sage to grant him this wish, and when he died he began to ascend to heaven in his body; but "Indra, the King of Heaven, pushed him down." While he was falling, the sage who had granted his wish broke his fall. But because he wasn't allowed to ascend, Trishanku ended up hanging upside down, suspended "in mid-air," belonging "neither to earth nor to heaven" (Kumar 2016, 1) for eternity.

Chapter 4

1. A version of this chapter was published as Williams 2013b.
2. Letter from Joshi to Provincial Hindu Sabhas, September 16, 1944, Papers of the All-India Hindu Mahasabha, Nehru Memorial Museum and Library, New Delhi (hereafter PAIHM), File C/51, p. 27.

3. Letter from Joshi to Provincial Hindu Sabhas, September 16, 1944, PAIHM, File C/51, p. 27.
4. Proceedings of the meeting of the Working Committee, January 23, 1945, PAIHM, File C/30, p. 4.
5. For a history of the AIWC, see Basu and Ray 1990. The AIWC still exists; see its website at http://www.aiwc.org.in/index.html.
6. Petition from Joshi to Linlithgow, PAIHM, File C/67, p. 47. Elsewhere Joshi specified that because Brahmos did not accept the authority of the Vedas, they could not be considered Hindus. She wrote: "I had raised an objection to the nomination of one of the women members of the All India Women's Conference Mrs. Renuka Ray of Brahmo faith as a representative of crores of Hindu women of India. The Brahmo religion does not believe in Vedas . . . but the Vedas are the very foundation of the Hindu religion. . . . It is, therefore, with formal protest against . . . the nomination of a Brahmo Lady to represent the cause of Hindu women of India in the Legislative Assembly." *Hindu Outlook*, April 20, 1943, p. 6, PAIHM, File C/67. On the Brahmo Samaj, see Bhushan 2017, Chapter 5; Wolpert 2006.
7. Letter from Joshi to Provincial Hindu Sabhas, August 26, 1943, PAIHM, File C/67, p. 44.
8. Reception Committee Meeting, 1949, PAIHM, File C/183, p. 16.
9. The literature on the RSS and the Samiti is vast. For a start, see Andersen and Damle 1987; T. Basu 1993. On the Samiti see Bacchetta 2004; Menon 2010.
10. Letter from Joshi to Sri Gokulchandji, February 21, 1944. PAIHM, File C/67, p. 31. The evolution of the relationship between the RSS and the Hindu Mahasabha is detailed in Chapter 1.
11. Letter from Joshi to V. G. Deshpande, January 16, 1944, PAIHM, File C/67, p. 46.
12. Letter from Joshi to all heads of provincial sabhas, August 26, 1943, PAIHM, File C/67, p. 44.
13. Letter from Joshi to N. B. Khare, March 5, 1950, PAIHM, File C/183, p. 14.
14. Several of her children followed Vijaya Raje Scindia into politics as well. Her only son, Madhavrao Scindia, became estranged from his mother and became a prominent Congress Party leader. His son, Jyotiraditya Scindia, has followed in his footsteps. The younger two of Vijaya Raje's daughters, however—Vasundhara Raje, the third daughter, and Yasudhara Raje, the youngest, followed their mother into BJP politics. Indeed, Vasundhara Raje is the current BJP chief minister of Rajasthan, her second turn in that position (2003–8; 2013–present).
15. It is important to note that the role of women's wings in political parties was fairly well defined and common across parties for most of their histories. The women's wing was critical to mobilizing voters (mostly women), feeding men party workers, and carrying out other support roles. In general women's wings were less about women's rights than about women's participation in the party. This was true from the 1930s through most of the postindependence period until some change began to take place in the 1990s. Women's wings did advocate for women to get party tickets and be elected (and we will see in the next chapter that the women's wing of the contemporary BJP continues this function); but feminist or women's right activists tended not

to come from the ranks of women's wings, especially in parties that enforced political discipline. I am grateful to Wendy Singer for these insights.
16. "Hindu Mahila-Sabhas," *Mahratta*, October 22, 1943, pp. 20–21. From Papers of S. P. Mookerjee (II-IV Institution), Sub. File-63. Nehru Memorial Museum and Library, New Delhi (hereafter PSPM).
17. Letter from Joshi to S. P. Mookerjee, September 23, 1944, PAIHM, File C/51, p. 25.
18. Resolutions for the All-India Hindu Mahasabha session at Gorakhpur, October 18, 1946, PAIHM, File C/132 Pt. I, p. 325.
19. Letter from Joshi to N. B. Khare, March 5, 1950, PAIHM, File C/183, p. 14.
20. "Hindu Mahila-Sabhas," *Mahratta*, October 22, 1943, PSPM, pp. 20–21.
21. Working Committee Meeting Resolution, Delhi, May 9, 1943, PAIHM C/183, p. 15.
22. Letter from Mookerjee to V. G. Deshpande, October 3, 1944, PAIHM, File C/51, p. 24.
23. Letter from Joshi to Mookerjee, February 1, 1944, PSPM, pp. 17–18.
24. Letter from Joshi to Sri Gokulchandji, February 21, 1944, PAIHM File C/67, pp. 30–31.
25. Working Committee Meeting Resolution, Delhi, May 9, 1943. PAIHM, File C/183, p. 15.
26. Letter from Joshi to Provincial Hindu Sabhas, September 16, 1944, PAIHM, File C/51, p. 27.
27. Letter from Joshi to Mookerjee, September 23, 1944. PAIHM, File C/51, p. 25.
28. Letter from Joshi to Secretary Hindu Mahasabha, New Delhi, March 4, 1949, PAIHM, File C/183, p. 16.
29. To be accurate, one might acknowledge that since the Hindu Mahasabha only won four seats in the First Lok Sabha, its representation of women MPs was actually 25 percent.
30. In this, the Hindu Mahasabha was certainly not alone; indeed, I have argued elsewhere that even Nehru's reforms of Hindu religious law in the 1950s were only secondarily about improving the status of women and primarily about building Indian nationalism. See Williams 2006, Chapter 4; 2010; 2013a.
31. https://www.inc.in/leadership/past-party-presidents. Accessed October 19, 2022.
32. These included a Women's Committee for the Gujarat Provincial Congress Committee (Basu 1995, 14); a Congress Mahila Sangh in 1939 (Kumar 1997, 92); and a Women's Branch of the Home Rule League (Agnew 1979, 35).
33. In a notable parallel with the Hindu Mahasabha, it seems that women trying to push for an active women's wing in the Congress Party also encountered particular resistance from the provincial levels of the party organization.
34. The Congress Party website lists the All India Mahila Congress as one of its frontal organizations along with workers, youth, and other organizations. The current president is listed as Ms. Sushmita Dev, Ex-MP, with no additional information to show the current status or activities of the organization. https://www.inc.in/all-india-mahila-congress. Accessed June 22, 2021.
35. See, for example, at https://www.hinduscriptures.com/hindu-lifestyle/lakshmibai-kelkar-mausiji/27107/. Accessed February 2, 2019.

36. Texts analyzed include Mathur 1996; Prakash 1938, 1942, 1966; Savarkar 1969, 1984. These represent the writings of Hindu nationalist ideologues, official party historians, and/or collected party documents of the Hindu Mahasabha.
37. For contemporary studies of the ongoing role of masculinity in Hindu nationalism see Anand 2007, 2011; Banerjee 2005.
38. On conversion policies in India, see L. Jenkins 2008, 2019.
39. Speech in Hyderabad, quoted in *Hindu Outlook* 2 (5) (March 30, 1938): 4.

Chapter 5

1. Foundational works on women in Hindu nationalism include Basu 1993b; Jeffery and Basu 1998; Sarkar 2001; Katju 2003; Bacchetta 2004; Sen 2007. More recent works include Menon 2010; Bedi 2016; Deo 2016. I cover this foundational literature in depth in Chapter 3.
2. Nirmala Sitharaman, interview with the author, New Delhi, October 3, 2013; Iyer and Bartwal 2007; Ravi and Sandhu 2014, 12.
3. Pinky Anand, interview with the author, New Delhi, October 28, 2013.
4. Sanyukta Bhatia, interview with the author, Lucknow, December 21, 2015.
5. Pinky Anand, interview with the author, New Delhi, January 5, 2016; Mohua Chatterjee, interview with the author, New Delhi (via phone), January 2016.
6. Pinky Anand, interview with the author, New Delhi, October 28, 2013.
7. Anita Agarwal, interview with the author, Lucknow, December 19, 2015; Sanyukta Bhatia, interview with the author, Lucknow, December 21, 2015; Vani Tripathi Tikoo, interview with the author, New Delhi, January 12, 2016.
8. Pushpa Singh Chauhan, interview with the author, Lucknow, December 16, 2015; Sanyukta Bhatia, interview with the author, Lucknow, December 21, 2015.
9. Pushpa Singh Chauhan, interview with the author, Lucknow, December 16, 2015.
10. Ranjana Dwivedi, interview with the author, Lucknow, December 18, 2015.
11. Sanyukta Bhatia, interview with the author, Lucknow, December 21, 2015.
12. http://164.100.47.192/Loksabha/Members/AlphabeticalList.aspx. Accessed February 20, 2016.
13. Vani Tripathi Tikoo, interview with the author, New Delhi, January 12, 2016.
14. The tension between Modi and Advani seemed to be ongoing; see for example Mohanty 2017. Modi's selection also led the chief minister of the state of Bihar, Nitish Kumar, to withdraw his Janata Dal (United) Party from a coalition government with the BJP in Bihar (Kumar 2013; TNN 2013). This break was later reversed as Nitish Kumar resurrected his alliance with the BJP. See Kumar and Singh 2017; Varshney 2017.
15. Pinky Anand, interview with the author, New Delhi, October 28, 2013.
16. Lalji Tandon, interview with the author, Lucknow, November 9, 2013; Pinky Anand, interview with the author, New Delhi, October 28, 2013.

17. Lalji Tandon, interview with the author, Lucknow, November 9, 2013; Shankar 2013, 222.
18. Vani Tripathi Tikoo, interview with the author, New Delhi, January 12, 2016.
19. Sunita Bhansal, interview with the author, Lucknow, December 17, 2015; Anita Agarwal, interview with the author, Lucknow, December 19, 2015; Sanyukta Bhatia, interview with the author, Lucknow, December 21, 2015.
20. Crowdsourcing their election manifestoes was presented as a democratizing maneuver by both the BJP and the Congress Party, a way to "popularize" the party's agenda and make sure it was in the hands of the party's supporters. Yet how the process actually worked—how the input was gathered and processed, and how much popular input made its way into the final documents—very much remains to be studied and theorized.
21. This is a bill to secure a 33 percent quota of seats for women in the national legislature. It has been introduced several times since 1996—most recently, passing the Rajya Sabha (upper house) but failing to pass the Lok Sabha in 2010. The BJP has claimed to support the bill, but since taking power in 2014 has done nothing to pursue it. See Randall 2006a; Krook 2009; Pandit 2018.
22. Pinky Anand, interview with the author, New Delhi, January 5, 2016.
23. A great deal of work has been done on gender quotas globally, in general, and in India in particular. For a publicly accessible database on gender quotas around the world, see http://www.quotaproject.org. For analysis of the ups and downs of gender quotas in India, see Randall 2006a and Krook 2009.
24. Pinky Anand, interview with the author, New Delhi, January 5, 2016; Vani Tripathi Tikoo, interview with the author, New Delhi, January 12, 2016; Anita Agarwal, interview with the author, Lucknow, December 19, 2015; Sanyukta Bhatia, interview with the author, Lucknow, December 21, 2015.
25. Pinky Anand, interview with the author, New Delhi, January 5, 2016.
26. Local governments, where 33 percent reservations have been in effect since 1993—long enough to have generated several studies of its effects and effectiveness. For an overview see Chattopadhyaya and Duflo 2004, Lama-Rewal 2005; for a recent study see Chauchard 2014.
27. Anita Agarwal, interview with the author, Lucknow, December 19, 2015.
28. Vani Tripathi Tikoo, interview with the author, New Delhi, January 12, 2016.
29. Kusum Rai, interview with the author, New Delhi, December 24, 2015.
30. Sanyukta Bhatia, interview with the author, Lucknow, December 21, 2015.
31. Sanyukta Bhatia, interview with the author, Lucknow, December 21, 2015; Sunita Bhansal, interview with the author, Lucknow, December 17, 2015; Ranjana Dwivedi, interview with the author, Lucknow, December 18, 2015.
32. Anita Agarwal, interview with the author, Lucknow, December 19, 2015; Sanjukta .Bhatia, interview with the author, Lucknow, December 21, 2015.
33. Sanyukta Bhatia, interview with the author, Lucknow, November 2013, December 21, 2015; Vani Tripathi Tikoo, interview with the author, New Delhi, January 12, 2016.
34. Ranjana Dwivedi, interview with the author, Lucknow, December 18, 2015; Vani Tripathi Tikoo, interview with the author, New Delhi, January 12, 2016.

35. http://www.rekhagupta.in. Accessed February 25, 2016.
36. Indeed, though my focus is on cisgender women, it is important to note that gender identity and sexuality are key among the ways incorporation is limited.
37. Deep Singh, interview with the author, New Delhi, September 28, 2015; Ranjana Dwivedi, interview with the author, Lucknow, December 18, 2015; Kusum Rai, interview with the author, New Delhi, December 24, 2015; Vani Tripathi Tikoo, interview with the author, New Delhi, January 12, 2016; Sanyukta Bhatia, interview with the author, Lucknow, December 21, 2015; Anita Agarwal, interview with the author, Lucknow, December 19, 2015.
38. Vani Tripathi Tikoo, interview with the author, New Delhi, January 12, 2016. These views have moved very little off the positions constructed and espoused by Gandhi during the independence movement. See Forbes 1996.
39. Nirmala Sitharaman, interview with the author, New Delhi, October 3, 2013.
40. Lalji Tandon, interview with the author, Lucknow, November 9, 2013.
41. Pinky Anand, interview with the author, New Delhi, January 5, 2016; Vani Tripathi Tikoo, interview with the author, New Delhi, January 12, 2016. "Dynastic" party politics in India refers to the overwhelming prominence of the Nehru-Gandhi lineage in the Congress Party.
42. Vani Tripathi Tikoo, interview with the author, New Delhi, January 12, 2016; Ranjana Dwivedi, interview with the author, Lucknow, December 18, 2015; Anita Agarwal, interview with the author, Lucknow, December 19, 2015.
43. Lalji Tandon, interview with the author, Lucknow, November 9, 2013; R. Balashankar, interview with the author, New Delhi, January 13, 2016. For my argument that they are in fact linked, see Chapter 1.

Chapter 6

1. Posted on Twitter, January 23, 2014.
2. Another died in police custody; the sixth was a minor and was given the maximum sentence of three years in a reform facility.
3. Similar arguments can and have been raised about Indian and South Asian feminism more broadly (Paik 2014; Jamal 2005). That remains a subject for further analysis.
4. Pinky Anand, interview with the author, New Delhi, January 5, 2016.
5. Other scholars advocating even more robust conceptions, such as deliberative and participatory democracy, "seek the participation of all sectors of society in decision-making over their lives" (Whetstone 2020, Chapter 2, p. 9; Davis 1964; Wolfe 1985; Pateman 1970). It is perhaps worth noting that some analysts have argued that even a more robust Indian democracy was far from ideal, in terms of full economic equality and social belonging (Jalal 1995). But no democracy has ever reached that ideal.

Bibliography

Abu-Lughod, Lila. 1998. *Remaking Women: Feminism and Modernity in the Middle East*. Princeton, NJ: Princeton University Press.

Abu-Lughod, Lila. 2013. *Do Muslim Women Need Saving?* Cambridge, MA: Harvard University Press.

Ackerly, Brooke A. and Jacqui True. 2010. *Doing Feminist Research in Political and Social Science*. New York: Palgrave Macmillan.

Adeney, Katharine and Lawrence Sáez. 2005. *Coalition Politics and Hindu Nationalism*. New York: Routledge.

Agnew, Vijay. 1979. *Elite Women in Indian Politics*. New Delhi: Vikas.

Akhil Bharat Hindu Mahasabha. 1942. *The History of the Bhagalpur Struggle; the 23rd Session of the A.I.H. Mahasabha*. Bangalpur: Madhukari.

Aldrich, John. 2011. "Political Parties in and out of Legislatures." In *The Oxford Handbook of Political Science*, edited by Robert E. Goodin. New York: Oxford University Press.

Ali, Azra Asghar. 2000. *The Emergence of Feminism among Indian Muslim Women, 1920– 1947*. New York: Oxford University Press.

Almond, Gabriel A. and Sidney Verba. 1963. *The Civic Culture: Political Attitudes and Democracy in Five Nations*. Princeton, NJ: Princeton University Press.

Almond, Gabriel A., R. Scott Appleby, and Emmanuel Sivan. 2003. *Strong Religion: The Rise of Fundamentalisms around the World*. Chicago: University of Chicago Press.

Anand, Dibyesh. 2007. "Anxious Sexualities: Masculinity, Nationalism and Violence." *British Journal of Politics & International Relations* 9 (2): 257–69.

Anand, Dibyesh. 2011. *Hindu Nationalism in India and the Politics of Fear*. New York: Palgrave Macmillan.

Andersen, Walter K. and Shridhar D. Damle. 1987. *The Brotherhood in Saffron: The Rashtriya Swayamsevak Sangh and Hindu Revivalism*. Boulder, CO: Westview Press.

Arat, Yeşim. 2005. *Rethinking Islam and Liberal Democracy: Islamist Women in Turkish Politics*. Albany: State University of New York Press.

Bacchetta, Paola. 1993. "All of Our Goddesses Are Armed: Religion, Resistance, and Revenge in the Life of a Militant in the Nationalist Woman." *Bulletin of Concerned Asian Scholars* 25 (4): 38–51.

Bacchetta, Paola. 2004. *Gender in the Hindu Nation: RSS Women as Ideologues*. New Delhi: Women Unlimited.

Bacchetta, Paola and Margaret Power, eds. 2002. *Right-Wing Women: From Conservatives to Extremists around the World*. New York: Routledge.

Baker, Graham. 2021. "Alternative Sources of Information: India, Poland, and Brazil." V-Dem Institute, March 2. https://www.v-dem.net/en/news/alternative-sources-information-india-poland-and-brazil/.

Banaszak, Lee Ann, Karen Beckwith, and Dieter Rucht. 2003. *Women's Movements Facing the Reconfigured State*. New York: Cambridge University Press.

Banerjee, Sikata. 1996. "The Feminization of Violence in Bombay: Women in the Politics of the Shiv Sena." *Asian Survey* 36 (12): 1213–25.

Banerjee, Sikata. 2005. *Make Me a Man! Masculinity, Hinduism, and Nationalism in India.* Albany: State University of New York Press.

Banerjee, Sikata. 2012. *Muscular Nationalism: Gender, Violence, and Empire in India and Ireland, 1914–2004.* New York: New York University Press.

Barnes, Samuel H. and Max Kaase. 1979. *Political Action: Mass Participation in Five Western Democracies.* Beverly Hills, CA: Sage.

Basu, Amrita. 1992. *Two Faces of Protest: Contrasting Modes of Women's Activism in India.* Berkeley: University of California Press.

Basu, Amrita. 1993a. "Feminism Inverted: The Real Women and Gendered Imagery of Hindu Nationalism." *Bulletin of Concerned Asian Scholars* 25 (4): 25–37.

Basu, Amrita, ed. 1993b. "Special Issue: Women and Religious Nationalism in India." *Bulletin of Concerned Asian Scholars* 25 (4): 3–52.

Basu, Amrita. 1998. "Hindu Women's Activism in India and the Questions it Raises." In *Appropriating Gender: Women's Activism and Politicized Religion in South Asia,* edited by Patricia Jeffery and Amrita Basu, 167–84. New York: Routledge.

Basu, Amrita. 2013. "The Changing Fortunes of the Bharatiya Janata Party." In *Routledge Handbook of Indian Politics,* edited by Atul Kohli and Prerna Singh, 81–90. New York: Routledge.

Basu, Amrita. 2015. *Violent Conjunctures in Democratic India.* New York: Cambridge University Press.

Basu, Amrita. 2016. "Women, Dynasties and Democracy in India." In *Democratic Dynasties: State, Party, and Family in Contemporary Indian Politics,* edited by Kanchan Chandra, 136–72. New York: Cambridge University Press.

Basu, Aparna. 1995. "A Nationalist Feminist: Mridula Sarabhai (1911–1974)." *Indian Journal of Gender Studies* 2 (1): 1–24.

Basu, Aparna and Bharati Ray. 1990. *Women's Struggle: A History of the All India Women's Conference, 1927–1990.* New Delhi: Manohar.

Basu, Srimati. 2018. "Hiding in Plain Sight: Disclosure, Identity, and the Indian Men's Rights Movement." *QED: A Journal in GLBTQ Worldmaking* 5 (3): 117–29.

Basu, Tapan. 1993. *Khaki Shorts and Saffron Flags: A Critique of the Hindu Right.* New Delhi: Orient Longman.

Baxter, Craig. 1969. *The Jana Sangh: A Biography of an Indian Political Party.* Philadelphia: University of Pennsylvania Press.

BBC News. 2013. "LK Advani: India BJP Leader Withdraws His Resignation." *BBC.com,* June 11. http://www.bbc.com/news/world-asia-india-22851915.

BBC News. 2019. "Triple Talaq: India Criminalises Muslim 'Instant Divorce.'" *BBC.com,* July 30. https://www.bbc.com/news/world-asia-india-49160818.

Bedi, Tarini. 2016. *The Dashing Ladies of Shiv Sena: Political Matronage in Urbanizing India.* Albany: State University of New York Press.

Behl, Natasha. 2017. "Diasporic Researcher: An Autoethnographic Analysis of Race and Gender in Political Science." *Politics, Groups, and Identities* 5 (4): 580–98.

Ben Shitrit, Lihi. 2016. "Authenticating Representation: Women's Quotas and Islamist Parties." *Politics & Gender* 12 (4): 781–806.

Benhabib, Seyla. 2002. *The Claims of Culture: Equality and Diversity in the Global Era.* Princeton, NJ: Princeton University Press.

Bennett, James. 2017. "In India, Low-Caste Dalits Put Dignity before Livelihood, by Leaving Cows Where They Die." *ABC News Australia*, January 27. https://www.abc.net.au/news/2017-01-28/indian-dalits-revolt-against-descrimination/7813970.

Bermeo, Nancy Gina and Deborah J. Yashar. 2016. "Parties, Movements and the Making of Democracy." In *Parties, Movements and Democracy in the Developing World*, edited by Nancy Gina Bermeo and Deborah J. Yashar, 1–27. New York: Cambridge University Press.

Bharatiya Janata Party. 2014. *Election Manifesto 2014: Sabka Saath, Sabka Vikaas*. https://www.bjp.org/images/pdf_2014/full_manifesto_english_07.04.2014.pdf. Accessed February 23, 2019.

Bhasin, Kamla and Ritu Menon. 1988. "The Problem." *Seminar* 342: 12–13.

Bhushan, Nalini. 2017. *Minds without Fear: Philosophy in the Indian Renaissance*. Oxford: Oxford University Press.

Biswas, Soutik. 2019. "Maharashtra: The Unravelling of India's BJP and Shiv Sena Alliance." BBC News, November 14. https://www.bbc.com/news/world-asia-india-50402748.

Blee, Kathleen M. 1993. "Evidence, Empathy, and Ethics: Lessons from Oral Histories of the Klan." *Journal of American History* 80 (2): 596–606.

Blee, Kathleen M. and Sandra McGee Deutsch, eds. 2012. *Women of the Right: Comparisons and Interplay across Borders*. University Park: Pennsylvania State University Press.

Bombay Union of Journalists. 1987. *Trial by Fire: A Report on Roop Kanwar's Death*. Bombay: Women and Media Committee, Bombay Union of Journalists.

Brechenmacher, Saskia and Caroline Hubbard, 2020. "Breaking the Cycle of Gender Exclusion in Political Party Development." Carnegie Endowment for International Peace Working Paper, March 24. https://carnegieendowment.org/2020/03/24/breaking-cycle-of-gender-exclusion-in-political-party-development-pub-81345.

Brocker, Manfred and Mirjam Kunkler. 2013. "Revisiting the Inclusion-Moderation Hypothesis: Introduction." *Party Politics* 19 (2): 171–86.

Burns, John F. 1994. "Riot Scars Are Gone, but Bombay Is Still Healing." *New York Times*, April 17. https://www.nytimes.com/1994/04/17/world/riot-scars-are-gone-but-bombay-is-still-healing.html.

Butalia, Urvashi. 2001. "Women and Communal Conflict." In *Victims, Perpetrators or Actors? Gender, Armed Conflict and Political Violence*, edited by Caroline O. N. Moser and Fiona C. Clark, 99–114. New York: Zed Books.

Carver, Terrell. 2008. "Men in the Feminist Gaze." *Millennium* 37 (1): 107–22.

Celis, Karen and Sarah Childs. 2012. "The Substantive Representation of Women: What to Do with Conservative Claims?" *Political Studies* 60 (1): 213–25.

Celis, Karen and Sarah Childs. 2018. "Introduction to Special Issue on Gender and Conservatism." *Politics & Gender* 14 (1): 1–4.

Celis, Karen and Liza M. Mugge. 2018. "Whose Equality? Measuring Group Representation." *Politics* 38 (2): 197–213.

Chadya, Joyce M. 2003. "Mother Politics: Anti-colonial Nationalism and the Women Question in Africa." *Journal of Women's History* 15 (3): 153–57.

Chakrabarty, Bidyut. 2006. *Forging Power: Coalition Politics in India*. New York: Oxford University Press.

Chakrabarty, Bidyut. 2014. *Coalition Politics in India*. New Delhi: Oxford University Press.

Chandra, Kanchan. 2016. *Democratic Dynasties: State, Party, and Family in Contemporary Indian Politics*. Cambridge: Cambridge University Press.

Charlton, Joy C. 2015. "Revisiting Gender and Religion." *Review of Religious Research* 57 (3): 331–39.

Charrad, M. 2001. *States and Women's Rights: The Making of Postcolonial Tunisia, Algeria, and Morocco*. Berkeley: University of California Press.

Chatterjee, Partha. 1993. *The Nation and Its Fragments: Colonial and Postcolonial Histories*. Princeton, NJ: Princeton University Press.

Chattopadhyay, Raghabendra and Esther Duflo. 2004. "Women as Policy Makers: Evidence from a Randomized Policy Experiment in India." *Econometrica* 72 (5): 1409–43.

Chauchard, Simon. 2014. "Can Descriptive Representation Change Beliefs about a Stigmatized Group? Evidence from Rural India." *American Political Science Review* 108 (2): 403–22.

Chhibber, Pradeep K. 1999. *Democracy without Associations: Transformation of the Party System and Social Cleavages in India*. Ann Arbor: University of Michigan Press.

Chhibber, Pradeep K. 2014. *Religious Practice and Democracy in India*. New York: Cambridge University Press.

Chhibber, Pradeep K. and Rahul Verma. 2018. *Ideology and Identity*. New York: Oxford University Press.

Childs, Sarah and Miki Caul Kittilson. 2016. "Feminizing Political Parties." *Party Politics* 22 (5): 598–608.

Chowdhry, Geeta. 2000. "Communalism, Nationalism and Gender: Bharatiya Janata Party (BJP) and the Hindu Right in India." In *Women, States, and Nationalism: At Home in the Nation?*, edited by Sita Ranchod-Nilsson and Mary Ann Tétreault, 98–118. New York: Routledge.

Clark, Janine and Jillian Schwedler. 2003. "Who Opened the Window? Women's Activism in Islamist Parties." *Comparative Politics* 35 (3): 293–312.

Courtright, Paul B. and Namita Goswami. 2001. "Who Was Roop Kanwar? Sati, Law, Religion, and Postcolonial Feminism." In *Religion and Personal Law in Secular India: A Call to Judgment*, edited by Gerald James Larson, 200–25. Bloomington: Indiana University Press.

CSDS (Centre for the Study of Developing Societies). 2017. *Crosstab of Gender by Party Vote for the 2014 Post Poll Election*. June. Sent via email.

CSWI (Committee on the Status of Women in India). 1975. *Towards Equality: Report of the Committee on the Status of Women in India*. New Delhi: Govt. of India, Ministry of Education & Social Welfare, Dept. of Social Welfare.

Daily Mail. 2013. "India's Literacy Rate Rises to 73 Per Cent as Population Growth Dips." *DailyMail.com India*, April 30. http://www.dailymail.co.uk/indiahome/indianews/article-2317341/Indias-literacy-rate-rises-73-cent-population-growth-dips.html.

Datta, Pradip Kumar. 1993. "'Dying Hindus': Production of Hindu Communal Common Sense in Early 20th Century Bengal." *Economic and Political Weekly* 28 (25): 1305–19.

Davis, L. 1964. "The Cost of Realism: Contemporary Restatements of Democracy." *Political Research Quarterly* 17 (1): 37–46.

Day, Graham and Andrew Thompson. 2004. *Theorizing Nationalism*. New York: Palgrave Macmillan.

Deo, Nandini. 2014. "The Sangh Parivar and Sexual Politics." Paper presented at the Annual Meeting of the Association for Asian Studies, Philadelphia, PA.

Deo, Nandini. 2016. *Mobilizing Gender and Religion in India: The Role of Activism*. New York: Routledge.

Deo, Nandini, ed. 2018. *Postsecular Feminisms*. London: Bloomsbury Academic.

Desai, P. and Jagdish N. Bhagwati. 1975. "Women in Indian Elections." In *Electoral Politics in the Indian States: Three Disadvantaged Sectors*, edited by Jagdish N. Bhagwati et al., 165–75. Delhi: Manohar Book Service.

Deshpande, Rajeshwari. 2004. "How Gendered Was Women's Participation in Election 2004?" *Economic and Political Weekly* 39 (51): 5431–36.

Deshpande, Rajeshwari. 2009. "How Did Women Vote in Lok Sabha Elections 2009?" *Economic and Political Weekly* 44 (39): 83–87.

Deshpande, Rajeshwari. 2014. "Women's Vote in 2014." *The Hindu*, June 25. https://www.thehindu.com/opinion/op-ed/womens-vote-in-2014/article6151723.ece.

Dhagamwar, Vasuda. 1988. "Saint, Victim or Criminal." *Seminar* 342: 34–39.

Donno, Daniela and Bruce Russett. 2004. "Islam, Authoritarianism, and Female Empowerment: What Are the Linkages?" *World Politics* 56 (4): 582–607.

Dovi, Suzanne. 2015. "Hannah Pitkin, The Concept of Representation." In *Oxford Handbook of Classics in Contemporary Political Theory*, edited by Jacob T. Levy. New York: Oxford University Press. DOI:10.1093/oxfordhb/9780198717133.013.24.

Dovi, Suzanne. 2018. "Political Representation." In *The Stanford Encyclopedia of Philosophy*, edited by Edward N. Zalta (Fall). https://plato.stanford.edu/archives/fall2018/entries/political-representation/.

Dutta, Prabhash. 2019. "35 Years of Shiv Sena-BJP Alliance: Hindutva Proposes, Rivalry Disposes." *India Today*, November 7. https://www.indiatoday.in/news-analysis/story/35-years-of-shiv-sena-bjp-alliance-hindutva-proposes-rivalry-disposes-1616546-2019-11-07.

Duverger, Maurice. 1955. *The Political Role of Women*. Paris: UNESCO.

Duverger, Maurice. 1963. *Political Parties, Their Organization and Activity in the Modern State*. 3rd ed. New York: Wiley.

Duverger, Maurice. 1972. *Party Politics and Pressure Groups: A Comparative Introduction*. New York: Crowell.

ECI (Election Commission of India). 2017. *Electoral Statistics Pocket Book 2017*. http://eci.nic.in/eci_main1/current/Electoral_Statistics_Pocket_Book2017_18052017.pdf. Accessed July 24, 2017.

Economic Times. 2011. "Uma Bharti Is Back in BJP, Wants to Forget Past 5 Years." June 8. https://m.economictimes.com/news/politics-and-nation/uma-bharati-is-back-in-bjp-wants-to-forget-past-5-years/articleshow/8768870.cms.

Eisenberg, Avigail I. 2009. *Reasons of Identity: A Normative Guide to the Political and Legal Assessment of Identity Claims*. New York: Oxford University Press.

Engels, Friedrich. [1884] 2010. "From 'The Origin of the Family, Private Property and the State.'" In *Feminist Theory: A Reader*, edited by Wendy K. Kolmar and Frances Bartkowski. 3rd ed., 90–92. Boston: McGraw-Hill Higher Education.

Engineer, Asghar Ali. 1987. *The Shah Bano Controversy*. Bombay: Orient Longman.

Evans, Elizabeth. 2016. "Feminist Allies and Strategic Partners." *Party Politics* 22 (5): 631–40.

Evans, Elizabeth and Meryl Kenny. 2019. "The Women's Equality Party: Emergence, Organisation and Challenges." *Political Studies* 67 (4): 855–71.

Farris, Sara R. 2017. *In the Name of Women's Rights: The Rise of Femonationalism*. Durham, NC: Duke University Press.

Feldman, Shelley. 1998. "(Re)presenting Islam: Manipulating Gender, Shifting State Practices, and Class Frustrations in Bangladesh." In *Appropriating Gender: Women's*

Activism and Politicized Religion in South Asia, edited by Patricia Jeffery and Amrita Basu, 33–52. New York: Routledge.

Ferber, Abby L. 2004. *Home-Grown Hate: Gender and Organized Racism*. New York: Routledge.

Fish, M. S. 2002. "Islam and Authoritarianism." *World Politics* 55 (1): 4–37.

Flåten, Lars Tore. 2019. "The Inclusion-Moderation Thesis: India's BJP." In *Oxford Research Encyclopedia of Politics*, edited by William R. Thompson, 1–31. New York: Oxford University Press.

Forbes, Geraldine. 1981. "The Indian Women's Movement: A Struggle for Women's Rights or National Liberation?" In *The Extended Family: Women and Political Participation in India and Pakistan*, edited by Gail Minault, 49–82. Columbia, MO: South Asia Books.

Forbes, Geraldine. 1988. "The Politics of Respectability: Indian Women and the Indian National Congress." In *The Indian National Congress: Centenary Hindsights*, edited by D. A. Low, 54–97. New Delhi: Oxford University Press.

Forbes, Geraldine. 1996. *Women in Modern India*. New York: Cambridge University Press.

Franceschet, Susan, Mona Lena Krook, and Jennifer M. Piscopo, eds. 2012. *The Impact of Gender Quotas*. New York: Oxford University Press.

Franda, Marcus F. 1962. "The Organizational Development of India's Congress Party." *Pacific Affairs* 35 (3): 248–60.

Freeman, Jo. 2000. *A Room at a Time: How Women Entered Party Politics*. Lanham, MD: Rowman & Littlefield.

Ganguly, Sumit. 2019. "India under Modi: Threats to Pluralism." *Journal of Democracy* 30 (1): 83–90.

Gettleman, Jeffrey and Hari Kumar. 2018. "India's Economic Woes Are Piercing Modi's Aura of Invulnerability." *New York Times*, January 6. https://www.nytimes.com/2018/01/06/world/asia/ india-modi-economy.html.

Gettleman, Jeffrey and Hari Kumar. [2020] 2021. "Modi Founds Temple on Mosque's Ruins, in Triumphal Moment for Hindu Base." *New York Times*, August 8, updated May 11. https://www.nytimes.com/2020/08/05/world/asia/modi-temple-ayodhya.html?referringSource=articleShare.

Gettleman, Jeffrey, Hari Kumar, and Shalini Venugopal. 2020. "Men Convicted in Delhi Bus Rape Are Hanged in India." *New York Times*, March 19. https://www.nytimes.com/2020/03/19/world/asia/india-bus-rape-convicts-hanged.html?searchResultPosition=2.

Gopal, Sarvepalli, ed. 1991. *Anatomy of a Confrontation: The Babri Masjid-Ramjanmabhumi Issue*. New York: Viking.

Gopalan, Sarala and National Commission for Women. 2001. *"Towards Equality." The Unfinished Agenda: Status of Women in India 2001*. New Delhi: National Commission for Women, Govt. of India.

Gordon, Richard. 1975. "The Hindu Mahasabha and the Indian National Congress, 1915 to 1926." *Modern Asian Studies* 9 (2): 145–203.

Gould, Harold. 1969. "Religion and Politics in a U.P. Constituency." In *South Asian Politics and Religion*, edited by Donald Eugene Smith, 51–73. Princeton, NJ: Princeton University Press.

Graham, Bruce D. 1968. "Syama Prasad Mukerjee and the Communalist Alternative." In *Soundings in Modern South Asian History*, edited by D. A. Low, 330–74. Berkeley: University of California Press.

Graham, Bruce D. 1990. *Hindu Nationalism and Indian Politics: The Origins and Development of the Bharatiya Jana Sangh*. New York: Cambridge University Press.

Grzymała-Busse, Anna. 2012. "Why Comparative Politics Should Take Religion (More) Seriously." *Annual Review of Political Science* 15: 421–42.

Grzymała-Busse, Anna. 2015. *Nations under God*. Princeton, NJ: Princeton University Press.

Guha, Ranajit. 1997. *A Subaltern Studies Reader, 1986–1995*. Minneapolis: University of Minnesota Press.

Haider, Faizan. 2013a. "2,000 Muslims to Be Seated Near Stage." *Hindustan Times*, September 29.

Haider, Faizan. 2013b. "BJP Cell Meets Target, Ropes in 15,000 Muslims to Rally." *Hindustan Times*, September 30.

Hansen, Thomas Blom. 1999. *The Saffron Wave: Democracy and Hindu Nationalism in Modern India*. Princeton, NJ: Princeton University Press.

Hardacre, Helen. 1993. "The Impact of Fundamentalisms on Women, the Family, and Interpersonal Relations." In *Fundamentalisms and Society: Reclaiming the Sciences, the Family, and Education*, edited by Martin E. Marty and R. Scott Appleby, 129–50. Chicago: University of Chicago Press.

Hasan, Zoya. 1993. "Communalism, State Policy, and the Question of Women's Rights in Contemporary India." *Bulletin of Concerned Asian Scholars Special Issue: Women and Religious Nationalism in India* 25 (4): 5–15.

Hasan, Zoya. 1998. "Gender Politics, Legal Reform, and the Muslim Community in India." In *Appropriating Gender: Women's Activism and Politicized Religion in South Asia*, edited by Patricia Jeffery and Amrita Basu, 71–88. New York: Routledge.

Hawley, John Stratton. 1994. *Fundamentalism and Gender*. New York: Oxford University Press.

Heath, Oliver. 1999. "Anatomy of BJP's Rise to Power: Social, Regional and Political Expansion in 1990s." *Economic and Political Weekly* 34 (34–35): 2511–17.

Heimsath, Charles Herman. 1964. *Indian Nationalism and Hindu Social Reform*. Princeton, NJ: Princeton University Press.

Hern, Erin. 2017. "The Trouble with Institutions: How Women's Policy Machineries can Undermine Women's Mass Participation." *Politics & Gender* 13 (3): 405–31.

Howells, Richard and Joaquim Negreiros. 2012. *Visual Culture*. Cambridge: Polity.

Hughes, Aaron W. 2012. *Abrahamic Religions: On the Uses and Abuses of History*. New York: Oxford University Press.

Huntington, Samuel P. 2011. *The Clash of Civilizations and the Remaking of World Order*. New York: Simon & Schuster.

Hurd, Elizabeth Shakman. 2015. *Beyond Religious Freedom*. Princeton, NJ: Princeton University Press.

Inglehart, Ronald and Pippa Norris. 2003. *Rising Tide: Gender Equality and Cultural Change around the World*. Cambridge: Cambridge University Press.

Iyer, Shekhar and Hemendra Singh Bartwal. 2007. "'33 Per Cent Quota for Women in BJP.'" *Hindustan Times*, June 27. http://www.hindustantimes.com/delhi-news/33-per-cent-quota-for-women-in-bjp/story-gHNuFtf8BH3d33RKBfiKOJ.html.

Jaffrelot, Christophe. 1996. *The Hindu Nationalist Movement in India*. New York: Columbia University Press.

Jaffrelot, Christophe. 2011. *Religion, Caste, and Politics in India*. New York: Columbia University Press.

Jaffrelot, Christophe. 2013. "Refining the Moderation Thesis. Two Religious Parties and Indian Democracy: The Jana Sangh and the BJP between Hindutva Radicalism and Coalition Politics." *Democratization* 20 (5): 876–94.

Jalal, Ayesha. 1991. "The Convenience of Subservience: Women and the State of Pakistan." In *Women, Islam and the State*, edited by Deniz Kandiyoti, 77–114. Philadelphia, PA: Temple University Press.

Jalal, Ayesha. 1995. *Democracy and Authoritarianism in South Asia: A Comparative and Historical Perspective*. New York: Cambridge University Press.

Jamal, Amaney and Vickie Langohr. 2014. "Women and the Middle East in the Political Science Discipline." In *Encyclopedia of Women & Islamic Cultures*, edited by Suad Joseph and Afsaneh Najmabadi. Berlin: Brill.

Jamal, Amina. 2005. "Feminist 'Selves' and Feminism's 'Others': Feminist Representation of Jamaat-e-Islami Women in Pakistan." *Feminist Review* 81: 52–73.

Jayawardena, Kumari. 1986. *Feminism and Nationalism in the Third World*. New Delhi: Kali for Women.

Jeffery, Patricia and Amrita Basu, eds. 1998. *Appropriating Gender: Women's Activism and Politicized Religion in South Asia*. New York: Routledge.

Jelen, Ted. 1998. "Research in Religion and Mass Political Behavior in the United States: Looking Both Ways after Two Decades of Scholarship." *American Politics Quarterly* 26 (1): 110–34.

Jenkins, Laura Dudley. 2008. "Legal Limits on Religious Conversion in India." *Law and Contemporary Problems* 71 (2): 109–27.

Jenkins, Laura Dudley. 2019. *Religious Freedom and Mass Conversion in India*. Philadelphia: University of Pennsylvania Press.

Jenkins, Laura Dudley and Rina Verma Williams. 2021. "Anti-Muslim Religious Communication in India and the U.S.: A Comparative and Interpretive Analysis." In *Exploring the Public Effects of Religious Communication on Politics*, edited by Brian Calfano, 97–129. Ann Arbor: University of Michigan Press.

Jenkins, Rob. 2019. "India 2019: A Transformative Election?" *Pacific Affairs* 92 (3): 475–96.

Jones, Kenneth W. 1989. *Socio-religious Reform Movements in British India*. New York: Cambridge University Press.

Kapoor, Mudit and Shamika Ravi. 2014. "Women Voters in Indian Democracy: A Silent Revolution." *Economic and Political Weekly* 49 (12): 63–67.

Katju, Manjari. 2003. *Vishva Hindu Parishad and Indian Politics*. Hyderabad: Orient Longman.

Key, V. O. [1942] 1964. *Politics, Parties, & Pressure Groups*. 5th ed. New York: Crowell.

Khan, Saeed. 2011. "My Mother Was Wronged, Gravely Wronged." *Hindustan Times*, November. http://www.hindustantimes.com/india-news/my-mother-was-wronged-gravely-wronged/article1-767905.aspx.

Kishwar, Madhu. 1986. "Pro Women Or Anti Muslim? The Shahbano Controversy." *Manushi: A Journal about Women in Society* 32 (4): 4–13.

Kishwar, Madhu. 1996. "Women and Politics: Beyond Quotas." *Economic and Political Weekly* 31 (43): 2867–74.

Kishwar, Madhu. 2008. *Zealous Reformers, Deadly Laws: Battling Stereotypes*. Thousand Oaks, CA: Sage.

Kishwar, Madhu and Ruth Vanita. 2007. "Manushi, 'the Burning of Roop Kanwar.'" In *Sati: A Historical Anthology*, edited by Andrea Major, 355–72. New York: Oxford University Press.

Kothari, Rajni. 1964. "The Congress 'System' in India." *Asian Survey* 4 (12): 1161–73.
Krook, Mona Lena. 2009. *Quotas for Women in Politics*. New York: Oxford University Press.
Krook, Mona Lena. 2014. "Electoral Gender Quotas: A Conceptual Analysis." *Comparative Political Studies* 47 (9): 1268–93.
Krook, Mona Lena and Par Zetterberg. 2014. "Electoral Quotas and Political Representation: Comparative Perspectives." *International Political Science Review* 35 (1): 3–11.
Kumar, Deepak. 2016. *The Trishanku Nation*. New Delhi: Oxford University Press.
Kumar, Devesh. 2014. "BJP + 29 Parties = National Democratic Alliance." May 20. http://www.ndtv.com/elections-news/bjp-29-parties-national-democratic-alliance-562972.
Kumar, Hari. 2013. "Does Nitish Kumar Need the B.J.P.?" *New York Times India Blog*, April 18. https://india.blogs.nytimes.com/2013/04/18/does-nitish-kumar-need-the-b-j-p/?_r=1.
Kumar, Manish and Suparna Singh. 2017. "For First Time since BJP Tie-Up, Nitish Kumar Asks to Meet PM Narendra Modi." *Ndtv.com*, August 10. http://www.ndtv.com/india-news/nitish-kumar-now-in-delhi-seeks-appointment-with-pm-narendra-modi-1736080.
Kumar, Radha. 1997. *The History of Doing: An Illustrated Account of Movements for Women's Rights and Feminism in India, 1800–1990*. 2nd ed. New Delhi: Kali for Women.
Kumar, Radha. 1999. "From Chipko to Sati: The Contemporary Indian Women's Movement." In *Gender and Politics in India*, edited by Nivedita Menon, 342–69. New Delhi: Oxford University Press.
Kumar, Sanjay and Pranav Gupta. 2015. "Changing Patterns of Women's Turnout in Indian Elections." *Studies in Indian Politics* 3 (1): 7–18.
Kuru, Ahmet T. 2019. *Islam, Authoritarianism, and Underdevelopment: A Global and Historical Comparison*. Cambridge: Cambridge University Press.
Lama-Rewal, Stéphanie Tawa. 2005. "Reservations for Women in Urban Local Bodies: A Tentative Assessment." In *Electoral Reservations, Political Representation, and Social Change in India: A Comparative Perspective*, edited by Stéphanie Tawa Lama-Rewal, 189–207. New Delhi: Manohar.
Lambert, Richard. 1959. "Hindu Communal Groups in Indian Politics." In *Leadership and Political Institutions in India*, edited by Richard Park and Irene Tinker, 211–24. Princeton, NJ: Princeton University Press.
LaPalombara, Joseph and Myron Weiner. 1966. *Political Parties and Political Development*. Princeton, NJ: Princeton University Press.
Lazarsfeld, Paul F., Bernard Berelson, and Hazel Gaudet. 1944. *The People's Choice: How the Voter Makes Up His Mind in a Presidential Campaign*. New York: Duell, Sloan and Pearce.
Lewis, Andrew R. 2017. *The Rights Turn in Conservative Christian Politics: How Abortion Transformed the Culture Wars*. New York: Cambridge University Press.
Liberhan Commission. 2009. *Report of the Liberhan Ayodhya Commission of Inquiry*. New Delhi: Ministry of Home Affairs, Govt. of India.
Lipset, Seymour Martin and Stein Rokkan. 1967. *Party Systems and Voter Alignments: Cross-National Perspectives*. New York: Free Press.
Loomba, Ania. 1993. "Dead Women Tell No Tales: Issues of Female Subjectivity, Subaltern Agency and Tradition in Colonial and Post-colonial Writings on Window Immolation in India." *History Workshop* 36 (1): 209–27.

Lovenduski, Joni. 1998. "Gendering Research in Political Science." *Annual Review of Political Science* 1: 333–56.
Ludden, David. 2002. *India and South Asia: A Short History*. London: OneWorld Publishers.
Lynch, Cecelia. 2020. *Wrestling with God: Ethical Precarity in Christianity and International Relations*. New York: Cambridge University Press.
Mackay, Fiona, Meryl Kenny, and Louise Chappell. 2010. "New Institutionalism through a Gender Lens: Towards a Feminist Institutionalism." *International Political Science Review* 31 (5): 573–88.
Mahajan, Gurpreet. 2005. "Can Intra-group Equality Co-exist with Cultural Diversity?" In *Minorities within Minorities: Equality, Rights, and Diversity*, edited by Avigail I. Eisenberg and Jeff Spinner-Halev, 90–112. New York: Cambridge University Press.
Mahmood, Saba. 2005. *Politics of Piety: The Islamic Revival and the Feminist Subject*. NJ: Princeton University Press.
Malik, Yogendra K. and V. B. Singh. 1994. *Hindu Nationalists in India: The Rise of the Bharatiya Janata Party*. Boulder, CO: Westview Press.
Mani, Lata. 1998. *Contentious Traditions: The Debate on Sati in Colonial India*. Berkeley: University of California Press.
Marty, Martin E., R. Scott Appleby, and American Academy of Arts and Sciences. 1991. *The Fundamentalism Project*. Chicago: University of Chicago Press.
Mathur, Sobhag. 1996. *Hindu Revivalism and the Indian National Movement: A Documentary Study of the Ideals and Policies of the Hindu Mahasabha, 1939–45*. Jodhpur: Kusumanjali Prakashan.
Mazumdar, Vina. 1978. "Comment on Suttee." *Signs* 4 (2): 269–73.
McClendon, Gwyneth H. and Rachel Beatty Riedl. 2019. *From Pews to Politics: Religious Sermons and Political Participation in Africa*. Cambridge: Cambridge University Press.
Mehra, Madhu. 2013. "India's CEDAW Story." In *Women's Human Rights: CEDAW in International, Regional, and National Law*, edited by Anne Hellum and Henriette Sinding Aasen, 385–409. Cambridge: Cambridge University Press.
Menon, Kalyani Devaki. 2010. *Everyday Nationalism: Women of the Hindu Right in India*. Philadelphia: University of Pennsylvania Press.
Menon, Nivedita. 2000. "State, Community and the Debate on the Uniform Civil Code in India." In *Beyond Rights Talk and Culture Talk: Comparative Essays on the Politics of Rights and Culture*, edited by Mahmood Mamdani, 75–95. New York: St. Martin's Press.
Menon, Nivedita. 2014. "A Uniform Civil Code in India: The State of the Debate in 2014." *Feminist Studies* 40 (2): 480–86.
Menon, Usha. 2003. "Do Women Participate in Riots? Exploring the Notion of 'Militancy' among Hindu Women." *Nationalism & Ethnic Politics* 9 (1): 20–51.
Mernissi, Fatima. 1987. *Beyond the Veil: Male-Female Dynamics in Modern Muslim Society*. Bloomington: Indiana University Press.
Mernissi, Fatima. 1992. *Islam and Democracy: Fear of the Modern World*. Reading, MA: Addison-Wesley.
Mitra, Subrata Kumar. 2017. *Politics in India*. 2nd ed. New York: Routledge.
Moghadam, Valentine M., ed. 1994. *Gender and National Identity: Women and Politics in Muslim Societies*. London: Zed Books.
Moghadam, Valentine M. 2003. *Modernizing Women: Gender and Social Change in the Middle East*. 2nd ed. Boulder, CO: Lynne Rienner.

Mohanty, N. R. 2017. "Advani Could Have Been a Presidential Candidate If the BJP Had a Leader Like Sardar Patel." *Huffpost India Blog*, June 24. http://www.huffingtonpost.in/n-r-mohanty/advani-could-have-been-a-presidential-candidate-if-the-bjp-had_a_22490228/.

Moitra, Mahua. 2021. "I Know What It Takes to Defeat Narendra Modi." *New York Times* Opinion Guest Essay, May 5. https://www.nytimes.com/2021/05/05/opinion/india-west-bengal-modi.html?referringSource=articleShare.

Momin, Sajeda. 2017. "When the Last Dome Fell: A First-Person Account of the Babri Masjid Demolition." *The Hindu*, December 6. https://www.thehindu.com/opinion/op-ed/when-the-last-dome-fell-a-first-person-account-of-the-babri-masjid-demolition/article21273367.ece.

Montero, José R. and Richard Gunther. 2002. "Introduction: Reviewing and Reassessing Parties." In *Political Parties: Old Concepts and New Challenges*, edited by Richard Gunther, José R. Montero, and Juan J. Linz, 1–38. New York: Oxford University Press.

Nandy, Ashis. 1983. *The Intimate Enemy: Loss and Recovery of Self under Colonialism*. Delhi: Oxford University Press.

Narayan, Uma. 1997. *Dislocating Cultures: Identities, Traditions, and Third-World Feminism*. New York: Routledge.

Noronha, Rahul. 2021. "Is Uma Bharti Planning a Return to MP Politics?" *India Today*, January 27. https://www.indiatoday.in/india-today-insight/story/is-uma-bharti-planning-a-return-to-mp-politics-1763352-2021-01-27.

Norris, Pippa and Ronald Inglehart. 2011. *Sacred and Secular: Religion and Politics Worldwide*. Cambridge: Cambridge University Press.

Nussbaum, Martha C. 2000. "Religion and Women's Equality: The Case of India." In *Obligations of Citizenship and Demands of Faith: Religious Accommodation in Pluralist Democracies*, edited by Nancy L. Rosenblum, 335–402. Princeton, NJ: Princeton University Press.

Och, Malliga and Shauna Lani Shames. 2018. *The Right Women: Republican Party Activists, Candidates, and Legislators*. Santa Barbara, CA: Praeger.

Och, Malliga and Rina Verma Williams. 2022. "Feminism, Identities, and the Substantive Representation of Women on the Right: Crafting a Global Dialogue." *Politics, Groups and Identities* 10 (1): 135–38.

Oldenburg, Veena. 2007. "The Roop Kanwar Case: Feminist Responses." In *Sati: A Historical Anthology*, edited by Andrea Major. New York: Oxford University Press.

OneIndia News. 2006. "Shah Bano's Husband Dead." April 4. http://news.oneindia.in/2006/04/04/shah-banos-husband-dead-1144147104.html.

Ozzano, Lucas. 2013. "The Many Faces of the Political God: A Typology of Religiously Oriented Parties." *Democratization* 20 (5): 807–30.

Paik, Shailaja. 2014. *Dalit Women's Education in Modern India: Double Discrimination*. New York: Routledge.

Panda, Sitakanta. 2019. "Political-Economic Determinants of Electoral Participation in India." *India Review* 18 (2): 184–219.

Pandit, Ambika. 2018. "Pass Long-Pending Women Reservation Bill, Demand Women Organizations." *Times of India* online, July 13. https://timesofindia.indiatimes.com/india/pass-long-pending-women-reservation-bill-demand-women-organisations/articleshow/64980701.cms.

Parsons, Talcott. 1964. *Social Structure and Personality*. New York: Free Press of Glencoe.

Pateman, Carole. 1970. *Participation and Democratic Theory*. Cambridge: Cambridge University Press.
Pateman, Carole. 1988. *The Sexual Contract*. Stanford, CA: Stanford University Press.
Pathak, Zakia and Rajeswari Sunder Rajan. 1989. "'Shahbano.'" *Signs* 14 (3): 558–82.
Pearson, Gail. 2004. "Tradition, Law and the Female Suffrage Movement in India." In *Women's Suffrage in Asia: Gender, Nationalism and Democracy*, edited by Louise Edwards and Mina Roces, 195–219. New York: Routledge.
Peterson, V. Spike. 1992. *Gendered States: Feminist (Re)visions of International Relations Theory*. Boulder, CO: Lynne Rienner.
Pirbhai, M. Reza. 2014. "Pakistan and the Awakening of a Muslim 'New Woman' 1937–1947." *Hawwa: Journal of Women of the Middle East and the Islamic World* 12 (1): 1–35.
Pirzada, Syed Sharifuddin, ed. 1970. *Foundations of Pakistan: All-India Muslim League Documents, 1906–1947*. Vol. 2. Karachi: National Publishing House.
Pitkin, Hanna Fenichel. 1967. *The Concept of Representation*. Berkeley: University of California Press.
Poornima, M. 2013. "Burqa-Clad Women Barred from Attending BJP's Rally." *Hindustan Times*, September 26.
Prakash, Indra. 1938. *A Review of the History & Work of the Hindu Mahasabha and the Hindu Sanghatan Movement*. New Delhi: Akhil Bharatiya Hindu Mahasabha.
Prakash, Indra. 1942. *Where We Differ? The Congress and the Hindu Mahasabha*. New Delhi: Hindu Mission Pustak Bhandar.
Prakash, Indra. 1966. *Hindu Mahasabha, Its Contribution to India's Politics*. New Delhi: Akhil Bharat Hindu Mahasabha.
PTI (Press Trust of India). 2013a. "'Burqa' Diktat by BJP for Narendra Modi Rally Raises Eyebrows." *Economic Times*, September 10. http://economictimes.indiatimes.com/news/politics-and-nation/burqa-diktat-by-bjp-for-narendra-modi-rally-raises-eyebrows/articleshow/22462610.cms.
PTI (Press Trust of India). 2013b. "Narendra Modi Anointed BJP PM Candidate, Advani Disappointed." *Times of India*, September 13. http://timesofindia.indiatimes.com/india/Narendra-Modi-anointed-BJP-PM-candidate-Advani-disappointed/articleshow/22554959.cms.
PTI (Press Trust of India). 2019. "Arrest of LK Advani, the Incident That Bled India but Gave BJP Political Heft." *India Today*, November 9. https://www.indiatoday.in/india/story/advani-arrest-lalu-prasad-bjp-mandir-mandal-hindu-politics-ayodhya-1617434-2019-11-09.
Puri, Geeta. 1980. *Bharatiya Jana Sangh, Organisation and Ideology: Delhi, a Case Study*. New Delhi: Sterling.
Qadeer, Imrana. 1988. "Roop Kanwar and Shah Bano." *Seminar* 342: 31–33.
Radhakrishnan, Sruti. 2019. "New Lok Sabha Has Highest Number of Women MPs." *The Hindu*, May 27. https://www.thehindu.com/news/national/new-lok-sabha-has-highest-number-of-women-mps/article27260506.ece.
Rai, Praveen. 2011. "Electoral Participation of Women in India: Key Determinants and Barriers." *Economic and Political Weekly* 46 (3): 47–55.
Rai, Praveen. 2014. "Election 2014: Imbalanced Participation of Women." *Reuters.com*, June 13. http://blogs.reuters.com/india-expertzone/2014/06/13/election-2014-imbalanced-participation-of-women/.
Rai, Praveen. 2017. "Women's Participation in Electoral Politics in India: Silent Feminisation." *South Asia Research* 37 (1): 58–77.

Raj, Suhasini and Kai Schultz. 2018. "Suspect Detained in Killing of the Indian Journalist Gauri Lankesh." *New York Times*, March 3. https://www.nytimes.com/2018/03/03/world/asia/india-gauri-lankesh-naveen-kumar.html?searchResultPosition=6.
Randall, Vicky. 2006a. "Legislative Gender Quotas and Indian Exceptionalism." *Comparative Politics* 39 (1): 63–82.
Randall, Vicky. 2006b. "Political Parties and Social Structure in the Developing World." In *Handbook of Party Politics*, edited by Richard S. Katz and William J. Crotty, 387–95. Thousand Oaks, CA: Sage.
Randall, Vicky and Georgina Waylen, eds. 1998. *Gender, Politics and the State*. New York: Routledge.
Ravi, Shamika and Rohan Sandhu. 2014. "Women in Party Politics." April. Working paper, Brookings India.
Rook-Koepsel, Emily. 2015. "Constructing Women's Citizenship: The Local, National and Global Civics Lessons of Rajkumari Amrit Kaur." *Journal of Women's History* 27 (3): 154–75.
Roy, Mary. 1999. "Three Generations of Women." *Indian Journal of Gender Studies* 6 (2): 203–19.
Ruparelia, Sanjay. 2006. "Rethinking Institutional Theories of Political Moderation: The Case of Hindu Nationalism in India, 1996–2004." *Comparative Politics* 38 (3): 317–36.
Salisbury, Robert H. 1975. "The Workshop: Research on Political Participation." *American Journal of Political Science* 19 (2): 323–41.
Sapiro, Virginia. 1998. "Feminist Studies and Political Science—and Vice Versa." In *Feminism and Politics*, edited by Anne Phillips, 67–89. New York: Oxford University Press.
Sarkar, Tanika. 1993a. "The Women of the Hindutva Brigade." *Bulletin of Concerned Asian Scholars* 25 (4): 16–24.
Sarkar, Tanika. 1993b. "Women's Agency within Authoritarian Communitarianism: The Rashtrasevika Samiti and Ram Janmabhoomi." In *Hindus and Others: The Question of Identity in India Today*, edited by Gyanendra Pandey, 24–45. New Delhi: Viking.
Sarkar, Tanika. 1998. "Woman, Community, and Nation: A Historical Trajectory for Hindu Identity Politics." In *Appropriating Gender: Women's Activism and Politicized Religion in South Asia*, edited by Patricia Jeffery and Amrita Basu, 89–106. New York: Routledge.
Sarkar, Tanika. 1999. "The Gender Predicament of the Hindu Right." In *The Concerned Indian's Guide to Communalism*, edited by K. N. Panikkar, 131–59. New Delhi: Penguin.
Sarkar, Tanika. 2001. *Hindu Wife, Hindu Nation: Community, Religion, and Cultural Nationalism*. Bloomington: Indiana University Press.
Sarkar, Tanika and Amrita Basu, eds. 2022. *Women, Gender and Religious Nationalism in India*. Cambridge: Cambridge University Press.
Sarkar, Tanika and Urvashi Butalia. 1995. *Women and Right-Wing Movements: Indian Experiences*. London: Zed Books.
Sathyamala, C. 2019. "Meat-Eating in India: Whose Food, Whose Politics, and Whose Rights?" *Policy Futures in Education* 17 (7) (October): 878–91.
Savarkar, Vinayak Damodar. 1969. *Hindutva; Who Is a Hindu?* 5th ed. Bombay: Veer Savarkar Prakashan.
Savarkar, Vinayak Damodar. 1984. *Hindu Rashtra Darshan*. 2nd ed. Bombay: Veer Savarkar Prakashan.
Schattschneider, E. E. 1942. *Party Government*. New York: Farrar and Rinehart.

Schlozman, Daniel. 2015. *When Movements Anchor Parties: Electoral Alignments in American History*. Princeton, NJ: Princeton University Press.

Schreiber, Ronnee. 2008. *Righting Feminism: Conservative Women and American Politics*. New York: Oxford University Press.

Schumpeter, Joseph A. [1942] 1987. *Capitalism, Socialism, and Democracy*. 6th ed. Boston: Unwin Paperbacks.

Schwartz-Shea, Peregrine and Dvora Yanow. 2012. *Interpretive Research Design: Concepts and Processes*. New York: Routledge.

Schwindt-Bayer, Leslie A. and William Mishler. 2005. "An Integrated Model of Women's Representation." *Journal of Politics* 67 (2): 407–28.

Scindia, Vijayaraje, with Manohar Malgonkar. 1987. *The Last Maharani of Gwalior: An Autobiography*. Albany: State University of New York Press.

Scott, Joan W. 2007. *The Politics of the Veil*. Princeton, NJ: Princeton University Press.

Sehgal, Meera. 2009. "The Veiled Feminist Ethnographer: Fieldwork among Women of India's Hindu Right." In *Women Fielding Danger: Negotiating Ethnographic Identities in Field Research*, edited by Martha Knisely Huggins and Marie-Louise Glebbeek, 325–52. Lanham, MD: Rowman & Littlefield.

Sen, Atreyee. 2006. "Reflecting on Resistance: Hindu Women 'Soldiers' and the Birth of Female Militancy." *Indian Journal of Gender Studies* 13 (1): 1–35.

Sen, Atreyee. 2007. *Shiv Sena Women: Violence and Communalism in a Bombay Slum*. Bloomington: Indiana University Press.

Sen, Atreyee and Rubina Jasani. 2014. "Mumbai (1992–93) and Ahmedabad (2002), A Tale of Two Cities: Narratives of Violent and Victimized Women Enduring Urban Riots in India." *Allegra Lab*, November 4. https://allegralaboratory.net/mumbai-1992-93-and-ahmedabad-2002-a-tale-of-two-cities-narratives-of-violent-and-victimized-women-enduring-urban-riots-in-india/.

Shah, Svati. 2015. "Queering Critiques of Neoliberalism in India: Urbanism and Inequality in the Era of Transnational 'LGBTQ' Rights." *Antipode* 47 (3): 635–51.

Shankar, Kalyani. 2013. *Pandora's Daughters*. New Delhi: Bloomsbury.

Sharafi, Mitra. 2014. *Law and Identity in Colonial South Asia: Parsi Legal Culture, 1772–1947*. New York: Cambridge University Press.

Sinha, Mrinalini. 1995. *Colonial Masculinity: The "Manly Englishman" and the "Effeminate Bengali" in the Late Nineteenth Century*. New York: St. Martin's Press.

Sinha, Mrinalini. 2000. "Suffragism and Internationalism: The Enfranchisement of British and Indian Women under an Imperial State." In *Women's Suffrage in the British Empire: Citizenship, Nation, and Race*, edited by Ian Christopher Fletcher, Laura E. Nym Mayhall, and Philippa Levine, 224–39. New York: Routledge.

Sirsikar, V. M. 1979. "Politicization of Women in India: An Overview." In *Symbols of Power: Studies on the Political Status of Women in India*, edited by Vina Mazumdar, 79–84. Bombay: Allied Publishers.

Smith, Amy Erica. 2019. *Religion and Brazilian Democracy: Mobilizing the People of God*. Cambridge: Cambridge University Press.

Soni, Alok. 2014. "How Well Do You Know These 7 Women Ministers in the New Indian Government?" *Yourstory.com*, May 27. https://yourstory.com/2014/05/women-ministers-narendra-modi-india-government/amp.

Spivak, Gayatri Chakravorty. 1988. "Can the Subaltern Speak?" In *Marxism and the Interpretation of Culture*, edited by Cary Nelson and Lawrence Grossberg, 271–313. Urbana: University of Illinois Press.

Spivak, Gayatri Chakravorty. 1999. *A Critique of Postcolonial Reason: Toward a History of the Vanishing Present.* Cambridge, MA: Harvard University Press.

Sridharan, Eswaran. 2014. "Behind Modi's Victory." *Journal of Democracy* 25 (4): 20–33.

Stein, Dorothy. 1978. "Women to Burn: Suttee as a Normative Institution." *Signs* 4 (2): 253–68.

Subramanian, Narendra. 2014. *Nation and Family: Personal Law, Cultural Pluralism, and Gendered Citizenship in India.* Stanford, CA: Stanford University Press.

Tepe, Sultan. 2019. "The Inclusion-Moderation Thesis: An Overview." In *Oxford Research Encyclopedia of Politics,* edited by William R. Thompson, 1–17. New York: Oxford University Press.

Thachil, Tariq. 2014. *Elite Parties, Poor Voters: How Social Services Win Votes in India.* New York: Cambridge University Press.

Thapar-Björkert, Suruchi. 2006. *Women in the Indian National Movement: Unseen Faces and Unheard Voices, 1930–42.* Thousand Oaks, CA: Sage.

Thukral, K. K. and Shafeeq Rahman. 2014. *India Elects 2014: A Comparative Analysis of General Election Results of India: 2009–2014.* New Delhi: Datanet India.

Tilly, Charles. 2006. "Afterword: Political Ethnography as Art and Science." *Qualitative Sociology* 29 (3): 409–12.

Times of India. 1986a. "'Ekjoot' Holds Morchas against 'Talaaq' Bill." March 3.

Times of India. 1986b. "BJP Stir against Art. 370 Likely." April 14.

Times of India. 1986c. "Copies of Bill Burnt in City." May 6.

TNN (Times News Network). 2013. "JD(U) Ends 17-Year-Old Alliance with BJP, Quits NDA." *Times of India,* June 16. http://timesofindia.indiatimes.com/india/JDU-ends-17-year-old-alliance-with-BJP-quits-NDA/articleshow/20616468.cms.

Tudor, Maya and Dan Slater. 2016. "The Content of Democracy: Nationalist Parties and Inclusive Ideologies in India and Indonesia." In *Parties, Movements and Democracy in the Developing World,* edited by Nancy Gina Bermeo and Deborah J. Yashar, 28–60. New York: Cambridge University Press.

Uhlaner, Carole Jean. 2015. "Politics and Participation." In *International Encyclopedia of the Social and Behavioral Sciences,* 2nd ed., edited by James D. Wright, 18:504–8. Amsterdam: Elsevier.

Vaishnav, M. and J. Hintson. 2019. "The Dawn of India's Fourth Party System." Carnegie Endowment for International Peace Working Paper, September 5. Downloaded from https://carnegieendowment.org/2019/09/05/dawn-of-india-s-fourth-party-system-pub-79759.

Varshney, Ashutosh. 2013. *Battles Half Won: India's Improbable Democracy.* New Delhi: Penguin Viking.

Varshney, Ashutosh. 2017. "The Nitish Echo." *Indian Express,* August 3. http://indianexpress.com/article/opinion/columns/nitish-kumar-bihar-jdu-bjp-alliance-lalu-prasad-yadav-corruption-4779525/.

Varshney, Ashutosh. 2018. "Taming Hubris." *Indian Express,* December 14. https://indianexpress.com/article/opinion/columns/state-assembly-election-result-2018-bjp-congress-democracy-5492733/.

Varshney, Ashutosh. 2021. "India's Democratic Exceptionalism Is Now Withering Away. The Impact Is Also External." *Indian Express,* February 23. https://indianexpress.com/article/opinion/columns/elected-government-death-of-democracy-india-7200030/.

Verba, Sidney, Norman H. Nie, and Jae-on Kim. 1978. *Participation and Political Equality: A Seven-Nation Comparison.* New York: Cambridge University Press.

Vickers, Jill. 2008. "Gendering the Hyphen: Gender Dimensions of Modern Nation-State Formation in Euro-American and Anti- and Post-colonial Contexts." In *Gendering the Nation-State: Canadian and Comparative Perspectives*, edited by Yasmeen Abu-Laban, 21–45. Vancouver: University of British Columbia Press.

Wald, Kenneth D. and Clyde Wilcox. 2006. "Getting Religion: Has Political Science Rediscovered the Faith Factor?" *American Political Science Review* 100 (4): 523–29.

Walsh, Denise M. 2011. *Women's Rights in Democratizing States: Just Debate and Gender Justice in the Public Sphere*. New York: Cambridge University Press.

Weiner, Myron. 1957. *Party Politics in India: the Development of a Multi-party System*. Princeton, NJ: Princeton University Press.

Whetstone, Crystal. 2020. "Nurturing Democracy in Armed Conflicts through Political Motherhood: A Comparative Study of Women's Political Participation in Argentina and Sri Lanka." PhD dissertation, University of Cincinnati.

Whetstone, Crystal and Rina Williams. 2019. "Globalizing Women's Political Participation: Beyond the State, Beyond the Global North." Paper presented at the Annual Meeting of the Western Political Science Association, San Diego, CA.

Williams, Rina Verma. 2006. *Postcolonial Politics and Personal Laws: Colonial Legal Legacies and the Indian State*. New Delhi: Oxford University Press.

Williams, Rina Verma. 2010. "Hindu Law as Personal Law: State and Identity in the Hindu Code Bills Debates, 1952–56." In *Hinduism and Law: An Introduction*, edited by Timothy Lubin, Donald R. Davis, and Jayanth Krishnan, 105–19. New York: Cambridge University Press.

Williams, Rina Verma. 2013a. "The More Things Change: Debating Gender and Religion in India's Hindu Laws, 1920–2006." *Gender & History* 25 (3): 711–24.

Williams, Rina Verma. 2013b. "Failure to Launch: Women and Hindu Nationalist Politics in Colonial India." *Politics, Religion & Ideology* 14 (4): 541–56.

Williams, Rina Verma. 2019. "Inconsistent Allies: Women's Issues, Feminism and Religious Nationalist Women in India." Paper presented at the Annual Meeting of the American Political Science Association, Washington, DC.

Williams, Rina Verma. 2022a. "Repeal and (Not) Replace"? Hindu Nationalist Women and Feminism in India." *Politics, Groups and Identities* 10 (1): 161–65.

Williams, Rina Verma. 2022b. "Track Changes: Women and the BJP from the 1990s to the 2010s." In *Women, Gender and Religious Nationalism in India*, edited by Tanika Sarkar and Amrita Basu. Cambridge: Cambridge University Press.

Williams, Rina Verma and Nandini Deo. 2018. "Hinduism and Democracy: Religion and Politicized Religion in India." In *Routledge Handbook of Asian Politics*, edited by Shiping Hua, 548–61. New York: Routledge.

Williams, Rina Verma and Laura Dudley Jenkins. 2015. "Secular Anxieties and Transnational Engagements in India." In *Multiple Secularities beyond the West: Religion and Modernity in the Global Age*, edited by Marian Burchardt, Monika Wohlrab-Sahr, and Matthias Middell, 19–38. Boston: de Gruyter.

Williams, Rina Verma, and Sayam Moktan. 2019. "Hinduism: India, Nepal, and Beyond." In *Oxford Research Encyclopedia of Politics*, edited by William Thompson. doi 10.1093/acrefore/9780190228637.013.764.

Williamson, D. G. 2002. *The Third Reich*. 3rd ed. New York: Longman.

Willmer, David. 1996. "Women as Participants in the Pakistan Movement: Modernization and the Promise of a Moral State." *Modern Asian Studies* 30 (3): 573–90.

Wolfe, Joel. 1985. "A Defense of Participatory Democracy." *Review of Politics* 47 (3): 370–89.
Wolpert, Stanley. 2006. "Brahmo Samaj." In *Encyclopedia of India*, edited by Stanley Wolpert, 1:165–66. Detroit, MI: Charles Scribner's Sons.
Yadav, Stacey Philbrick. 2012. "Segmented Publics and Islamist Women in Yemen: Rethinking Space and Activism." *Journal of Middle East Women's Studies* 6 (2): 1–30.
Yadav, Yogendra. 1999. "Electoral Politics in the Time of Change: India's Third Electoral System, 1989–99." *Economic and Political Weekly* 34 (34–35): 2393–99.
Yadav, Yogendra. 2000. "Understanding the Second Democratic Upsurge." In *Transforming India*, edited by Francine Frankel et al., 120–45. New Delhi: Oxford University Press.
Yadav, Yogendra. 2003. "The New Congress Voter." *Seminar India* 526: n.p.
Yanow, Dvora and Peregrine Schwartz-Shea. 2014. *Interpretation and Method: Empirical Research Methods and the Interpretive Turn*. Armonk, NY: M.E. Sharpe.
Yasir, Sameer, Kai Schultz, and Hari Kumar. 2018. "Kashmiri Journalist Shujaat Bukhari, a Voice for Peace, Is Killed." *New York Times*, June 24. https://www.nytimes.com/2018/06/14/world/asia/kashmir-journalist-killed.html?searchResultPosition=4.
Yuval-Davis, Nira. 1997. *Gender & Nation*. Thousand Oaks, CA: Sage.
Zavos, John. 2000. *The Emergence of Hindu Nationalism in India*. New York: Oxford University Press.

Index

For the benefit of digital users, indexed terms that span two pages (e.g., 52–53) may, on occasion, appear on only one of those pages.
Tables and figures are indicated by *t* and *f* following the page number

Aam Aadmi Party, 36–37
Abrahamic religions, 9–10, 74, 84–
  85, 165n.7
academic scholarship on women in Hindu
    nationalism
  generally, 15, 72–73
  BJP, on, 80, 87–88, 93
  Congress Party, on, 87
  disciplinary literature, 15, 72–76, 81–89,
    93–94 (*see also* religion and women,
    academic scholarship on)
  empowerment of women and, 3–4, 72–
    73, 78, 80–81, 93
  feminist scholarship (*see* feminist
    scholarship on women in Hindu
    nationalism)
  "first phase," 76, 93
  Global South, historical neglect of,
    75, 88–89
  historical neglect of women, 75
  India, on, 9–11
  interdisciplinary literature, 15, 72–
    81, 93–94
  masculinity and, 80
  nationalist political parties, on, 5–
    8, 74–75
  participation by women, on, 73–74
  positionality and (*see* positionality)
  reasons for participation by women,
    3–4, 72–73, 78, 80–81, 93–94
  religion and women, on (*see*
    religion and women, academic
    scholarship on)
  RSS, on, 80
  sati controversy and, 58–59
  "second phase," 80, 93
  Shiv Sena, on, 80
  VHP, on, 80
Adivasis, 87–88
Advani, Lal Kishan
  campaign posters of, 134
  electoral incorporation of women
    and, 125–26
  extremist, as, 150
  Modi and, 171n.14
  rath yatra and, 30, 60–62, 61*f*
  uniform civil code, on, 53–54
  women and, 66
agency of women, 12–13, 78–79, 89
alimony under Islamic law. *See*
  maintenance under Islamic law
All Hindu Babri Masjid Action
    Committee, 60
All-India Anna Dravida Munnetra
    Kazhagam (AIA-DMK), 166n.11
All-India Conference of Hindus
    (1915), 21–22
All India Congress Committee, 109
All-India Hindu Mahasabha. *See* Hindu
  Mahasabha
All-India Trinamool Congress Party, 158–
  59, 166n.11
All-India Women's Conference (AIWC)
    (1937), 54, 100, 104, 109–10
All India Women's Cow Protection
    Conference (1942), 106
authoritarianism, 151–52
Ayodhya
  Babri Masjid mosque incident (*see*
    Babri Masjid mosque incident
    [1992])
  Ram temple at, 30, 151, 153

Babri Masjid mosque incident (1992)
  generally, 1, 15, 49, 68–69, 76
  BJP and, 61–64
  Congress Party and, 60
  international law, lack of discussion of, 70
  maintenance under Islamic law compared, 62
  masculinity, role of, 69
  "nationalized" nature of controversy, 69–70
  rallying women in streets and, 49–50, 50*t*, 51, 59–64, 155–56
  rath yatra and, 30, 60–62, 61*f*
  rioting in connection with, 59–60, 61–63, 69, 76, 77–78, 167–68n.10
  sati controversy compared, 62
  secularism and, 62
  VHP and, 60
Babur (Mughal emperor), 60
Bacchetta, Paola, 65–66
Bannerjee, Mamta, 158–59
Basu, Amrita, 6–7, 12, 65, 67–68, 77, 120–21, 146
Baxter, Craig, 28
Bedi, Tarini, 80
Begum, Shah Bano, 52–53. *See also* maintenance under Islamic law
Besant, Annie, 108–9
Bharatiya Jana Sangh. *See* Jana Sangh
Bharatiya Janata Party (BJP)
  generally, 14, 95–96
  academic scholarship on, 80, 87–88, 93
  authoritarianism and, 151–52
  Babri Masjid mosque incident and, 61–64
  cabinet positions, women in, 43–44, 125, 126
  campaign posters, 132–36, 138*f*, 139*f*
  campaign rallies, 130–32, 131*f*, 132*f*, 133*f*, 134*f*, 135*f*, 136*f*
  candidates, women as, 40–41, 41*f*, 42–43, 46–47, 125–26
  caste and, 135–36, 139–40
  Central Election Committee, 42
  challenging feminism (*see* challenging feminism)
  colonialism and, 140–41
  complementarity and, 142–43, 146
  Congress Party and, 35, 140–41
  continuity with Hindu Mahasabha, 20, 27–29, 46
  data collection, 19
  democracy and, 16–17, 140–42
  effect of incorporation on, 137–42, 145
  electoral incorporation of women in, 125–29
  electoral performance of, 20, 30–32, 48, 87–88, 107–8, 119, 120, 125–26, 137–39, 158–59, 165n.4
  empowerment of women and, 158
  ethnographic observation of, 13–14, 145
  extremism in, 152
  family support and, 143–44
  founding of, 1, 5–6, 29–30
  Gandhian socialism and, 29–30
  gender difference in voting and, 36–37, 37*f*
  gendered discourses (*see* gendered discourses)
  "gender gap" and, 35–36
  hegemony of, 75
  Hindu Mahasabha and, 120, 122–23, 129, 146, 158
  Hindu nationalism and, 9, 30–32, 146, 150–51
  historical background, 29–32
  inclusion-moderation hypothesis and, 151–52
  incorporation of women in, 12, 16, 95–96, 149, 155–57 (*see also* incorporation of women)
  internal incorporation of women in, 122–25
  interviews with, 13, 121–22, 128–29, 143, 161, 162
  Jammu and Kashmir, on, 151, 152, 153
  Jana Sangh and, 29–30, 48, 103
  Janata Party and, 48, 103
  Lok Sabha, in, 7–8, 30–32, 40, 42–43, 45, 48, 93, 119, 120, 125, 137–38, 165n.4
  Mahila Morcha (MM), 41–42, 122, 124–25, 129–30, 133–34, 137, 145

maintenance under Islamic law, on, 53–54
majoritarian nature of, 150–51
manifestos, women's issues in, 45, 126–29, 172n.20
media spokespersons, 123–24
mobilization of women in, 3, 11–12, 47, 48–51, 76, 119, 149, 156–57 (*see also* mobilization of women)
Muslim League and, 140–41
National Executive Committee, 42
as "national" organization, 18
NDA, in, 30–31, 48, 79–80, 119, 128–29, 166n.11
Parliamentary Board, 42
participation by women in, 86–87
party functionaries, women as, 41–42
rallying women in streets (*see* rallying women in streets)
Ram temple in Ayodhya, on, 151, 153
religious family laws, on, 151, 153–54
religious minorities and, 167n.7
religious politics in, 9
rise of, 94
RSS and, 30, 46, 144
secularism versus, 16–17, 152–54
social movement organizations and, 6–7
tethering of women and, 65–68, 142–44, 145–46
uniform civil code, on, 153–54
VHP and, 30
visual analysis of, 129–36
voters, women as, 35–36, 36*f*
women generally, 1–2, 8, 32, 48, 64–65, 66–67, 88, 148–49
Bharti, Uma, 63–64, 65, 66–67, 150
Bhopatkar, L.B., 105
Biju Janata Dal, 166n.11
BJP. *See* Bharatiya Janata Party (BJP)
Bombay Union of Journalists, 56–57
Buddhism
Hindu nationalism and, 2
origins of, 165n.2

cabinet positions, women in, 43–44, 125, 126
campaign posters, 132–36, 138*f*, 139*f*

campaign rallies, 130–32, 131*f*, 132*f*, 133*f*, 134*f*, 135*f*, 136*f*
candidates, women as
generally, 32–33, 37–41, 42–43, 46–47
BJP, 40–41, 41*f*, 42–43, 46–47, 125–26
Congress Party, 40–41, 40*f*, 41*f*
CPI, 40–41, 40*f*, 41*f*
CPI-M, 40–41, 40*f*, 41*f*
gender differences in win rate, 43, 43*t*
relatives of male candidates, 98
caste
Adivasis, 87–88
BJP and, 135–36, 139–40
Dalits, 29–30, 68, 87–88, 131–32
Hinduism and, 9–10
Hindu Mahasabha and, 24–25, 117
positionality, effect on, 90
quotas, 38–39
Rajputs, 57, 69
celibacy, 65
Census of India, 19
Center for the Study of Developing Societies in India (CSDS), 19
challenging feminism
generally, 11–12, 14–15, 49, 64, 68, 69, 149
participation by women in Hindu nationalism as, 77–78, 79
sati controversy and, 49–50, 50*t*, 51, 55–59, 155–56
Chandra, Kanchan, 168n.6
Chatterjee, Partha, 129
Chhibber, Pradeep K., 8, 84–85, 87–88, 140, 141–42
Christianity
codification of personal laws, 52
Hindu nationalism versus, 2, 116–17
colonialism
BJP and, 140–41
Global South and, 118–19
Hindu Mahasabha and, 22–23
Islamic law and, 69
marginalization of women and, 10–11, 108
personal laws and, 52, 54
positionality and, 91–92
sati and, 56–57, 58
women and, 118–19

Commission of Sati (Prevention) Act (Rajasthan), 56
Commission on the Status of Women in India, 38–39
Communist Party of India (CPI)
  BJP compared, 35
  candidates, women as, 40–41, 40f, 41f
  gender difference in voting and, 36–37, 37f
  voters, women as, 36f
  women in, 88
Communist Party of India–Marxist (CPI–M)
  BJP compared, 35
  candidates, women as, 40–41, 40f, 41f
  gender difference in voting and, 36–37, 37f
  voters, women as, 36f
  women in, 88
complementarity, 120–21, 142–43, 146
Congress Party. *See* Indian National Congress (Congress Party)
Convention on the Elimination of All Forms of Discrimination against Women, 70
COVID-19 pandemic, 158–59
crowdsourcing, 172n.20

Dalits, 29–30, 68, 87–88, 131–32
data collection, 2–3, 19
Delhi Pact, 26
deliberative democracy, 173n.5
democracy
  BJP and, 16–17, 140–42
  deliberative democracy, 173n.5
  Hindu nationalism and, 16–17
  India, in, 148, 154–55
  minimalist school, 154
  participatory democracy, 173n.5
  realignment in, 140–42
  robust definitions of, 154–55
demography, 116–18
Deo, Nandini, 4, 64, 80
Deshpande, Rajeshwari, 34–36, 38–39
Deshpande, V.G., 105
Dev, Sushmita, 170n.34
Directive Principle, 22
dynastic politics, 8, 88, 98, 120

Egypt, Hindu nationalism compared, 78–79
electoral incorporation of women, 125–29
electoral marginalization of women, 98, 99, 106–14
electoral performance
  BJP, of, 20, 30–32, 48, 87–88, 107–8, 119, 120, 125–26, 137–39, 158–59, 165n.4
  Hindu Mahasabha, of, 20–21, 22, 25–26, 97–98, 107–8, 170n.29
  incorporation of women, relation to, 158
  Jana Sangh, of, 20–21, 26–29, 107–8
  Lok Sabha, electoral performance of parties in, 20, 21f
  marginalization of women, relation to, 158
  mobilization of women, relation to, 158
  nationalist political parties, of, 20, 21f
Emergency of 1975-1977, 27–28
empirical methodology of study, 13–14
Engels, Friedrich, 129
ethnographic observation of incorporation of women, 129–36, 145
extremism, 152

family support, 143–44
feminism
  challenging (*see* challenging feminism)
  Hindu nationalism and, 68
  Islam and, 88–89
  sati controversy, on, 56–58
  scholarship on women in Hindu nationalism (*see* feminist scholarship on women in Hindu nationalism)
  second-wave feminism, 77
  secularism and, 121
  uniform civil code, on, 54–55, 79
feminist scholarship on women in Hindu nationalism
  generally, 15, 20–21
  positionality and, 76, 89–90, 92–93 (*see also* positionality)
  reassessment of assumptions, 79
  religion and women, on, 82–83

INDEX

Gandhi, Indira
   assassination of, 137–38
   Congress Party and, 8, 27–28, 29, 88, 108–9
   dynastic politics and, 120
   Prime Minister, as, 37–38
   religion and, 141
Gandhi, Mahatma, 22, 24, 25, 110
Gandhi, Rajiv, 53–54, 60, 137–38, 141, 167n.8
Gandhi, Sonia, 108–9
Gandhian socialism, 29–30, 93
gang rape, 147–48
gendered discourses
   generally, 11–12, 14–15, 49, 64, 68, 69, 149
   maintenance under Islamic law and, 49–50, 50*t*, 51–55, 155–56
"gender gap," 34, 35–36
gender quotas, 45
gender studies, 10–11
Global South
   academic scholarship on, 73–74, 75, 81
   colonialism and, 118–19
   India in, 10–11
Godse, Nathuram, 24
Goods and Services Tax, 31
Government of India Act (1935), 102
Govindacharya, K.N., 66–67
Graham, Bruce, 26–27, 28–29
Gunther, Richard, 86
Gupta, Pranav, 34–35
Gupta, Rekha, 133–35, 136

Haryana Vikas Party, 166n.11
Hasan, Zoya, 58–59
health care, 127
Hedgewar, K.B., 23, 113
Heptullah, Najmah, 125
Hinduism
   Abrahamic religions contrasted, 9–10, 84–85
   caste and, 9–10
   mobilization, lack of basis for, 4, 84–85
Hindu Mahasabha
   generally, 5–6, 14
   All-India Hindu Mahila Sabha, 99, 103–4, 105–6, 155–56

archival materials, 13–14
Arya Samaj faction, 24–25
BJP and, 120, 122–23, 129, 146, 158
caste and, 24–25, 117
colonialism and, 22–23
Congress Party and, 22–23, 99–100, 102, 110, 119
continuity of BJP, 20, 27–29, 46
decline of, 26
demography and, 117–18
electoral marginalization of women in, 106–7
electoral performance of, 20–21, 22, 25–26, 97–98, 107–8, 170n.29
failure of, 24–26
founding of, 21–22
fundamentalist religious movement, as, 146
Gandhi assassination and, 24
historical background, 21–26
internal contradictions, 24–26, 97–98
internal marginalization of women in, 98, 99–106
Islam and, 116–17
Jana Sangh and, 26, 27
Joshi in, 99–102, 103–6, 110, 155–56
Lok Sabha, in, 25–26, 106, 170n.29
manifestos, women's issues in, 106–7
marginalization of women in, 3, 11, 16, 95, 97, 98–99, 114–15, 118–19, 141, 149, 156 (*see also* marginalization of women)
Muslim League and, 110–11, 112–13, 119
as "national" organization, 18
participation by women in, 86–87
RSS and, 23–24, 102, 113, 114
Sanatan Dharma faction, 24–25
Scindia and, 103
secularism versus, 26
tethering of women and, 114–18, 142, 145, 156
violence, on, 25
women generally, 2, 88
Working Committee, 106, 110
Hindu nationalism *(Hindutva). See also specific topic*
   generally, 2

Hindu nationalism (*cont.*)
  academic scholarship on women in (*see* academic scholarship on women in Hindu nationalism)
  BJP and, 9, 30–32, 146, 150–51
  Buddhism and, 2
  challenging feminism, participation by women as, 77–78, 79
  Christianity versus, 2, 116–17
  complementarity and, 120–21
  Congress Party and, 100
  democracy and, 16–17
  demography and, 116–18
  Egypt compared, 78–79
  feminism and, 68
  feminist scholarship on women in (*see* feminist scholarship on women in Hindu nationalism)
  gender-progressive ideology, lack of, 4
  historical background, 18–19, 45–46
  Islam versus, 2
  Jainism and, 2
  Judaism versus, 2
  maintenance under Islamic law, on, 53–54
  masculinity and, 115–16
  mobilization of women, role of in rise of, 70–71
  Muslim League and, 45–46
  resistance to, 141–42
  secularism versus, 31–32
  Sikhism and, 2
  translation of, 166n.10
  unrepresentative nature of Hindu nationalist women, 148–49, 157
  women generally, 48, 64–65, 115–16, 148–50
Hindutva. *See* Hindu nationalism (*Hindutva*)
Huntington, Samuel, 84

immolation. *See sati* (widow immolation) controversy
implications of study, 16, 157–59
inclusion–moderation hypothesis, 7–8, 151–52
incorporation of women
  generally, 2, 119, 120–22, 145–46
  BJP, in, 12, 16, 95–96, 149, 155–57
  defined, 12
  effect on BJP, 137–42, 145
  effect on women, 142–44, 145
  electoral incorporation, 125–29
  electoral performance, relation to, 158
  empowerment of women and, 121
  ethnographic observation of, 129–36, 145
  internal incorporation, 122–25
  interrelationship with other forms of participation, 156–57
  tethering of women and, 142–44
  visual analysis of, 129–36
India. *See also specific topic*
  academic scholarship on, 9–11
  democracy in, 148, 154–55
  Global South, in, 10–11
  secularism in, 9
  universal suffrage in, 10–11, 33
Indian Constitution
  Directive Principle, 22
  discrimination under, 69–70
  Jammu and Kashmir, 152, 153
Indian Election Commission, 19, 26, 27, 39–40
Indian National Congress (Congress Party)
  generally, 8, 24
  All India Mahila Congress, 170n.34
  Babri Masjid mosque incident and, 60
  BJP and, 35, 140–41
  candidates, women as, 40–41, 40*f*, 41*f*
  Congress Mahila Sangh, 170n.32
  dynastic politics and, 88, 98
  electoral marginalization of women in, 108–10
  erosion of dominance, 27, 75, 93, 120
  gender difference in voting and, 36–37, 37*f*
  "gender gap" and, 35–36
  Hindu Mahasabha and, 22–23, 99–100, 102, 110, 119
  Hindu nationalism and, 100
  Indira Gandhi and, 8, 27–28, 29, 88, 108–9
  Jana Sangh and, 27
  maintenance under Islamic law, on, 53

INDEX 199

manifestos, women's issues in, 172n.20
Muslim League and, 112–13
Quit India movement, 25, 109
sati controversy, on, 58–59
Scindia and, 103
secularism and, 24, 58–59, 110–11, 116–17
voters, women as, 34–36, 36*f*
women and, 99–100
Women's Branch of the Home Rule League, 170n.32
Women's Committee for the Gujarat Provincial Congress Committee, 170n.32
Working Committee, 110
Indian Penal Code, 56
Indo–China War, 27
Indra (deity), 168n.9
instant divorce, 153–54
integral humanism, 27
internal incorporation of women, 122–25
internal marginalization of women, 98, 99–106
international law, lack of discussion of, 70
Irani, Smriti, 124
Iranian Revolution (1979), 84
Islam
  Babri Masjid mosque incident (*see* Babri Masjid mosque incident [1992])
  feminism and, 88–89
  Hindu Mahasabha and, 116–17
  Hindu nationalism versus, 2, 116–17
  mahr, 167n.5
  maintenance and (*see* maintenance under Islamic law)
  women and, 10–11, 74, 85–86, 88–89

Jaffrelot, Christophe, 24–25, 151–52
Jainism
  Hindu nationalism and, 2
  origins of, 165n.2
Jammu and Kashmir, 151, 152, 153
Jana Sangh
  generally, 5–6, 165n.3
  BJP and, 29–30, 48, 103
  bridging character of, 20, 27–29
  Congress Party and, 27

dissolution of, 20–21, 27–28, 29
electoral performance of, 20–21, 26–29, 107–8
founding of, 26
hegemony of, 8
Hindu Mahasabha and, 26, 27
historical background, 26–29
inclusion–moderation hypothesis and, 7–8
internal contradictions, 28–29
internal succession crisis, 27
Janata Party and, 27–30
Lok Sabha, in, 27–28
Mahila Sammelan, 28
as "national" organization, 18
RSS and, 26–27, 46
women and, 28
Working Committee, 28
Janata Dal (United) Party, 171n.14
Janata Party
  generally, 20–21
  BJP and, 48, 103
  Jana Sangh and, 27–30
  NDA, in, 166n.11
Jeffery, Patricia, 77
Jinnah, Fatima, 111–12
Jinnah, Mohammad Ali, 111–12
Joshi, Jankibai, 169n.6
  generally, 16, 98, 114, 118
  Hindu Mahasabha, in, 99–102, 103–6, 110, 155–56
  letter of, 101*f*
  resistance faced by, 122–23
Judaism
  codification of personal laws, 52
  Hindu nationalism versus, 2

Kamlabehn (Hindu nationalist women leader), 65–66
Kanwar, Roop, 55–57. See also *sati* (widow immolation) controversy
Kaur, Rajkumari Amrit, 106
Kelkar, Lakshmibai, 113–14, 114*f*
Key, V.O., 15–16, 86, 96, 98
Khan, Mohammed Ahmed, 52–53, 167n.5
Kumar, Nitish, 171n.14
Kumar, Sanjay, 34–35

legislators, women as, 32–33, 38–39, 38*t*,
    See also Lok Sabha
Lekhi, Meenakshi, 100
Liberhan Commission, 63–64
Lok Sabha
    Bharti in, 63–64, 66
    BJP in, 7–8, 30–32, 40, 42–43, 45, 48, 93, 119, 120, 125, 137–38, 165n.4
    electoral performance of parties in, 20, 21*f*
    "gender gap" in, 34
    Hindu Mahasabha in, 25–26, 106, 170n.29
    instant divorce and, 153–54
    Jana Sangh in, 27–28
    Muslim Women Bill in, 53
    quotas in, 172n.21
    Scindia in, 103
    Swaraj in, 125–26
    women in, 37–38, 38*t*, 43*t*
    Women's Reservation Bill in, 39, 128–29
Lok Shakti, 166n.11
Loomba, Ania, 58

Mahmood, Saba, 11, 12–13, 68, 78–79, 88–89, 121
maintenance under Islamic law
    generally, 15, 49, 68–69, 76
    Babri Masjid mosque incident compared, 62
    family law, 22
    gendered discourses and, 49–50, 50*t*, 51–55, 155–56
    international law, lack of discussion of, 70
    maintenance under, 52–55
    masculinity, role of, 69
    multiculturalism and, 168n.11
    "nationalized" nature of controversy, 69–70
    sati controversy compared, 58–59
Malaviya, Madan Mohan, 22
Malkani, K.R., 54
manifestos, women's issues in
    generally, 44–45, 163
    BJP, 126–29, 172n.20
    Congress Party, 172n.20

crowdsourcing, 172n.20
Hindu Mahasabha, 106–7
marginalization of women
    generally, 2, 14, 97–99, 118–19, 155–56
    colonialism and, 10–11, 108
    Congress Party, in, 108–10
    defined, 11, 99
    effect of, 114–18
    electoral marginalization, 98, 99, 106–14
    electoral performance, relation to, 158
    framework, 15–16
    Hindu Mahasabha, in, 3, 11, 16, 95, 97, 98–99, 114–15, 118–19, 141, 149, 156
    internal marginalization, 98, 99–106
    interrelationship with other forms of participation, 156–57
    Muslim League, in, 108, 110–13
    RSS, in, 113–14
    tethering of women and, 114–18
    West, in, 10–11
    Western phenomenon, as, 108
Marumalarchi Deravida Munnetra Kazhagam (MDMK), 166n.11
masculinity
    academic scholarship on, 80
    Babri Masjid mosque incident, role in, 69
    Hindu nationalism and, 115–16
    maintenance under Islamic law, role in, 69
    sati controversy, role in, 69
Menon, Kalyani Devaki, 76, 80
mobilization of women
    generally, 2, 14–15, 48–51, 68–71
    BJP, in, 3, 11–12, 47, 48–51, 76, 119, 149, 156–57
    challenging feminism (*see* challenging feminism)
    defined, 11–12
    effect of, 64–68
    electoral performance, relation to, 158
    gendered discourses (*see* gendered discourses)
    Hinduism, lack of basis for in, 4, 84–85
    Hindu nationalism, role in rise of, 70–71

interrelationship with other forms of participation, 156–57
rallying women in streets (*see* rallying women in streets)
restrictions in BJP, 64–65
tethering of women and, 65–68
Modi, Narendra
   Advani and, 171n.14
   campaign posters, 133–34
   campaign rallies, 130, 131–32
   challenges facing, 141–42
   COVID-19 pandemic and, 158–59
   popularity of, 120
   Prime Minister, as, 30–32
   secularism versus, 152
   uniform civil code, on, 44–45
   women and, 124–26
   Women's Reservation Bill and, 128–29
Montero, José R., 86
Mookerjee, Shyama Prasad, 24, 26–27, 98, 101*f*, 105, 166n.5
multiculturalism, 168n.11
Muslim League
   All-India Muslim Women's Subcommittee, 111–12
   BJP and, 140–41
   Congress Party and, 112–13
   Council, 111–12
   electoral marginalization of women in, 108, 110–13
   founding of, 21–22
   Hindu Mahasabha and, 110–11, 112–13, 119
   Hindu nationalism and, 45–46
   Lahore Resolution (1940), 112
   Pakistan and, 111, 112–13
   War Council, 112
   Women's National Guard, 112
Muslim Women (Protection of Rights on Divorce) Bill, 53–54, 58–59, 167n.8

Naidu, Sarojini, 37–38, 108–9
Narang, Gokulchand, 105
nataks (traveling plays), 129–30
National Democratic Alliance (NDA)
   BJP in, 30–31, 46, 48, 79–80, 119, 128–29, 166n.11
   duration of, 167n.1
   RSS and, 46
National Election Studies (NES), 19
nationalism. *See* Hindu nationalism (*Hindutva*)
nationalist political parties. *See also specific party*
   academic scholarship on, 5–8, 74–75
   electoral performance of, 20, 21*f*
   "gatekeepers," as, 41
   historical background, 18–19, 20–21, 45–46
   inclusion–moderation hypothesis and, 7–8
   lack of women in, 88
   manifestos, women's issues in (*see* manifestos, women's issues in)
   party functionaries, women as, 32–33, 41–42
   rightist parties, women in, 8
   social movement organizations contrasted, 5–7, 18–19
   women's wings, 169–70n.15
Nawaz, Jahan Ara Shah, 111–12
Nayar, K.K., 28, 106
Nayar, Shakuntala, 28, 106, 118
Nehru, Jawaharlal
   Congress Party and, 8, 88, 110, 137–38
   death of, 27
   dynastic politics and, 120
   Prime Minister, as, 24, 26, 60
   religious law and, 170n.30
   secular nationalism, 141
Nehru Memorial Museum and Library, 98
9/11 attacks (2001), 84

Obama, Barack, 147

Pakistan
   Muslim League and, 111, 112–13
   women in, 77
Panchayati Raj, 128–29
Pandit, Vijayalakshmi, 37–38
Parmanand, Bhai, 117–18
Parsis (Zoroastrianism)
   codification of personal laws, 52
   Hindu nationalism versus, 2
Parsons, Talcott, 142–43

participation by women
  generally, 15
  academic scholarship on, 73–74
  BJP, in, 86–87
  cabinet positions, 43–44, 126
  campaigners, as, 32–33
  candidates, as (*see* candidates, women as)
  challenging feminism, as, 77–78, 79
  "gender gap," 34, 35–36
  Hindu Mahasabha, in, 86–87
  incorporation of women (*see* incorporation of women)
  increase in, 33–34
  interrelationship among forms of, 156–57
  legislators, as, 32–33, 38–39, 38*t*
  manifestos, women's issues in (*see* manifestos, women's issues in)
  measurement of, 5
  mobilization of women (*see* mobilization of women)
  party functionaries, as, 32–33, 41–42
  reasons for, 3–4, 72–73, 78, 80–81, 93–94
  religion and women, academic scholarship on, 82–84
  voters, as (*see* voters, women as)
participatory democracy, 173n.5
Pateman, Carole, 10–11, 107–8
Pattali Makkal Katchi, 166n.11
personal laws, 52, 54
platforms, women's issues in. See manifestos, women's issues in
political parties. *See also specific party*
  lack of academic scholarship on women in, 88
  nationalist political parties (*see* nationalist political parties)
  party-as-organization, 86, 98, 122
  party-in-electorate, 86, 98
  party-in-government, 86
  religion and women, academic scholarship on, 86–89
  Western bias in academic scholarship on, 86–87
positionality, 89–93
  generally, 76
  caste, effect of, 90
  clothing, effect of, 90–91
  colonialism and, 91–92
  feminist scholarship on women in Hindu nationalism and, 76, 89–90, 92–93
  gender, effect of, 90
  insider-outsider status, effect of, 91–92
  reflexivity and, 76, 89–90
Prasad, Rajendra, 22
property rights, 127
Punjab Hindu Sabha, 21–22

Quit India movement, 25, 109
quotas, 33, 38–39, 45, 123, 158, 172n.21, 172n.23

Rai, Lala Lajpat, 22
Rai, Praveen, 32–33, 41, 43, 44
Rajputs, 57, 69
Rajya Sabha, 39, 103, 125, 172n.21
rallying women in streets
  generally, 11–12, 14–15, 49, 64, 68, 69, 149
  Babri Masjid mosque incident and, 49–50, 50*t*, 51, 59–64, 155–56
Ram (deity), 60, 168n.9
Rashtriya Swayamsevak Sangh (RSS)
  generally, 5–8, 106
  academic scholarship on, 80
  BJP and, 30, 46, 144
  electoral marginalization of women in, 108, 113–14
  founding of, 23, 113
  Gandhi assassination and, 24
  Hindu Mahasabha and, 23–24, 102, 113, 114
  Jana Sangh and, 26–27, 46
  kin-like structures in, 144, 149, 156
  marginalization of women in, 113–14
  Modi and, 125–26
  NDA and, 46
  Rashtra Sevika Samiti, 80, 102, 113–14, 114*f*, 166n.3
  tethering of women and, 144
  women and, 16
rath yatra (procession), 30, 60–62, 61*f*
Ravi, Shamika, 39, 40–42

Ray, Renuka, 100, 169n.6
reflexivity, 76, 89–90
religion and women, academic scholarship on
　generally, 74, 81
　Abrahamic conception of, 84
　feminist scholarship, 82–83
　historical neglect of, 83–84, 85–86
　ideational versus institutional factors, 85
　participation by women and, 82–84
　political parties and, 86–89
　politics and, 84–86
　Western conception of, 84
religious communalism, 67–68
religious family laws, 151, 153–54
religious politics, 9, 141
remarriage, 117
Rithambara, Sadhivi, 63–64, 65, 150
Roop Kanwar controversy. *See sati* (widow immolation) controversy
RSS. *See* Rashtriya Swayamsevak Sangh (RSS)

Samajwadi Party, 36–37
Samata Party, 166n.11
Sandhu, Rohan, 39, 40–42
Sangh Parivar, 5–6
Sati Prevention Act (1987), 56–57
sati (widow immolation) controversy
　generally, 15, 49, 68–69, 76, 165n.9
　academic scholarship and, 58–59
　Babri Masjid mosque incident compared, 62
　challenging feminism and, 49–50, 50*t*, 51, 55–59, 155–56
　colonialism and, 56–57, 58
　feminism on, 56–58
　international law, lack of discussion of, 70
　maintenance under Islamic law compared, 58–59
　masculinity, role of, 69
　"nationalized" nature of controversy, 69–70
　pro-*sati* forces, 57–58
Savarkar, Vinayak Damodar "Veer," 22–23, 24, 150–51

scholarly research. *See* academic scholarship on women in Hindu nationalism
Scindia, Jivajirao, 103
Scindia, Jyotiraditya, 169n.14
Scindia, Madhavrao, 169n.14
Scindia, Vasundhara Raje, 169n.14
Scindia, Vijaya Raje, 63–64, 65, 66, 103, 118, 169n.14
Scindia, Yasudhara Raje, 169n.14
secularism
　Babri Masjid mosque incident and, 62
　BJP versus, 16–17, 151, 152–54
　Congress Party and, 24, 58–59, 110–11, 116–17
　feminism and, 121
　Hindu Mahasabha versus, 26
　Hindu nationalism versus, 31–32
　India, in, 9
　Modi versus, 152
　Nehruvian secular nationalism, 141
　personal laws and, 52
　religion and women and, 84
Shafi, Mia Muhammad, 111–12
Shah Bano controversy. *See* maintenance under Islamic law
Sharma, M.C., 27
Shiromani Akali Dal, 166n.11
Shiv Sena
　generally, 165n.6, 166n.1
　academic scholarship on, 80
　adjustment and, 143–44
　Mahila Aghadi, 62–63
　NDA, in, 166n.11
　"sons of the soil" and, 166n.1, 167n.9
Sikhism
　Hindu nationalism and, 2
　origins of, 165n.2
Singh, Mal, 55–56
Singh, Manmohan, 120
Singh, Pushpender, 56
Singh, Rajnath, 122–23, 155–56
Sitharaman, Nirmala, 100, 125
social movement organizations, nationalist political parties contrasted, 5–7, 18–19
Swaraj, Sushma, 41–42, 122–24, 125–26, 134–35, 136, 150

Tamizhaga Rajiv Congress, 166n.11
tethering of women
   BJP and, 65–68, 142–44, 145–46
   family support and, 143–44
   Hindu Mahasabha and, 114–18, 142, 145, 156
   incorporation of women and, 142–44
   marginalization of women and, 114–18
   mobilization of women and, 65–68
   RSS and, 144
Thachil, Tariq, 87–88
Thakur, Pragya, 150
Tilly, Charles, 3–4, 75, 80–81
Trishanku (mythological figure), 168n.9

uniform civil code, 44–45, 54–55, 79, 153–54
United Progressive Alliance, 120
Universal Declaration of Human Rights, 70
Upadhyay, Deen Dayal, 27, 28

Vajpayee, Atal Bihari, 29–30, 93, 128–29, 134, 144, 150, 152
Vedas, 169n.6
Verma, Rahul, 8, 87–88, 140, 141–42
Vickers, Jill, 10–11, 108, 118–19
violence against women, 127–28
Vishwa Hindu Parishad (VHP)
   generally, 5–7
   academic scholarship on, 80
   Babri Masjid mosque incident and, 60
   BJP and, 30
visual analysis of incorporation of women, 129–36
voters, women as
   generally, 32–35, 46–47
   BJP, 35–36, 36*f*
   Congress Party, 34–36, 36*f*
   CPI, 36*f*
   CPI-M, 36*f*

Weiner, Myron, 87
widow immolation. See *sati* (widow immolation) controversy
women. See also *specific topic*
   academic scholarship on, 3–5
   agency of, 12–13, 78–79, 89
   BJP generally, 1–2, 8, 32, 48, 64–65, 66–67, 88, 148–49
   cabinet positions in, 43–44
   candidates, as (*see* candidates, women as)
   celibacy and, 65
   colonialism and, 118–19
   complementarity and, 120–21, 142–43, 146
   Congress Party and, 99–100
   CPI, in, 88
   CPI-M, in, 88
   demography and, 116–18
   effect of incorporation on, 142–44, 145
   family support and, 143–44
   Hindu Mahasabha generally, 2, 88
   Hindu nationalism generally, 48, 64–65, 115–16, 148–50
   historical neglect in academic scholarship, 75
   incorporation of (*see* incorporation of women)
   Islam and, 10–11, 74, 85–86, 88–89
   legislators, as, 32–33, 38–39, 38*t*
   manifestos, women's issues in (*see* manifestos, women's issues in)
   marginalization of (*see* marginalization of women)
   mobilization of (*see* mobilization of women)
   participation by (*see* participation by women)
   party functionaries, as, 32–33, 41–42
   political parties, lack of women in, 88
   religion and women, academic scholarship on (*see* religion and women, academic scholarship on)
   rightist parties, in, 8
   RSS and, 16
   tethering of (*see* tethering of women)
   universal suffrage, 10–11, 33
   unrepresentative nature of Hindu nationalist women, 148–49, 157
   voters, as (*see* voters, women as)
   weak, portrayal as, 115
Women's Indian Association, 109

Women's Indian Association of Madras, 33
Women's Reservation Bill (WRB), 39, 45, 127, 128–29

Yadav, Yogendra, 33–34, 35–36, 87
Yuval-Davis, Nira, 116, 129

Zoroastrianism. *See* Parsis (Zoroastrianism)

Printed in the USA/Agawam, MA
April 5, 2023

808007.014